DATE DUE		
APR 0 9 1998		

FEMINIST PERSPECTIVES

Philosophical Essays on Method and Morals

Feminist-informed inquiry is presenting new insights and new challenges to all areas of contemporary study. The essays in this collection focus on scholarship in philosophy and its relationship to feminism. The contributors are all currently engaged in writing and teaching philosophy at the university level; all are committed feminists. Their essays begin from the principles that 'the philosophical project' is transformed by feminist inquiry and that feminist philosophers bring to the larger 'feminist project' a unique contribution, shaped by the philosophical tradition in which they have been trained, and which they are now coming to challenge.

The essays raise questions about the nature of knowledge, and about standards of justification and credibility previously taken for granted. They demonstrate that claims to knowledge hitherto suppressed and invalidated are, in fact, important and illuminating. Other issues raised include the notion of objectivity; these essays show that the nature of moral inquiry, along with a number of questions that have long preoccupied ethicists, has been developed from a narrow perspective which often fails to account for women's experiences.

This collection raises important questions for scholarship in philosophy, and offers a new perspective in both methodology and morals from which to consider them.

LORRAINE CODE is Canada Research Fellow, Department of Philosophy and Women's Studies Research Group, York University.

SHEILA MULLETT is Associate Professor of Philosophy, Concordia University.

CHRISTINE OVERALL is Associate Professor of Philosophy and Queen's National Scholar, Queen's University.

FEMINIST PERSPECTIVES

Philosophical Essays on Method and Morals

Edited by

LORRAINE CODE, SHEILA MULLETT,
AND CHRISTINE OVERALL

UNIVERSITY OF TORONTO PRESS

Toronto Buffalo London

© University of Toronto Press 1988
Toronto Buffalo London
Printed in Canada

ISBN 0-8020-2627-3 (cloth)
ISBN 0-8020-6668-2 (paper)

Canadian Cataloguing in Publication Data

Main entry under title:

Feminist perspectives : philosophical essays on
method and morals

Papers presented at conferences of the Canadian
Society for Women in Philosophy.
Includes bibliographical references.
ISBN 0-8020-2627-3 (bound) ISBN 0-8020-6668-2 (pbk.)

1. Feminism – Philosophy. 2. Woman (Philosophy).
3. Methodology. 4. Ethics. I. Code, Lorraine.
II. Mullett, Sheila, 1943– . III. Overall,
Christine, 1949– . IV. Canadian Society for
Women in Philosophy.

HQ1206.F45 1988   305.401   c88-093367-4

This book has been published with the help of
a grant from the Canadian Federation for the Humanities,
using funds provided by the Social Sciences and Humanities
Research Council of Canada.

Contents

vi Contents

Acknowledgments

We wish to thank the Canadian Society for Women in Philosophy, the Social Sciences and Humanities Research Council of Canada, and the Canadian Federation for the Humanities, without whose help this book could not have been published.

We are grateful to Joanne Yamaguchi for initiating this project and to Virgil Duff for his help in seeing it through.

FEMINIST PERSPECTIVES

Philosophical Essays on Method and Morals

Editors' Introduction

Feminist philosophy poses serious and sustained challenges to many of the most cherished assumptions of the philosophical tradition. Even such seemingly unassailable ideals as those of objectivity and autonomy come to be recognized as products of certain ways of viewing the world, from within specific and contingent sets of social structures, rather than as having the timeless, absolute value they have long been taken to have. *Re-vision*[1] is a central theme: a painstaking scrutiny and explication of reasons for the hegemony of certain theoretical principles, and an exploration of how structures of thought and action might be transformed if they were considered from a radically different perspective. Broadly speaking, this perspective is based in the *experiences* of feeling, thinking, temporally located human beings. A guiding conviction is that it is instructive to consider how theoretical structures look when their practical origins are emphasized. Such an emphasis resists attempts to superimpose theory upon experiences. It rejects claims to the effect that theory must transcend experience.

In philosophical practice, the experiences of women have long been overlooked, repressed, ignored, or denigrated. In feminist philosophy, by contrast, women's experiences are highlighted and used as material for philosophical discussion, though without begging the important question as to whether, in concentrating upon those experiences, one must assume that female and male natures are inherently different. Women's emotions, bodily awareness, moral reasoning, and social practices become legitimate foci of this discussion. It is out of a conviction that such explorations will have wide-ranging effects upon the structure and content of most belief systems and institutions that feminist philosophers describe women's experiences and examine their implications.

Philosophy grows through and articulates itself in dialogue, and the Canadian Society for Women in Philosophy (C-SWIP) has, for a decade, provided a remarkably fertile space for the dialogue of feminist philosophy to develop. Perhaps the most notable feature that distinguishes C-SWIP conferences from many other philosophy conferences is the way in which women share their philosophical reflections and collaborate in the formulation of more satisfactory ways of thinking and talking about vital issues. A spirit of enquiry guides these discussions. That spirit contrasts with the adversarial tone of much academic philosophy. It is not unusual for a presenter at a C-SWIP meeting to confess to ignorance about how a searching question put to her argument might be answered, nor for other participants to join in seeking possible lines of approach. Simple and obvious as such responses might seem to be, they are remarkably rare in academic philosophy. They recapture something of the Socratic spirit in which genuine enquiry should begin, marked by a just assessment of the limitations of one's own vision (in observation of the Socratic 'know thyself' injunction), and by a recognition of the value of communal, co-operative enquiry. It is less important to appear to be right than it is to explore ideas with other thinkers equally concerned to understand. Such exploration is marked by a principle of charity whereby participants attempt to see the point of one another's work, and to extend its scope. Salient features of these conferences, then, are the solidarity and commitment of the participants, who are collectively articulating a new approach to philosophy. This solidarity is a self-critical one, constantly wary of the danger of blinding itself with its own ideology: aware of 'the way of all ideology' (to borrow Susan Griffin's phrase) – its liberating *and* its constraining possibilities[2]

Reading, hearing, and discussing ideas developed by C-SWIP participants and other feminist philosophers, one comes to realize that this new approach to philosophy has truly revolutionary implications. In presenting this collection of papers on two themes central to discussions at recent conferences, we hope to convey to our readers something of this revolutionary spirit. Gradually, feminist philosophers are coming to understand some of the complex and subtle ways in which socially constructed institutions and theories have contributed to the public invisibility of women, and hence the inaudibility of female voices in the philosophical forum. Articulation of these common experiences of being invisible and inaudible, and analyses of their roots in social practices, in thought and language, are having the effect of enabling feminist philosophers to see that there are genuinely *new* ways of thinking, and that it is important to find these ways instead of trying simply to adapt the old ways so that they include and accommodate women. Necessary changes cannot be wrought simply by altering every occurrence of 'he' and 'man' in the literature to 'she' and 'woman,' for the problems that need to be addressed are resistant to simple semantic solutions. These problems demand profound reflection not only upon language usage, but upon the patterns of perception and thought manifested in language. Philosophy's semantic suppression of women's experiences reflects a more general exclusion of women from full personhood. Hence the introduction of women's experiences and of a feminist perspective into philosophical discourse would transform philosophy itself.

However difficult it may be to reconcile feminist and 'received' philosophical methodology, all of the contributors to this volume are committed to the project of developing a feminist approach to philosophy. Yet, to speak of 'feminist philosophy' is to use an open-textured concept still very much in the process of articulation. Certain of its features can be indicated, but it would be a serious mistake to consider these to be constitutive of a *definition* of feminist philosophy. Many of the concerns implicit or explicit in what it is now appropriate to designate as 'part' of feminist philosophy are continuous with broader feminist endeavours and, like them, are not confined within the boundaries of any discipline. Noteworthy among these concerns are, first, that kind of consciousness-raising that emerges out of political praxis, manifested in the way struggles for equal rights, for access to contraception and abortion, and for equal pay for work of equal value lead women to new understandings of their situation. Second, there is a continuity with social and political analysis, as ethical implications of such issues as rape, pornography, prostitution, reproductive freedom and reproductive technology, war, and arms proliferation are elaborated. And a third feature of feminist theoretical endeavour, especially evident in this volume, is the construction of more systematic philosophical analyses of the limitations and distortions inherent in traditional thought structures. In their re-visionary aspect, these analyses produce what Sandra Lee Bartky has called 'ontological shock,'[3] showing that the situations and preoccupations that have produced women's invisibility and inaudibility are neither necessary nor inescapable. In consequence of this shock, taken-for-granted assumptions shift, and much that has hitherto seemed immune from doubt is shown to be but another product of fallible, historically contingent – and hence alterable – human gropings towards making sense of the world.

In feminist philosophy there is a constant awareness of history, process, and change. Indeed, one might venture to declare that a thoughtful historicism pervades these philosophical approaches: a realization that there are no timeless truths, and that the alleged truths by which philosophers have been living and conducting their enquiries have the form they do at least in part because of the circumstances of their articulation. To understand something about these circumstances is neither to yield to temptations of relativism, nor simply to explain the circumstances themselves away. Rather, it is to see with growing clarity just how deeply rooted are the structures that have created female oppression, and how constantly vigilant an informed feminist consciousness must be to recognize practical and theoretical assumptions for what they are and to uncover possible explanations for them.

The discussions undertaken in these papers attempt to go to the roots of some presuppositions upon which moral and political debate are based. Such presuppositions shape both the structure and the content of any treatment of substantive issues; they must be unmasked if progress is to be made either in philosophical discussion per se, or in the social-political praxis to be based upon this re-visioned philosophical approach. Indeed, it becomes increasingly clear that political moves, such as preferential hiring or the provision of freer access to abortion and day care, made in response to feminist political pressure, should not be taken as signs of genuine improvement in the absence of evidence that patriarchal attitudes themselves are being obliterated, and that this obliteration is reflected in those practical measures that one might be inclined to applaud. Hence the ontological and epistemological dimensions of patriarchal structures are most in need of demolition. But ontological and epistemological questions are in no sense separate or separable either from one another or from the moral and political discussions to which they give rise. Rather, all of these matters are interrelated in a complex network of reciprocal influence. What a person *is* affects what that person can know, which in turn structures and restructures what she is, giving rise, then, to altered modes of being. These modes of being, in turn, create possibilities for different modes of knowing. Moral and political theories and decisions emerge out of ways of perceiving and knowing the world: such theories, then, can only be as good, as accurate, and as just as are the modes of perceiving and knowing in which they originate.

Hence, although the papers in this volume have been divided into two sections whose primary focus is either methodology or morality, readers will discover that there is considerable continuity from one section to the other, just as there is a commonality of themes in the papers in each section. Methodological issues are addressed in the papers on morals, and it is often apparent that methodological choices themselves have moral implications. The fact that the papers are not clearly differentiated by subject-matter reflects another recurring feminist theme: a resistance to dichotomous, dualistic, divisive modes of thinking. This resistance grows out of the conviction that such thinking imposes unnecessarily artificial distinctions upon experience, and often draws unwarranted evaluative conclusions from them. In keeping with the re-visionary spirit of the volume is the persistent underlying question about what difference it might make, both in practice and in theory, if such dichotomies were dissolved or abandoned.

Dichotomies are deeply entrenched in the philosophical tradition. Yet such dichotomies as abstract/concrete, reason/emotion, universal/particular, subjective/objective, knowledge/experience, public/private, theory/practice, and mind/body, long taken to mark distinctions discoverable in the 'real' world, are shown instead to be products of ways of thinking that could well have been different. In many of the papers the suggestion is made that the two 'sides' of these dichotomies need not be taken to be polar opposites of each other, but might rather be understood as points in constant interplay.

In the papers in part one of this volume, a number of methodological shifts are proposed that might restructure philosophical reflection by removing constraints that have systematically, if often imperceptibly, obscured the meanings of certain crucial aspects of experience. Susan Sherwin's description of her 'dual identity' as a philosopher and a feminist, and of the different methodological constraints that are imposed upon her work according to which 'hat' she happens to be wearing, vividly illustrates what it means to try to reconcile such artificially differentiated identities. A shift such as Sherwin envisages, where a rapprochement is effected between these allegedly disparate modes of enquiry, can enrich both feminism and philosophy.

Marsha Hanen engages in a critique of the 'objectivist' epistemology in which legal theory has long been based. She shows how its claims to objectivity have tended, under a rhetoric of equality, to mask ideologies that enforce women's powerlessness. To entertain the pluralistic possibilities she envisages is to acquire a more general understanding of the implications of a long-standing epistemological insistence upon an ideal of virtually unrealizable objectivity. Such an ideal can be striven for only at the expense of denying much of the meaning of particular, individual experiences.

Petra von Morstein and Lorraine Code are concerned with the theme of the meaning of experience. Von Morstein takes her inspiration from Cassandra's valiant attempt to find a voice in which to articulate her own peculiarly private perspective. In her paper, the dichotomy between concrete experiences and concepts used for description and explanation is put into question with the contention that much experiential knowledge is non-propositional. Because it is not amenable to objective, propositional formulation except at the expense of its experiential quality, it cannot become part of the domain of 'knowledge' as that domain has hitherto been designated. Hence there is no way of counting its deliverances among those things that one knows. Out of a concern with a related problem, Code draws attention to a curious dichotomy between knowledge and experience that creates a rift between the two such that experience, again, cannot count as a source of knowledge. Traditionally, knowledge that would merit its title must prescind from experience, rather than take root in it. And this artificial separation from experience is quite at odds with the pre-philosophical sense that one is knowledgeable precisely *because* of one's experience. Here again, much of what it means to be a human knower – and particularly, as it happens, to be a *female* human knower – is lost in the analysis.

Reflecting upon standard philosophical approaches to the problem of other minds, Christine Overall suggests that the ground be shifted from focus on 'minds,' 'otherness,' and 'belief' to the 'self/other' relationship. In making this move from 'minds' to 'self,' Overall argues for the dissolution of the problem: experiences common to many women (and some men) render the usual terms in which the problem is posed untenable. Philosophical problems regarding the constitution of individuals require solutions that involve relations between individuals.

The papers on morals express a related set of concerns. The broadest suggestion is that the moral universe as it is construed in the philosophical tradition is not one in which women can live. It is a universe that denies value to the fundamental experience of caring for other human beings, and erects standards of moral maturity according to which female moral responses are accorded minimal esteem. The impossibly divisive standards of this moral universe may drive women to 'moral madness,' or require of them an implausible and saintly self-abnegation.

Sheila Mullett examines the ethical ideals embedded in the theories of Iris Murdoch and Nel Noddings, both of which involve shifting perspective from self to other. She argues that such a shift in perspective falls short of affording a feminist perspective, and then delineates what such a perspective might entail. Central to her discussion is a concept of caring, which has at its core a cultivated ability to apprehend the world through the eyes of another. And in a related vein, Jacqueline Davies proposes a shift of perspective in discussions of pornography, showing how pornography assaults conditions necessary for the development of a consensual process of articulating what it is to be human. By showing how a process like this requires dialogue, and how such dialogue cannot separate beliefs from speech and action, she clarifies the way in which this integrated understanding might contribute to a positive restructuring of 'forms of life.' The usual terms in which discussions of pornography are conducted are shown to be untenable.

It would seem, at least in the light of Barbara Houston's analysis, that the kind of caring Mullett describes and the kind of dialogue Davies advocates are possible only for persons who have achieved a certain self-consciousness, one that enables them to hear and acknowledge their own moral voice. Such a sense of self would be no mean achievement for women who have long acquiesced in the assessment that they are morally inferior, and whose 'different' voice has been heard as one that speaks from inchoate, irrational immaturity, when it has been heard at all. When this voice is allowed, rather, to speak and to generate its own 'unpredictable utterances,' as Houston puts it, it may be possible to see the end of what Kathryn Morgan aptly describes as women's 'moral madness.' If women are indeed to escape such madness, Morgan argues, they require nothing less than new models of the self, in terms of which moral imagination, empathy, and feeling are taken at least as seriously as autonomy, rationality, and detachedness long have been taken. The emergent 'other-connected' self will clearly care about others and find in that caring a valued part of her moral experience. It is evident, then, that such *positive* caring will not be manifested in self-abnegation of the sort that requires one to lose oneself in devotion to the good of others. Not all self-abnegation is to be deplored, in Bonnelle Strickling's view, but it can only be positively valued when it is practised by a person who has achieved a certain level of self-development. One must have a well-established sense of self if one is to trust in one's chosen forms of abnegation.

It is an affirmative new voice, then, that is heard in these papers, the voice of a collective endeavour to create a philosophical universe where the male/female dichotomy is seen to be as pernicious and constraining in its effects as are all of the other dichotomies discussed here and throughout this volume. We invite our readers to join us in the creation of this new philosophical approach. In it, artificial boundaries will no longer circumscribe possibilities of understanding and co-operation.

NOTES

1 The term 're-vision' was introduced into feminist theory by Adrienne Rich, in her article 'When We Dead Awaken: Writing as Re-Vision,' published in her *On Lies, Secrets, and Silence* (New York: W.W. Norton & Co., 1979).

2 See Susan Griffin, 'The Way of All Ideology,' in *Feminist Theory: A Critique of Ideology*, ed. N. Keohane, M. Rosaldo, and B. Gelpi (Chicago: University of Chicago Press, 1982).

3 See Sandra Lee Bartky, 'Toward a Phenomenology of Feminist Consciousness,' in *Feminism and Philosophy*, ed. M. Vetterling-Braggin, F. Elliston, and J. English (Totowa, NJ: Littlefield, Adams & Co., 1977), p. 29.

METHOD

Philosophical Methodology and Feminist Methodology: Are They Compatible?

SUSAN SHERWIN

Both 'philosophy' and 'feminism' are broad terms covering a variety of activities and subject-matter. Each identifies an area of central concern to me: I frequently tend, in fact, to define myself in terms of them (I *do* philosophy; I *am* a feminist – though, curiously, I seldom say I *am* a philosopher; never, I *do* feminism). But, more and more, I find myself wondering just how compatible these two interests are. They often seem to present different, and conflicting, demands.

The tension I experience revolves around the question of method. This issue is a particularly serious one, since some philosophers recommend that we make method the defining characteristic of philosophy. Jay Rosenberg, for instance, says in *The Practice of Philosophy*: 'Philosophy as a discipline is perhaps thought of most fruitfully as being distinguished by its method rather than by a subject matter.'[1] The question then naturally arises of what that methodology is, and, whether it is compatible with the methodology of feminism.

In 'Feminism, Marxism, Method, and the State,' Catharine A. MacKinnon defines feminist methodology as consciousness-raising: 'consciousness raising is the major technique of analysis, structure of organization, method of practice, and theory of social change of the women's movement.'[2] We must ask, then, whether this methodology of consciousness-raising falls within the scope of acceptable philosophical methodology.

Immediately, we are confronted by the problem of which methodology to use to examine, without distortions, the question of the compatibility of philosophical and feminist method. As a reflection of my deep ambivalence on this matter, I have chosen to consider various aspects of the question alternately from each perspective to see what insight I can derive as to whether I may keep both hats, only one, or – perish the thought – none. (Hence, as some critics have noticed, this paper at various points, rather schizophrenically reflects virtues and vices of both approaches. I see no way to avoid that dilemma in this particular task.)

I am not addressing a disinterested or 'purely academic' question. This paper is motivated by a particular personal experience. Hence, following feminist methodology, I shall begin by describing and interpreting that experience. Here we come quickly to the first point of departure from philosophy, for there is no comparable beginning from a philosophical orientation. Philosophy does not encourage focusing on particular personal experiences such as this one.

THE EXPERIENCE: A paper I submitted to the Canadian Philosophical Association (CPA) in 1984, entitled 'Ethics: A Feminist Approach,' was rejected by the CPA; it was, however, enthusiastically received by the Canadian Society for Women in Philosophy (C-SWIP). An earlier draft was also read at the national Canadian Research Institute for the Advancement of Women (CRIAW) meeting, where it received a great deal of encouragement (and two requests for publication.)[3]

Among the referees' comments from the CPA were the following remarks:

[Referee 1] The discussion at the bottom on p. 4 implies that there is 'a common experience of being female' that women generally share, that is distinctive of the sex, and that is morally significant so that a correct moral theory must take it into account. What is this 'common experience' and what is the evidence for its prevalence? Also, why is it morally relevant? [These questions are precisely the ones addressed by the paper.]

[Referee 2] This essay is ... not up to the standards we should expect for CPA philosophy papers. ... The author's thesis is likely false. Much of contemporary feminism *is* individualistic in ways criticized by the author ...

[Referee 3] 1. Exactly what thesis does the paper profess? 2. Is it a philosophical thesis? (To put the question differently, does the paper seek to *prescribe a morality* different from those it identifies as dominant or traditional? Or does it seek to produce a *moral theory which describes* morality more accurately than the disfavoured theories?) 3. If (as it seems to this reader) the paper seeks to do the first, what is its relevance to a philosophical congress? (I am asking) [In fact, it was a first step toward developing a feminist approach to a normative theory; I continue to consider such a project relevant to a philo-sophical congress.]

The experience of receiving such scathing reviews is painful. Like many women, I am inclined to accept the deprecating judgment of my limited philosophcal ability. I've certainly made similar judgments myself often enough. But, under my feminist hat, I know that I am obliged to look more deeply. The personal may just be political, even here.

I consider it significant that I continue to run into non-feminist philosophers who insist that what I (and other feminist philosophers) do is 'not philosophy.' The viciousness with which our feminist work is dismissed by some philosophers is a frequent source of concern. It is helpful though, to note that this hostility is not directed exclusively at me; other feminist philosophers have experienced similar sorts of attack from the pens and word-processors of mainstream (malestream) philosophers. The target of this rage is often difficult to determine, for the objectors usually insist that they have no problem with the feminist content of the work per se; they are always very eager to make clear their tolerance for radical thought. Rather, they say, the problem is with the sloppiness, the ignorance, the incompetence of the author qua philosopher. If they were to write feminist philosophy, they suggest, they would do a far more 'professional' job of it. I believe they might, but would it be equally good by feminist standards?

I imagine they would produce work something like the books on feminist themes that have been published over the last few years by writers who are clear about their philosophical identity, and who are prepared to use their certified philosophic expertise unquestioningly to provide helpful guides for feminists, showing *them* how philosophy can clarify their thinking; I have in mind such works as *Women's Choices* by Mary Midgley and Judith Hughes, and *Women, Reason, and Nature* by Carol Macmillan. Implicit in the promise of such writers to bring the clear light of philosophy to feminist thought is a patronizing attitude – recognizable by the third-person references to feminism by which they dissociate themselves from most feminist thought; the distancing, patronizing tone limits the value of their work to feminists. Janet Radcliffe Richards provides a borderline case in *The Sceptical Feminist*, for she oscillates between including herself in and distancing herself from feminist thinkers. There is a striking contrast in tone and content of these books from those by explicitly self-identified feminist philoso-phers, such as Marilyn Frye, Alison Jagger, or the authors of the papers collected in the volume edited by Sandra Harding and Merrill Hintikka.[4] The latter set of books, produced by self-proclaimed *feminist* philosophers, expands and deepens feminist thought rather than constraining and reducing it. There are important differences in approach between the two models that reflect divergent paradigms.

Feminist methodology directs us to look for the political significance of personal experience. What is the political message underlying the scorn with which our individual work is frequently received within the profession? Clearly, the work of feminist philosophers is not of lower quality than the norm for mainstream philosophical meetings, so it is puzzling that a paper welcomed at feminist forums is not even worthy of a hearing at 'regular' philosophical association meetings. Hence, we are left to wonder whether the feminist content is so threatening that the men who dominate the standards of scholarship in philosophy cannot bear to allow it a hearing, or whether there are different methodological criteria operating in the different forums.

These questions are partly empirical, and in that sense, they are already suspect by purely philosophical standards. Philosophy assumes that there exist objective criteria by virtue of which any paper, whatever its political orientation, could be evaluated. Most philosophers would be profoundly offended by suspicions of political resistance on the part of referees.

It may just be, however, that there is no way to do genuinely feminist research and have it thoroughly respected by one's non-feminist colleagues. Feminism, after all, is ultimately extremely radical, insofar as it challenges the status quo in thought as well as in practice. Feminist philosophy does not just offer new truths, or new perspectives on truth, nor is it simply another point of view in these relativistic philosophic times. I believe that feminism demands a distinct way of doing philosophy and challenges the very practice most philosophers pride themselves on having mastered. Hence, I shall explore this philosophically disturbing intuition to see whether or not it is possible to discuss feminism in a way that is 'philosophically respectable.'

What, then, are the methods that characterize philosophy and are they compatible with feminist methodology? As they do with most things, philosophers tend to disagree about *the* method. Throughout this paper, the style of philosophy that I refer to is the one that is characteristic of the Anglo-American approach, a method that has its roots in analytic philosophy and prizes a 'scientific' approach to thought. This tradition is dominant in Anglophone Canadian philosophy departments, and the philosophic community to which the feminist writings I refer to are addressed. There are significant differences in other approaches to philosophy, and some of my specific comments may not be applicable to those other approaches. Although I suspect there are specific barriers between modern feminist methodology and those that characterize various other styles of philosophy, I shall not attempt to review them here. (This limited focus is itself reflective of my philosophic roots.)

Even within the Anglo-American style of philosophy, there are variations in views about what constitutes appropriate methodology. Rosenberg characterizes the method of philosophy as 'the application of reason to its own operations, the rational study of rational practices' (p. 6). He considers philosophy to be primarily a 'second-order' activity occupied with abstract 'radical generalizations.' He recommends that we appeal to the history of philosophy as a major methodological tool, seeing it as our common 'medium' of inquiry. That history 'provides philosophers with a common expository idiom, a shared vocabulary of *concepts*, and a set of paradigms of philosophical reasoning, which can serve as shared starting points for contemporary reexplorations of central philosophical concerns' (p. 11). In other words, we do philosophy by learning the traditions the masters have handed down to us and carrying on in a similar vein: philosophy is defined by what philosophers have done.

If we take Rosenberg's advice seriously and look to the history of philosophy for the common assumptions of method and concepts, feminists are bound to have some concerns. The first thing feminists are sure to notice is that there are seldom any women listed among the philosophic greats, and, as Genevieve Lloyd puts it, the female philosophers we find in the history of philosophy 'have been philosophers despite, rather than because of, their femaleness; there has been no input of femaleness into the formation of ideals of Reason.'[5] The tradition, it would seem, has long been biased against the perspective of women.

The next thing feminists observe is that the work of the leading historical figures is embarrassingly filled with powerful misogynistic statements. Apart from Plato, Augustine, and Mill, it is difficult to find a major historical figure who had a good word to say about women; and the claims of equality from these three are so qualified that they, too, are offensive to some feminists. Most contemporary philosophers are more careful in their discussions of gender than the historical figures were; they tend to be 'liberal' on such matters, and generally excuse their predecessors as being naively misguided by the culture of their times when it came to the question of women. It is commonly accepted that we can simply excise the offensive empirical claims from their philosophy and maintain the pure intellectual core. Feminist historians are far less certain about the externality of an author's views on women. Many feminists have argued that the misogyny runs right through to the core of the views of most major philosophers.[6] Again quoting Lloyd: 'It is clear that what we have in the history of philosophical thought is no mere succession of surface misogynist attitudes, which can now be shed, while leaving intact the deeper structures of our ideals of Reason ... women cannot easily be accommodated into a cultural ideal which has defined itself in opposition to the feminine' (pp. 103–4).

If we look to the method recommended by history we find that although philosophers disagree about the best method of doing philosophy, their debates include agreement about certain principles that psychologists have identified as male oriented. Descartes, for instance, urged a method which he expressly claimed would be suitable 'even for women.' It was the method of pure thought, moving privately from general universals to particulars by the pure activity of the mind uncontaminated by the influence of the body. Being more generous than many other philosophers, he assumed that women had minds as well as bodies; hence, apparently, he genuinely believed that women, too, were capable of truth. Unfortunately, in advocating this method he did not take into account his own further claims that such activity required a concentration that necessitates freedom from concern with practical demands. It is still common to think that philosophic activity demands total concentration: for example: 'The real philosopher, it might be said, exhibits a full, intense commitment to *his* work, as Socrates did ... the "real" philosopher, it might be argued, spends most of *his* time doing philosophy'[7] (italics added). Yet, as Virginia Woolf observed,[8] such a luxury was/is available only to men, since culture dictates that women must see to the demands of practical living, leaving men free for the 'important work.' Given our socialization and the real demands on our time for non-theoretical tasks, it is hardly surprising that few women are perceived as engaged in 'real philosophy.' In contrast, we should note, within feminist circles, practical work is an important component of one's contribution to theory.

Moreover, in our society at least, men are inclined towards abstract general thought and tend to find universals clearer and more comfortable than particulars, just as Descartes imagined. Women, however, seem to think most readily in terms of particulars. Universal, abstract ideas are things they can think towards, but seldom are they the place where thought begins for women.[9] In this sense, perhaps the Socratic model of reasoning from the particular to the general is more suitable for women. If so, it is unfortunate that it passed out of philosophic style so many centuries ago.

When we turn to feminism, we become aware of several important differences in norms. The methodology of consciousness-raising is very much a 'first-order' methodology, where we begin by focusing on the concrete and the specific and delay abstraction and generalization to a later stage. Consciousness-raising involves 'collective critical reconstitution of the meaning of women's social experience, as women live through it' (MacKinnon, p. 29). Thus, where philosophers are encouraged to seek abstract generalization, feminists try to learn to uncover the personal. So, while philosophers seek objective truth, defined as truth valid from any possible viewpoint, feminists consider it important to look to the actual point of view of the individual speaking. Philosophers believe that emotion and personal feeling are impediments to truth, since they can seldom be generalized objectively, but feminists, who consider direct, personal experience an important component of truth, pay particular attention to the emotional content of claims. The quest for abstract universality is reflected in the fascination philosophers have with hypothetical counter-examples. Feminists, however, tend to concentrate on the texture of a complex range of different but related real experiences.

Psychologists have observed that women tend to prefer social, interactive processes, unlike men, who long for the isolation of completely private thought.[10] In this sense, then, the methodology of feminism is the methodology of women's thought: consciousness-raising begins with personal experience, focusing on the details of that experience, and then collectively moves to a broader analysis. Generalizations emerge after a number of particulars are presented. This activity is interactive and not the sort of private process Descartes envisioned.

Feminists do not assume that the truth is readily accessible if only we concentrate hard enough. Recognizing that what has been claimed to be objective and universal is in reality the male point of view, feminists concentrate on women's own experience and explicitly avoid any claims of being 'objective, abstract or universal.'[11] Feminists acknowledge that their perspective is not universal or unpremised, recognizing that women's perspectives might in fact be different if the world were different. After all, women's experience is experience within patriarchy, and 'the male perspective is systematic and hegonomic' (MacKinnon [1983] p. 636). Philosophers, in contrast, continue to hope to find the pure, general, universal point of view. Thus, feminists readily admit to bias in their perspective, while philosophers continue to assume bias should and *can* be avoided. This is, then, a point of serious conflict between the two approaches.

Another area of difference is that feminist scholarship is explicitly interdisciplinary. Feminist scholars have argued that they are constrained in their work by limits connected with the established frameworks of existing disciplines. Such constraint has been cited as constituting one of the most insidious barriers to the development of feminist thought,[12] and it is of as much concern to those with a background in philosophy as it is to those from other disciplines. Hence, by definition, feminists will rely on an eclectic methodology, having its roots in various disciplines, and will not restrict themselves entirely to any single disciplinary approach, neither that of philosophy, nor any other. Although there is a sense in which philosophy is also interdisciplinary, it views its relation to other disciplines in meta-theoretic terms, and so it is not interdisciplinary in the methodological sense of involving genuine collective cross-disciplinary thought. Philosophy maintains its own sense of method and sees its task as criticizing, not adopting, the methods of the disciplines it examines (though, in fact, scientific methodology has been highly attractive to modern philosophers).

Another area of apparent difference is in the definition of criteria of acceptability and criticism within each field. In philosophy, the emphasis on universality makes positive claims virtually impossible to prove and renders counter-examples potentially devastating; hence, commenting on a philosopher's thought is often taken to require a furious search for the decisive counter-example, however hypothetical it may be. Advancing negative theses, to disprove the analysis someone else has offered, is the most natural route for a 'critical' philosopher to take. The logic of the argument is the most important feature of a philosophical position, far more important than the plausibility of the claims or the usefulness of the insight to other questions. In commenting on a philosophical thesis, one may identify a logical flaw in it, challenge its underlying assumptions, or note the inadequacy of its explanatory power. It is taken for granted that the task of colleagues discussing this work is to test the thesis along these logical dimensions, seeking to demolish it to make room for their own clever innovations.

In feminist scholarship, logic is also important – as Richards et al take great pains to point out – and theories which are logically flawed, or clearly false, or lacking in explanatory power are subject to criticism among feminists as well. But feminists have political as well as intellectual aims, which they are quite willing to admit to. (Feminists have provided powerful arguments to show that, historically, philosophers commonly have political agendas as well, but, apart from Marxists and feminists, few philosophers will admit that politics shapes their work.) What this means in practice is that a theoretical claim in feminism must be consistent with overall feminist values, and, in fact, it should further the pursuit of those values. The effect, as well as the logic, of a theory is significant. A theory that does not contribute to political change is of only limited interest. In other words, feminists view political effects as one measure of acceptability, though certainly not the *only* measure. Philosophers tend to be appalled by such frank admissions of bias.

Moreover, it is commonly accepted among feminists that theory alone is not sufficient – that the theorist should also be directly involved in social activism. In this way, we guard against the danger of ungrounded theory. So, where philosophers are deeply suspicious of explicit political concerns shaping one's intellectual exploration, feminists are suspicious of theoretic arguments that deny any political implications. Philosophers, for the most part, now recognize that value-free reasoning is an impossible goal in science, yet they continue to aspire to it within their own discipline.

Feminists are also unlikely to tolerate a theory that rejects or denies personal experience. Philosophers, for their part, seem to take a perverse delight in shocking others by providing an analysis that appears to fly in the face of experience. And where feminists consider it important to fit their ideas into the broader picture of developing feminist thought, philosophers are often most pleased if they can turn existing philosophical thought on its head and present some radically original position that brings much prior work into question.

This difference in standards of acceptability and grounds of criticism leads to differences in style of interaction within the area of study. Janice Moulton has provided a clear feminist critique of a standard model of interaction among modern philosophers. As she argues in 'A Paradigm of Philosophy: The Adversary Method,'[13] the model of philosophic debate is that of a contest of adversaries, where aggression is at least as important as truth to the outcome. Aggression, however, is not an attractive or desirable model for anyone to pursue in professional debates, and it is particularly alien and dangerous for women, let alone feminists. There are clear defects in this approach as a means of arriving at the goal of philosophical activity – truth. By making debating skill a chief criterion of success, the profession of philosophy rewards traits such as aggression and competitiveness; but feminists reject the view that these traits are desirable, for they see them as being central to patriarchy. By making truth an all-or-nothing affair, and encouraging us to seek any hole in a colleague's argument by which her/his position might be demolished, we foster a rather frightening model of the pursuit of truth. More than one clever philosopher has abandoned the profession because s/he lacks the taste for the combative search for truth. Moreover, debating skill is a difficult tool to use in the pursuit of truth. Recognizing that the truth is complex and elusive, philosophers none the less expect one another to pursue it at all stages with air-tight arguments and supreme confidence. It often is the case, though, that one's first attempts in a new direction are tentative and exploratory, and not best pursued by pitting them, alone and unassisted, against the criticism of the strongest opponent.

Feminist scholarship, in contrast, holds onto an ideal of co-operative, collective work. Scholarship in pursuit of a shared goal is to be undertaken as a collective enterprise where different people do piece-work on different aspects of the problem. Ideas are shared as part of this collective enterprise, and, as long as those ideas contribute to the overall goals of feminist activity and are not thoroughly false, the goal of criticism is to help develop those ideas further in the direction begun. Assumptions are shared and, hence, one can get immediately to the business at hand of furthering the argument, rather than reviewing it yet again. Each contribution is related to the larger system of ideas, the larger project, and is not offered as a private theory then to bear one's name. (It is a *feminist* view of justice we seek, not a Kantian, Marxist, Rawlsian, or Nozikian one.)

This description of feminist work is, of course, an idealized one. There are different approaches to feminism, and the disputes between various interpretations can be quite significant. Certainly many feminist scholars have felt shocked and betrayed to find their work (and often themselves) under attack by other feminists. The reason for the shock, however, is that it really is a violation of feminist values and norms to *attack* another's work destructively (rather than criticize it in some constructive way). It happens, but debate as a pitched battle is not an explicit ideal of the discipline. Feminists consciously aim at co-operative solutions and seek to avoid personally devastating attacks.

My philosophy colleagues sometimes express puzzlement over how to criticize feminist work if the adversary system is not acceptable. One approach is to try to understand how the paper at issue fits into the larger picture of feminist goals, and the broad view of social and political or ethical (or epistemological, metaphysical, etc.) thought. Feminists begin with a spirit of charity in trying to decipher the thrust of a colleague's work. For feminists, the nit-picking inherent in the current Anglo-American approaches to philosophy comes after a general consideration of the plausibility of the position. In fairness, I must add that it does seem to be true, lately, that many non-feminist philosophers are recognizing the limits of the adversary method; more and more sessions at philosophy conferences seem to eschew that approach and see the task at hand as a collective search for the truth. (I think, in fact, feminist philosophers can take some of the credit for this shift in style. We really do offer a more attractive paradigm.)

Consider now, from both perspectives, another aspect of academic activity, namely teaching. Here, too, the ideal envisioned in philosophy classes differs from that in feminist studies. In academic contexts, feminist teaching does not proceed by the Socratic method where the wise but humble teacher skilfully directs the unreflective student to the truth s/he has overlooked; rather it involves a co-operative exploration of perceptions and experience towards a new understanding for all members of the 'class.' Feminist teaching incorporates feminist values. Hence, feminist class-rooms are noted for 'an acceptance of, and even emphasis on, the personal/affective element in learning; and a warm human relationship among persons in the class, students and teachers.'[14] Feminist teachers are conscious of the politics of the class-room. As Marilyn Webb writes: 'When we teach about sexual politics, it's a class hierarchy we are attacking. If we recreate this class division within our teaching, our analysis is "devoid of form." That's why as feminist teachers, it's just as important for us to look at how we teach as to look at what we teach.'[15] More precisely, Webb goes on to sketch the methods of achieving these ideals, including: the attempt to teach without imposing authoritarian structures; the attempt to build a 'consciousness of an alternative, e.g., collective learning and action' rather than individual isolation and competition; an attempt to incorporate 'actual experience of what we are talking about in our teaching'; and a general commitment to an emphasis on the experimental (p. 417). These aspects of feminist teaching are not explicitly rejected in general philosophic pedagogy, but they are certainly not accepted as central to the enterprise either. In fact, in philosophy, as in other disciplines, feminist pedagogy tends to contradict mainstream methods, creating hostility to and rejection of our approach within the model of other academic classes.[16]

It seems, then, that there are many important differences in the approaches I see taken by philosophers and feminists. None the less, there are many of us who believe ourselves to be both feminists and philosophers, and much high-quality work has been produced that seems to satisfy the norms of both disciplines. There must, then, be room for overlap. Hence, what I am really seeking here is a way of characterizing that area of overlap, of identifying the method of feminist philosophy that is acceptable from both perspectives.

One aspect I can perceive of shared approach is the important fact that both are committed to a strong and general scepticism about authoritative pronouncements of the truth. Both disciplines train initiates not to accept statements of fact without question. It is not really such a surprise that some philosophers are pursuing radical feminist alternatives to the standard problems of philosophy. Philosophy has always tolerated, and perhaps from time to time has even encouraged, radical rethinking of its underlying assumptions. It is not unreasonable for feminists to align themselves with this time-honoured philosophic tradition.

Moreover, philosophers have never actually agreed on any single method. While individual philosophers and schools have identified particular methods as paradigmatic, other philosophers have always challenged such restrictions and introduced different approaches as legitimate. There is no single 'authorized method,' wholly original and unique to the discipline, that does not have counterparts and inspiration in other disciplines. In feminism, also, there is a great diversity of opinion on the best approach. In fact, both philosophy and feminism have always involved rather an eclectic variety of methods. Thus, there is no single, accepted method by which philosophers can reject feminist methodology out of hand.

Perhaps what is more important, it would be a violation of feminist principles to reject philosophic methods. Feminism relies on whatever morally and epistemologically acceptable methods are available that can contribute to its overall ends, and surely philosophy can help in that enterprise. Those feminists who have expressed scepticism over 'rational methods' of philosophy are recording a well-deserved distrust of methods and ideas that have been used to limit women's freedom and imagination. But, as philosophers never tire of pointing out, feminists can only express their case by use of such rational methods themselves, and in most cases, their distrust of 'rationality' can be attributed in part to their unexamined – and mistaken – assumptions about what rationality involves. What is seen by some feminists as a methodological barrier is actually the result of abuses of a rational approach by mysogynistic practitioners.

One of the dangers that feminists have pointed to within traditional methodologies is that of accepting dichotomies. Dichotomous thinking forces ideas, persons, roles, and disciplines into rigid polarities. It reduces richness and complexity in the interest of logical neatness, and, in doing so, it distorts truth. Moreover, the creation and use of dichotomies seem to be important elements in the very structure of patriarchy: the institution of patriarchy involves power relations that rest on the assumption of fundamental and unbridgeable differences between the sexes reflected in multiple forms of polarity. Hence I believe that it is important for feminists to resist the temptation to pursue dichotomies from their own perspective; i.e., we should take care not to define philosophical methodology as inherently opposed to feminist thought or to imagine the differences in approach to involve a schism that cannot be crossed.

I cannot, therefore, conclude that feminist and philosophical methodologies are incompatible. They are, however, made compatible only with significant effort from each end. Many standard approaches and assumptions in philosophy are not acceptable from a feminist point of view; therefore, not all of philosophy can be seen as compatible with feminism. Philosophers, from their perspective, must make some noticeable effort to understand the feminist enterprise rather than dismissing it as not meeting the usual professional norms. They must recognize that feminists have much ground to cover in rethinking the philosophical activity of the past 2,500 years, and they should be prepared to tolerate a bit of sketchiness and hand-waving as feminists explore the ways in which ethics, epistemology, and metaphysics may have to be revised when we change their underlying political assumptions. Perhaps the greatest challenge comes from the need to pay attention to the genuine criticisms of their discipline that feminists have to offer. Philosophers should consider whether the particular approaches feminists take to philosophical questions can in fact serve philosophical ends. I still believe that feminism can enrich philosophy and it behooves philosophers to learn to be open to feminist style and commitments.[17]

For our part as feminists, in order to help philosophers make such modifications in their usual methods of evaluation, we should continue to try to put our thoughts into a language they can understand and relate our analysis to familiar issues when possible. In doing so, though, I believe we must remain conscious of the risks involved. It is important to be able to rely on one another for the support necessary when philosophers fail to notice the significant differences involved in adopting a feminist perspective. We should never forget that philosophical gatherings and journals are still predominantly hostile environments for feminists, and we ought not to venture far into such terrain without adequate support from one another.

POSTSCRIPT. I noticed as I concluded this paper that I experienced a familiar sense of unease about the ideas seeming tentative and lacking in surprise and drama. Writing this paper was a valuable cathartic exercise for me, for I now realize that this déjà vu feeling of dissatisfaction is in fact yet another symptom of my ambivalence about appropriate standards. Under my philosopher's hat, the ideal is to come up with the decisive conclusion, settling the question once and for all; I feel that I should now be prepared to defend my view against all comers. On that criterion, this paper, like the earlier one so disliked by the referees, is flawed.

But as a feminist paper, the agenda is different. Under my feminist hat, I see my task to be an exploration of my views and feelings on this broadly abstract and deeply personal question. Having done that, I am quite prepared to pass the issue on to others who will share the responsibility of following these ideas through, taking it in directions I cannot clearly foresee. From that perspective, it is acceptable to be reflective about a matter that troubles me without presuming to have entirely settled it. Clearly, this dilemma is a piece of a greater puzzle, and it is open to modification in light of the experience and insight of others who approach it constructively. Or, in other words, this is a paper I could only have read at a conference for feminist philosophers.

NOTES

This paper was originally written for the meeting of the Canadian Society for Women in Philosophy, held in Vancouver, BC, in October 1985. I am very grateful for the encouragement and helpful feedback received there, and for thoughtful suggestions offered by Ann Garry.
1 Jay Rosenberg, *The Practice of Philosophy*, 2nd ed. (Englewood Cliffs, NJ: Prentice-Hall, 1984), p. 6

2 Catherine MacKinnon, 'Feminism, Marxism, Method, and the State,' *Feminist Theory*, ed. N. Keohane, M. Rosaldo, and B. Gelpi (Brighton: The Harvester Press, 1982), p. 5

3 The paper, called 'From Feminism to a New Conception of Ethics,' was published in a collection of selected papers from the proceedings of that CRIAW meeting, called *Knowledge Reconsidered: A Feminist Overview* (Vancouver: CRIAW, 1984). An abridged version, called 'Ethics: Towards a Feminist Approach,' was published in *Canadian Women's Studies* 6, no. 2 (Spring 1985). Since then, I have developed these ideas further and an extension appears as 'A Feminist Approach to Ethics,' *The Dalhousie Review*, Winter 1984–5.

4 Marilyn Frye, *The Politics of Reality: Essays in Feminist Theory* (Trumansburg: The Crossing Press, 1983); Alison M. Jagger, *Feminist Politics and Human Nature* (Totowa, NJ: Rowman & Allenheld, 1983); Sandra Harding and Merrill Hintikka, eds., *Discovering Reality: Feminist Perspectives on Epistemology, Metaphysics, Methodology, and Philosophy of Science* (Boston: D. Reidel Publishing Co., 1983)

5 Genevieve Lloyd, *The Man of Reason: 'Male' and 'Female' in Western Culture* (Minneapolis: University of Minnesota Press, 1984), p. 108

6 See, for instance, articles in Sandra Harding and Merrill Hintikka, eds., *Discovering Reality* and in Lorenne M.G. Clark and Lynda Lange, eds., *The Sexism of Social and Political Theory* (Toronto: University of Toronto Press, 1979).

7 'Introduction: Some Approaches to Philosophy,' *The Owl of Minerva*, ed. Charles J. Bontempo and S. Jack Odell (New York: McGraw-Hill Paperbacks, 1975), p. 27

8 Virginia Woolf, *A Room of One's Own*

9 Some of this evidence is provided by Carol Gilligan in *In a Different Voice: Psychological Theories and Women's Development* (Cambridge, Mass: Harvard University Press, 1982). To see how it applies specifically to the philosophic context see Annette Baier's 'What Do Women Want in a Moral Theory?' *Nous* XIX, no. 1 (March 1985) and Virginia Held's *Rights and Goods* (New York: The Free Press, 1984).

10 Again, see Gilligan, *In a Different Voice*.

11 Catherine MacKinnon, 'Feminism, Marxism, Method, and the State: Toward Feminist Jurisprudence,' *Signs* 8, no. 4 (1983): 636

12 Toni Laidlaw and Gisele Thibault, 'Women and Schooling: The Importance of a Multi-disciplinary Approach,' unpublished paper presented to the Canadian Society for Studies in Education at the Learned Societies Meetings, Vancouver, 1983

13 Janice Moulton, in *Discovering Reality*

14 Sheila Tobias, ed., *Issues in Feminism: A First Course in Women's Studies* (Boston: Houghton Mifflin, 1980), p. 15
15 Marilyn Webb, 'Feminist Studies: Frill or Necessity?' *And Jill Came Tumbling After* (New York: Dell Publishing, 1974), p. 412
16 Gisele Thibault, 'The Dissenting Academy: A History of the Barriers to Feminist Scholarship,' PH D dissertation, Dalhousie University, 1985, pp. 29–139
17 I believe that a feminist approach does result in different analyses of philosophical questions. Such a contention is best evaluated by reviewing the evidence. Most essays in this volume would serve to provide such evidence. My own work arguing concretely for the significance of the different perspective feminism offers is developed in two recent papers: 'Feminism and Theoretical Perspectives on Peace,' *Atlantis* 12, 1 (Summer 1986) and 'Feminist Ethics and In Vitro Fertilization,' *Canadian Journal of Philosophy* 12, no. 3 (September 1987).

Feminism, Objectivity,
and Legal Truth

MARSHA P. HANEN

Various forms of the feminist critique of science and its objectivity are familiar to all of us. One aspect of this critique is the picture of scientific objectivity as expressing an essentially male approach to knowledge and the world. Thus, Ruth Bleier tells us that: 'Science is the male intellect: the active, knowing subject; its relationship to nature – the passive object of knowledge – is one of manipulation, control, and domination; it is the relationship of man to woman, of culture to nature.'[1] And Catharine MacKinnon speaks of objectivity, 'the ostensibly non-involved stance' as the male epistemological stance, which 'does not comprehend its own perspectivity.'[2] The idea is that what has traditionally been seen as objective, neutral, and unbiased is itself caught up in a particular perspective on the world – a perspective that is specifically male and that tends to exclude or devalue the experiences and the points of view of women. Clearly there is much that is being presupposed in these critiques about the nature and significance of sexual differences, but that is not the topic of this paper. The important point for the moment is just that standard claims to objectivity are being challenged by feminist writers as embodying a bias that has long gone virtually unnoticed.

The other aspect of the critique that is relevant for my purposes is the suggestion that part of the problem about objectivity and thus about how women have traditionally been perceived and described may well have to do with the dualistic categories into which we have tried to place all knowledge. The claim here is that science rests on and is defined by the assumption of a polarity between man and woman that structures our views of and investigations into what constitutes men's and women's natures. Even more generally, these polarities underlie all of our views about what constitutes knowledge and, indeed, structure our investigations of the nature of human thought, behaviour, and organization. The consistency with which our culture accepts these dualisms as constituting not only science but art, philosophy, literature, and indeed our customs and institutions, is standardly taken to reflect the fact that these dualisms really exist in the world, and specifically in the natures of men and women – a kind of realism with respect to the male/female polarity. But some writers have argued that the truth of the matter is the exact converse: that these dualisms are more properly seen, not as existing in nature, but as ways of describing, ordering, categorizing, and analysing our perceptions and experience. Though it is not entirely clear why this bifurcation occurred, the division of virtually all of our knowledge into two contradictory domains required or at least supported the development of a dualistic mode of thought. Thus the oppositions between male and female, culture and nature, subject and object, public and private can be seen as expressing and reinforcing the basic assumption of duality, but as themselves products of the human intellectual need to order and classify experience rather than as features of the world itself. As Bleier says: 'We tend to mistake our cognitive techniques to comprehend the universe for the universe itself. They are cultural constructions that, like all other such constructions, are intimately related to our experiences and perceptions within the particular social, economic, and political context of our lives. Dualisms that could be posed as hypotheses to be investigated were established as though self-evident truths, inherent to the human phenomena being examined.'[3]

Feminist argument usually goes on to claim that to treat these dualisms as representing contradictory and mutually exclusive spheres is to propound false dichotomies, not because these ways of classifying fail to order our perceptions (for they do this), but because they order them in a way that leaves out or underrepresents or undervalues women's experience. Such dualisms really represent continua whose extremes are not separable but interact with one another to achieve some sort of balance; furthermore, they are, to a greater or lesser extent, culturally variant.

Thus, one version of the critique sees the traditional understanding of objectivity as itself not objective, but as capable of being improved by a filling in of the gaps – an inclusion of women's experience in scientific and other research that will ultimately make that research and the knowledge that results from it more objective. Another version of the critique is more radical, however. It argues that the standard view of objectivity and, for that matter, of rationality is a male construction that fails to recognize its own dependence on a point of view. Furthermore, being pessimistic about the possibility of freeing these notions from the male perspective, it argues for the abandonment by feminist scholars of objectivity and rationality, and the construction of knowledge without the dualisms that attribute, even if only implicitly, a lesser value to the pole associated with the female. A mode of thinking more congenial to women would stress the realities of interconnectedness and contextuality, would not treat male experience as the norm for both sexes, and would be less bound by the need to be in control, to dominate.[4]

I do not intend, in this paper, to argue explicitly for the accuracy of any of these perceptions. Each of them has received detailed treatment by many feminist writers, and will no doubt receive more. Interestingly, feminist critique is by no means limited to science. Catherine MacKinnon[5] views it as extending to epistemology generally, and one can certainly argue that the traditional bifurcation between reason and emotion, with knowledge made dependent upon reason alone, has led to a very incomplete account of knowing. Similarly in ethics, as Annette Baier has pointed out,[6] a male perspective has led to an emphasis on rather sterile decision-theoretic exercises as opposed to the emphasis on trust and relationship one might wish to have included, and indeed does find if one tries to understand the perspective present in the work of many women in moral philosophy.

One question that leaps to mind is whether and to what extent this kind of critique of objectivity is limited to the feminist perspective. No doubt the answer to this question depends upon the particular aspects of the critique being emphasized, but if there were strong parallels between even some of its aspects and developments in other areas of the philosophical literature, this fact would itself be illuminating in that it would suggest directions for exploring possibilities for a broader view of objectivity. Such a view might bring together a feminist perspective and some other current perspectives that seem more promising than the old (for lack of a better term) foundationalist models. The advantage, of course, would be an ultimate integration of these more promising perspectives with a feminist approach, which would, I suggest, strengthen both.

Clearly, such integration is a long-term project, but one way to begin would be to explore some of the relevant similarities and dissimilarities. What I want to do in this paper, then, is to examine some of the issues and arguments concerning objectivity that have arisen in another area, independently of feminist approaches, and then to consider whether there might be any common ground between those accounts of objectivity and a feminist critique, assuming that the rather loose characterization of the latter that I have given will do for these purposes. The area from which I draw my lessons is legal theory – specifically, recent attempts to construct a theory or theories that will explain settled law (in general or in a specific area such as contract law) and will predict how future cases will or ought to be settled.

Two models for achieving legal coherence – roughly distinguishable as the scientific and the literary – have been much discussed in recent years. The scientific picture is perhaps most easily characterized as the one arising from Dworkin's natural model of reflective equilibrium wherein theories of justice 'describe an objective moral reality; they are not, that is, created by men or societies but are rather discovered by them, as they discover laws of physics.'[7] But discovering principles in the law, as opposed to creating them, is not meant by Dworkin in the scientific sense. Legal principles do not mirror some independent reality in the way that scientific laws do, he might say, for whereas scientific laws are descriptive, legal ones are fundamentally prescriptive. Legal reasoning, instead, can be captured in another – the constructive – model. This second model, he says, 'treats intuitions of justice not as clues to the existence of independent principles, but rather as stipulated features of a general theory to be constructed, as if a sculptor set himself to carve the animal that best fits a pile of bones he happened to find together. This 'constructive' model does not assume, as the natural model does, that principles of justice have some fixed, objective existence, so that descriptions of these principles must be true or false in some standard way. It does not assume that the animal it matches to the bones actually exists.'[8] I think that the picture of science as fitting the natural model in the way that Dworkin characterizes it is a false one. The problem is that this conception of science requires that we believe our observations put us in touch with some transcendent reality, and this is surely questionable. But even if we think of science as ultimately directed towards discovering the truth, it obviously does not follow that we have attained that truth at any particular stage, or that there is a clear and unassailable correspondence between our observations and certain features of an external reality, as Dworkin apparently believes.

Indeed, it seems patent that Dworkin accepts some fairly naive version of scientific realism. He refers to an 'astronomer who has clear observational data that he is as yet unable to reconcile in any coherent account, for example, of the origin of the solar system. He continues to accept and employ his observational data, placing his faith in the idea that some reconciling explanation does exist though it has not been, and for all he knows may never be, discovered by men.'9 That both the sculptor and the astronomer are male is surely not without significance, even if unintended, for each fits a rather sharply defined and inflexible pattern. By contrast, I want to claim that the distinction that Dworkin draws between the natural and constructive models is too sharp, and that some composite of the two would better fit both scientific and legal theorizing.10 Put another way, to the extent that the natural model fits scientific theorizing, it equally well fits the judicial enterprise; and to the extent that the constructive model fits the latter, it equally well fits science. Dworkin's picture of the natural model presupposes existence assumptions that are much too strong for science as we know it; and the adjustment between theory and intuition can come out either way, for science as much as for law.

The difficulty, for Dworkin, with the claim that legal reasoning fits the constructive model revolves around his wanting to say both that there is no external reality in virtue of which legal propositions are correct *and* that there is a single right answer in every (or almost every) legal case. He wants to argue against the thesis that if a proposition is true, it must be demonstrable as true, presumably on the basis of the facts available. To do this, he introduces what I have referred to above as the literary model, using the example of the interpretive game played by a group of Dickens scholars in 'No Right Answer?'11 That game, it will be remembered, can be played with a number of different sets of ground rules, some of which will have the result that certain propositions about David Copperfield, the person, will be neither assertable as true nor deniable as false. The version of the game that is most like the actual practice of literary criticism is one where 'a further proposition about David [beyond what is in the novel] is assertable as true (or deniable as false) if that further proposition provides a better (or worse) fit than its negation with propositions already established, because it explains in a more satisfactory way why David was what he was, or said what he said, or did what he did, according to those already established propositions.'12

More recently, Dworkin has developed this model further,13 arguing that 'legal practice is an exercise in interpretation'14 that can be il-luminatingly compared with literary interpretation. Propositions of law are interpretations of legal history that combine elements of both description and evaluation without being limited to either one. He puts forward the 'aesthetic hypothesis' as follows: 'an interpretation of a piece of literature attempts to show which way of reading (or speaking or directing or acting) the text reveals it as the best work of art.'[15] Such a judgment relies on beliefs about art of both a theoretical and normative sort, and 'academic theories of interpretation are no longer seen as ... analyses of the very idea of interpretation ... Interpretation becomes a concept of which different theories are competing conceptions.'[16] This distinction between the concept of interpretation and various conceptions of it is meant to highlight the difference between an appeal to the meaning of 'interpretation' and an appeal to particular *views* of interpretation – of what will count as an interpretation. A theory of interpretation, Dworkin thus argues, differs primarily in level of abstraction from an interpretation of a particular work of art, and both depend upon normative theories of art.

In order to draw the analogy between literary interpretation and legal analysis, Dworkin imagines a group of novelists each writing one chapter of a novel, the order of play being determined by lot. Each writer after the first must interpret what has gone before in order to continue it and is therefore constrained in certain ways that the first novelist is not. The suggestion is that deciding hard cases at law is a similar sort of chain enterprise: the interpretation must both fit the practice and show its value, but in this case in political rather than artistic terms. There is some flexibility of interpretation, and some previously decided cases may be argued to have been mistakes; but Dworkin insists on the distinction between interpretation and 'fresh, clean-slate decision about what the law ought to be.'[17] Where no unique interpretation emerges, substantive political theory (or artistic theory, in the literary case) will be decisive. Thus conservative or liberal or radical interpretations of crucial and difficult parts of law may be expected to differ, and the interpretive question concerns which conception is the best in the context of the whole of law.

The problem with all of this, of course, is that a certain scepticism about whether there is always (or even often) a 'best conception' in the sense in which Dworkin intends it is not only plausible but quite appealing. Such scepticism ranges all the way from a position only slightly less insistent than Dworkin on a single best interpretation all the way to the complete anarchy of 'anything goes.' Radical pluralism, for example, holds that there is no basis for preferring one interpretation over others and that we must, therefore, accept all views as on an equal footing from the standpoint of rationality or objectivity. Clearly, such a view is in direct opposition to Dworkin's interpretive monism.

Perhaps the most interesting critique of that monism is provided by Stanley Fish.[18] Essentially, Fish wants to 'argue that Dworkin repeatedly falls away from his own best insights into a version of the fallacies [of pure objectivity and pure subjectivity] he so forcefully challenges.'[19] Fish insists that, in the chain novel-writing exercise, all participants are equally constrained, and so the distinction between the first author and later ones will not hold up. Dworkin's positing of almost complete freedom for the first novelist and virtually none for later ones commits him to both 'the Scylla of legal realism ("making it up wholesale") and the Charybdis of strict constructionism ("finding the law just 'there'").'[20] According to Fish, Dworkin

repeatedly makes two related and mutually reinforcing assumptions: he assumes that history in the form of a chain of decisions has, at some level, the status of a brute fact; and he assumes that wayward or arbitrary behavior in relation to that fact is an institutional possibility. Together these two assumptions give him his project, the project of explaining how a free and potentially irresponsible agent is held in check by the self-executing constraints of an independent text. Of course by conceiving his project in this way – that is, by reifying the mind in its freedom and the text in its independence – he commits himself to the very alternatives of legal realism on the one hand and positivism on the other.[21]

The claim, thus, is that Dworkin's dichotomies are artificial and distort the nature of interpretation.

Dworkin is, of course, well aware that interpretation is not simply a matter of finding similarities lying about 'on the surface' as it were. As Fish argues,[22] similarities are not properties of texts or objects, but rather are conferred by relational arguments which, in pointing out that A is similar to B, provide a partial characterization of both A and B. To see a legal case as similar in relevant respects to a chain of earlier ones is usually to see that chain in a new way. Similarly, to explain a work of art or literature is to see it in a new way, or to see features of it that had previously gone unnoticed. Interpretation thus takes on a constantly changing aspect, with no one view being seen as correct, particularly over time. Indeed, it is not too extreme on this view to say that interpretation constructs the text. But Dworkin does not seem to be comfortable giving free reign to this relativism, with the result that there is a tension in his work. He wants to say both that creation is free while interpretation is constrained and that 'the artist can create nothing without interpreting as he creates,'[23] but if we take both views seriously, it is not clear that he is left with any coherent theory of interpretation.

What, then, if anything, does this tell us about Dworkin's view of uniquely correct answers and truth in law and literature? Dworkin particularly in 'No Right Answer?'[24] espouses a view of truth that fits with what Dummett and others have described as a realist position. A statement such as 'Jones was brave,' spoken of someone now dead who never encountered danger in his life, might be said to be true only if there is something in virtue of which it is true. Dummett claims that both the realist and anti-realist could accept the following principle: 'that a statement cannot be true unless it is in principle capable of being known to be true.'[25] Then the fundamental difference between realist and anti-realist comes to this: that 'the anti-realist interprets "capable of being known" to mean "capable of being known *by us*", whereas the realist interprets it to mean "capable of being known by some hypothetical being whose intellectual capacities and powers of observation may exceed our own".'[26] Now, such a hypothetical being could very well be Dworkin's Hercules, for Dworkin wishes to count as true propositions of law that could not be determined to be true by any actual judge or lawyer and about which, in fact, there might be considerable controversy among equally intelligent and sincere judges.

This is not the place to engage in a detailed discussion of realism, but, of course, it is well known that the realist position has not gone unchallenged, in a number of areas. Thus van Fraassen's 'constructive' empiricism takes the view that 'scientific activity is one of construction rather than discovery: construction of models that must be adequate to the phenomena, and not discovery of truth concerning the unobservable.'[27] And Nelson Goodman argues in his two most recent books (*Ways of Worldmaking* and *Of Mind and Other Matters*) for a view he calls 'irrealism,' which is even more radical than the original anti-realism of Dummett or van Fraassen. He says, 'I am convinced that there is no one correct way of describing or picturing or perceiving "*the world*", but rather that there are many equally right but conflicting ways – and thus, in effect, many actual worlds. We must, then, inquire into the standards, compatible with such multiplicity, of rightness of rendering of all sorts, in all media, in symbol systems of every variety.'[28] And again, he tells us that there is no one true description of the world compatible with all true descriptions – no independent world to match a version against. 'Any notion of a reality consisting of objects and events and kinds established independently of discourse and unaffected by how they are described or otherwise presented must give way to the recognition that these, too, are parts of the story.'[29] Thus reality depends upon discourse and other means of symbolization, the correctness of which derives not from correspondence with the 'external world,' but from appropriate categorization and related things.

The existence of these various positions suggests, then, that we can identify a variety of stances about truth or correctness in interpretation ranging from the absolutism of Dworkin's 'one right answer' thesis to a complete relativism to the point of arbitrariness – a sort of 'anything goes' attitude that denies the possibility of any selection criteria that are anything but purely subjective. Such a view is familiar to us in philosophy of science from the work of Paul Feyerabend and in literature from that of the radical literary critics; and many people writing in this vein cite Kuhn and Rorty, among others. In law, too, there has been much recent discussion of various respects in which law is to be seen as pure ideology rather than as rational and principle-governed. Thus law is sometimes seen as a tool of a particular social class, or of commercial or political interests, rather than as a working out of underlying principles that express the moral fabric of society. An intermediate possibility that attempts to avoid both absolutism and arbitrariness is the alternative that there are many right or acceptable interpretations, some of which may even be incompatible with one another, though this does not imply that we cannot identify some interpretations as wrong. Perhaps the simplest example of such a state of affairs occurs in the theatre, where many different and even incompatible versions of *Hamlet* or *Hedda Gabler* may strike us as interesting, illuminating, and correct while yet others will be totally unacceptable.

It is thus clear that we have an ample supply of philosophical voices to argue that there is no such thing as a neutral description of the world and even that the existence of conflicting or irreconcilable true descriptions points to the existence of many worlds, each with an internally consistent but incomplete description. The difficulty is that if there is no independent world against which to match a description, it is hard to know what constitutes truth and what are the tests for it. If we are not satisfied with complete relativism in this matter, it is incumbent on us to try to explain what makes for correctness in science, literature, or law, and one context for exploring this, given the absence of an external touchstone for accuracy, has been sought in a focus on hermeneutic concerns that is based on a belief, at least, in shared canons of correctness, understanding, or morality. This focus is what is behind the 'law as interpretation' approach so central to Dworkin's attempt to establish his 'uniquely correct answer' thesis in terms other than the standard scientific ones.

There is a certain delicious irony about this, for, a little over a hundred years ago, Christopher Columbus Langdell, invariably described as the driving force behind the view that law is actually a science not unlike chemistry (the library was the laboratory, and the data were the reported cases), saw law also as a matter of interpretation. According to Sanford Levinson, 'For Langdell law was essentially a literary enterprise, a science of extracting meaning from words that would enable one to believe in law as a process of submission to the commands of authoritative texts (the rule of law) rather than as the creation of willful intepreters (with submission concomitantly producing the rule of men).'[30] The legitimacy of law is thus linked to the interpretation of texts, whether of cases, statutes, or a constitution; but the history of theorizing in the law provides an instructive example of the different forms such interpretation can take over time. One place where this change in interpretation can be seen most clearly is in theorizing about the law of contract.

The idea of law as science, put forward by Langdell about 1870, was developed for contract by Holmes and Williston. There are a number of ways of viewing contract theory of that period, but the usual one is to take as fundamental the idea that the imposition of contractual liability should be avoided where possible, and confined within the narrowest possible limits where such avoidance is not possible. Within those limits, liability was to be absolute, so that, in cases where a promisor does not fulfil his or her legally binding promise, he or she will be required to pay damages to the promisee. Such monetary damages were, however, to be strictly compensatory, never punitive; and the motivation of the promise breaker was to be legally irrelevant. Intent, whether evil or otherwise, was to make no difference. Indeed, the theory even went so far as to imply that it was perfectly acceptable to break one's contracts, the only consequence being that one would have to pay damages. No particular opprobrium was attached to the breaking of contracts beyond this requirement of compensation.

All of the necessary features of contract – offer, acceptance, consideration – were made formal and external; without the formalities, there was no contract and no liability. Initially, the idea had been that, for a contract to be binding, there had to be a 'meeting of the minds,' but this soon came to be thought too 'subjective.' Holmes and his successors substituted an 'objective' approach, believing that the natural process of development in the law moved from a situation in which rules of law are based on judgments of moral fault or guilt towards one in which all that matters is external manifestations. Moral guilt and the state of mind of the contract breaker become irrelevant: the question becomes simply whether expectations have been frustrated and, if so, compensation is owed. This move to 'objectivism' in law is, of course, not surprising, and it is interesting to note that it coincides with the rise of a positivistic conception of science, with behaviourism in psychology, and with the growth of large corporations requiring that behaviour be externalized and criteria for accountability developed. This coincidence needs to be explored further, but this is a topic for another time. Questions which began as questions of *fact* – what was 'intended,' 'meant,' 'believed,' or what was the 'actual state of the parties' minds' – came to be resolved in terms of what would be taken as permissible or impermissible *conduct*, and thus became questions of *law*. This had the general effect of placing these important matters in the hands of the judge rather than the trier-of-fact, of narrowing the range of excuses that could relieve a party of contractual responsibility, and thus of moving the system more in the direction of absolute liability. Thus, Williston wrote, around 1920: 'Under the guise of conclusive presumptions of mental assent from external acts, the law has been so built up that it can be expressed accurately only by saying that the elements requisite for the formation of a contract are exclusively external ... Thus ... it is clear that the great majority of courts have discarded the impractical and unrealistic subjective standard (using the cliché "meeting of the minds") which seemed so appropriate and fitting a century or more ago in favor of an objective approach based on the *external* manifestation of mutual assent.'[31] And Learned Hand, who had been a student of Williston's, said in 1911: 'A contract has, strictly speaking, nothing to do with the personal, or individual, intent of the parties. A contract is an obligation attached by the mere force of law to certain acts of the parties, usually words, which ordinarily accompany and represent a known intent.'[32]

This neat, tidy theory, needless to say, never bore any very close relation to the actual goings-on in the courts, and the subsequent history of contract law led away from the idea of a scientific system towards wider and wider grounds for liability, just so long as a reasonable case could be made for the existence of a good-faith agreement. The tight, rule-governed classical theory failed in its own terms, much as positivism failed as a theory of science; and so in law as in science, it is not surprising to find moves towards the incorporation of new perspectives earlier thought insufficiently 'objective' to count as genuine theory. But whether the current stance is so much more enlightened, and possessed of so much more verisimilitude than our earlier ones, or whether these swings are merely cyclical, with little relation to ultimate truth and meaning, is debatable. Here is Grant Gilmore on this point:

We have become used to the idea that, in literature and the arts, there are alternating rhythms of classicism and romanticism. During classical periods, which are, typically, of brief duration, everything is neat, tidy and logical; theorists and critics reign supreme; formal rules of structure and composition are stated to the general acclaim. During classical periods, which are, among other things, extremely dull, it seems that nothing interesting is ever going to happen again. But the classical aesthetic, once it has been formu- lated, regularly breaks down in a protracted romantic agony. The romantics spurn the exquisitely stated rules of the preceding period; they experi- ment, they improvise; they deny the existence of any rules; they churn around in an ecstasy of self-expression. At the height of a romantic period, everything is confused, sprawling, formless and chaotic – as well as, frequent- ly, extremely interesting. Then, the romantic energy having spent itself, there is a new classical reformulation – and so the rhythms continue.[33]

Gilmore thinks that such alternating rhythms may characterize legal theory as well. What this tells us about the correctness or incorrectness of particular views is unclear, but at least I think it suggests that we need to be more sensitive about the historical and cultural context in which theories are put forward than we sometimes are. We might then be better able to evaluate the swing away from narrow conceptions of rationality without supposing that the only alternative is a mindless romanticism: we may even be able to find ways of transcending the traditional oppositions.

What is interesting about the currently popular analogy between law and literature is the extent to which these dualisms are not tran- scended, and the old tensions between subjectivity and objectivity simply re-emerge. We might have hoped that the comparison with literature would be salutary because the literary context always presumes a point of view; but this does not seem to be carried over in the analogies. Dworkin, for example, wants to argue that there is a correct or 'best' interpretation of any legal or literary text even if there is no theory-independent fact of the matter against which to check our interpretations. Interpretive claims in law and literature are more like scientific judgments in that they are parts of very complex systems of belief with many levels and 'internal tensions, checks and balances'[34] than they are like simple judgments of taste. He wants to argue, further, that interpretive judgments can be objective without our being able to claim that everyone agrees to them, and that objectivity here has no further meaning than that we believe our judgments to be correct and are prepared to offer arguments for them. The standard understanding of objectivity is thus, in this context, a red herring, for the idea that a body of knowledge cannot be objective unless it can be shown to correspond with some external reality, and a theory cannot be objective unless it would 'wring assent from a stone,'[35] sets standards that cannot be met by any body of knowledge or theory. What this suggests at least is that the traditional view of objectivity is not the only possible one; and if this is so, then it may be that the less narrow understanding that seems to emerge would also fit a feminist conception of knowledge and interpretation.

One of the things that is troubling about Dworkin's insistence on the 'single right answer' thesis is that, given that we cannot know what that answer is, and equally competent lawyers may disagree about what it is, it is hard to see what practical difference there is between this thesis and the 'no right answer' thesis. No doubt there is something reassuring about there being a right answer and it may be that if the judge believes there is, she is more likely to work hard to find it than she would be if she believed she had discretion in the matter. The right answer for Dworkin is the one that best accords with institutional history and political morality, which is to say that the answer is meant to flow from our existing conceptions of what settled law is and of the political morality underlying it. But even if we grant the 'right answer' thesis, the question that leaps to mind is whether those existing conceptions of settled law and political morality are as they should be. To the extent that they are not, Dworkin's right answer may well be a morally incorrect one. The emphasis on history, or entrenchment in the legal system, is thus troubling, not least because the law has not historically always treated women and minorities the way we would wish. Dworkin, of course, thinks that he can give arguments within the legal system for the morally correct outcomes, but whether he is right about this is at least controversial.

Certainly some feminist writers believe not. Catharine MacKinnon, for example, argues that both the liberal and marxist approaches to law embody ideologies that have enforced women's powerlessness and subjugation. She claims that both are based on objectivist epistemologies that rationalize male power by presuming that equality between the sexes is really the basic ideology underlying social structures and that deviations from this ideal are not central. The truth is that our society is anti-feminist both in fact and in ideology, according to MacKinnon, and this is revealed particularly clearly if we look carefully at legal norms and structures:

If objectivity is the epistemological stance of which women's sexual objectification is the social process, its imposition the paradigm of power in the
male form, then the state will appear most relentless in imposing the male
point of view when it comes closest to achieving its highest formal criterion of
distanced aperspectivity. When it is most ruthlessly neutral, it will be most
male; when it is most sex blind, it will be most blind to the sex of the standard
being applied. When it most closely conforms to precedent, to 'facts,' to
legislative intent, it will most closely enforce socially male norms and most
thoroughly preclude questioning their content as having a point of view at
all ... Once masculinity appears as a specific position, not just as the way things
are, its judgments will be revealed in process and procedure, as well as
adjudication and legislation.[36]

This, I take it, is part of the feminist claim with respect to what are seen as objectively correct answers in both law and science, even if it is stated more contentiously than need be. The framework within which a certain answer is correct may itself be too narrow to take account of different and emerging perspectives. Among the valuable lessons we have learned from the last fifteen or so years of feminist scholarship is that frameworks vary and need to be made explicit and that not all are equally acceptable; furthermore, there may be no way of incorporating all of knowledge into a single consistent framework – there may be no single truth to be discovered as people once thought of acquiring knowledge as uncovering what is in God's mind. It is not, though, simply a matter of moving from some sort of monism to an epistemo-logical pluralism or relativism; rather, I think it is important to try to recognize the extent to which a given account is conditioned by perspectives – historical and social context, class, gender, age, even individual psychology. Feminist attempts to break down, or at least to question, traditional ways of categorizing have been an important part of this movement. But the material and the structures have been extremely resistant.

Consider an example central to the lives of most academic feminists. Universities are structured according to academic disciplines that are viewed by most academics as carving both substantive and methodological knowledge 'along the joints.' Credentials for teaching and research are issued by those steeped in this way of categorizing. Virtually everything works against crossing the boundaries or understanding anyone on the other side. Even within traditional disciplines there is little understanding between persons trained in different approaches: think how long it has taken for there to begin to be any understanding between philosophers working in the (for lack of a better term) 'continental' tradition and those working in the analytic one. It is easy to despair of ever bridging any gaps when knowledge is seen as a commodity to be owned exclusively by those with the proper pedigreed title. All of this has much to do with control and power, and the whole system preys on our understandable insecurities about venturing outside our own narrow areas of expertise. Academic imperialism with all of its territoriality, protectionism, and conflict strikes me as a natural, if not inevitable, outgrowth of the sort of realism writ large that characterizes the traditional picture of our categorizations as mirroring nature.

Academic feminism has probably recognized these pitfalls better than most other outlooks; but they are hard to avoid when our ways of seeing are so much determined by a disciplinary perspective. We are neither very good at recognizing the limitations, nor, when we do recognize them, at integrating different perspectives, partly because we are usually too locked into our own approach even to understand different ones very well. Much feminist theorizing speaks of the desirability of such integration, often basing its recommendations on a recognition that the standard classifications have imposed a way of seeing human nature that has been a way of not seeing women. Interestingly, the move away from the view that traditional categories necessarily describe the world as it really is seems also to have become part of a relatively mainstream intellectual outlook in the last few years, espoused by a fair number of male as well as female philosophers, not to mention lawyers, literary critics, and others. It is important not to lose sight of the tremendous variability within any culture – it is hard sometimes to know even what 'same culture' could mean when we look at the vast individual differences – but it is equally important not to lose sight of the similarities. In some sense, we do share an intellectual context, not all of which is wrongheaded, and one might even venture to speculate that the turn away from a narrow understanding of objectivity may be part of the temper of the times. This does not mean, of course, that the new understandings that emerge will, in a very widespread way, be explicitly feminist. Procedural justice does not necessarily yield substantive justice, and neither does a correct method-ological approach necessarily yield correct results, even if these are indispensable means to the ends we desire. Merely to break down rigid and unproductive systems of classification will not, by itself, lead to the more humane and co-operative forms of knowledge, which is ulti-mately what we need, rather than just to new or altered frameworks. But the questioning of the categorizations, and the serious consideration (and even trying) of some alternatives, probably represent a necessary first step; and that work, notwithstanding all that *has* been done, is still, I suggest, at a fairly early stage.

NOTES

1 Ruth Bleier, *Science and Gender* (New York: Pergamon Press, 1984), p. 196
2 Catharine MacKinnon, 'Feminism, Marxism, Method, and the State: An Agenda for Theory,' *Signs* 7 (1982): 538
3 Bleier, *Science and Gender*, p. 197
4 Bleier, *Science and Gender* and Evelyn Fox Keller in her *Reflections on Gender and Science* (New Haven: Yale University Press, 1985) make this point with respect to science. Carol Gilligan makes a similar one with respect to morality in her book *In a Different Voice: Psychological Theory and Women's Development* (Cambridge, Mass.: Harvard University Press, 1982).
5 MacKinnon, 'Feminism, Marxism, Method, and the State'
6 Annette Baier, 'What Do Women Want in a Moral Theory?' *Nous* XIX, no. 1 (1985): 53–63
7 Ronald Dworkin, *Taking Rights Seriously* (Cambridge, Mass.: Harvard University Press, 1977), p. 160
8 Ibid.
9 Ibid., p. 161
10 See my 'Justification as Coherence,' in *Law, Morality and Rights*, ed. M.A. Stewart (Boston: D. Reidel Publishing Company, 1983), pp. 67–92
11 In P.M.S. Hacker and Joseph Raz, eds., *Law, Mortality and Society* (London: Oxford University Press, 1977), pp. 58–84
12 Ibid., p. 75
13 R. Dworkin in 'Law as Interpretation,' *Texas Law Review* 60 (1981–2), pp. 527–50
14 Ibid., p. 527
15 Ibid., p. 531
16 Ibid., p. 534

17 Ibid., p. 544
18 Stanley Fish in 'Working on the Chain Gang,' *Texas Law Review* 60 (1981–2), pp. 551–67
19 Ibid., p. 552
20 Ibid., p. 555
21 Ibid., p. 559
22 Ibid., pp. 558–62
23 Dworkin, 'Law as Interpretation,' p. 540
24 'No Right Answer?' in Hacker and Raz, *Law, Morality and Society*
25 M. Dummett, 'Truth,' in *Truth and Other Enigmas* (Cambridge, Mass.: Harvard University Press, 1978), p. 24
26 Ibid.
27 Bas van Fraassen, *The Scientific Image* (London: Oxford University Press, 1980), p. 5
28 Nelson Goodman, *Of Mind and Other Matters* (Cambridge, Mass.: Harvard University Press, 1984), p. 14
29 Ibid., p. 67
30 Sanford Levinson, 'Law as Literature,' *Texas Law Review* 60 (1981–2), p. 374
31 Grant Gilmore, *The Death of Contract* (Columbus: Ohio State University Press, 1974), p. 43
32 Ibid., p. 123
33 Ibid., p. 102
34 Dworkin, *A Matter of Principle* (Cambridge, Mass.: Harvard University Press, 1985), p. 170
35 Ibid., p. 162
36 MacKinnon, 'Feminism, Marxism, Method, and the State,' p. 658

A Message from Cassandra –
Experience and Knowledge:
Dichotomy and Unity

PETRA VON MORSTEIN

Christa Wolf's *Cassandra* is set at the end of the Trojan war. The surviving Greeks return home with their prey. Cassandra, daughter of Priamos, fallen king of Troy, is among the prey of Agamemnon, king of Mycenae. She, a seer, knows that Agamemnon will be killed by his wife, Clytemnestra, a few hours after his home-coming, and that she too will die by Clytemnestra's hand. The novel consists in Cassandra's inner monologue spoken during the last hours before her death, while she is still outside Agamemnon's castle, sitting on a cart in which she has been brought.

I

For the last twenty years women in philosophy have been developing vital changes in philosophical enquiry and method. Philosophical techniques and ideas, in the analytic and other traditions, were generated almost exclusively from men's perspectives. Further, much of the history of Western philosophy rests on the assumption of a dichotomous relation between concrete experiences on the one hand, and concepts for description and explanation on the other.

Necessarily women cannot assume perspectives that are essentially men's; nor can men assume perspectives which are essentially women's.

The changes that feminist philosophers find necessary presuppose the unity of concrete experiences and descriptive as well as explanatory concepts, the unity of feeling and thought. Those changes integrate experiences determined by women's perspectives.

Women's experiences and feminist viewpoints are new to philosophy. They require thorough revisions of established methods of philosophical enquiry and a search for new methods.

Kant was the first philosopher in the history of Western philosophy to rely on the unity of concrete experiences and concepts and to account for it. For him that unity was the rock-bottom basis for establishing his philosophical system. Hegel, Schopenhauer, Kierkegaard, Nietzsche, Heidegger, Merleau-Ponty, et al followed suit. Although these philosophers are to be criticized for implicit or explicit sexist views, their works are important sources for feminist philosophical enquiry. Feminist philosophy not only rests on the assumption of the unity of feeling and thought but, with women's experiences, brings a new orientation to all philosophical enquiry so far based on this assumption.

In philosophy and other areas of discourse, women's experiences have been traditionally described and explained by men, from men's perspectives. The language used to describe and explain women's experiences was based on men's experiences of women's experiences, rather than on women's experiences themselves. Thus, in this respect, as of course in others, women's experiences and their lives were other-determined rather than self-determined. Even women writing on women's experiences were inclined to use language determined by men's perspectives.

The question how, exactly, the distinction between men's and women's perspectives is to be drawn has not yet been fully resolved. A satisfactory answer to this question depends on descriptions of women's experiences that have been determined by women from their own perspectives. It depends on the creative enterprise of self-determination through telling one's own stories of one's own experiences.

As women's perspectives are being integrated into philosophical enquiry, it is becoming clearer and clearer that philosophy cannot be governed by rules of reason alone. Rather it must be acknowledged that concrete experiences generate the constitution or reconstitution of concepts. Established analytic procedures or explanatory systems must be re-examined, eliminated, or replaced.

This requirement arose not only from feminist philosophy. Also, for instance, according to both Nietzsche[1] and Merleau-Ponty[2] every description or theory is strictly tied to the viewpoint from which it is issued. Nietzsche's perspectivism requires the reconstruction of concepts and revaluation of values. Merleau-Ponty argues for the necessity for creative language in consequence of his version of perspectivism.

However, this paper will not delve into the historical connections of feminist philosophy. Rather, it will focus on story-telling as a necessary component of philosophical enquiry into the nature of knowledge, and supply a case study.

Christa Wolf's *Cassandra* presents the case of a woman in search of her 'own voice' with which to tell her own story. In an environment in which discourse and other behaviour are governed by rules devised by men in power, such a search must be revolutionary, and communication in one's own voice an original and creative act. That story-telling from a woman's point of view is a revolutionary act has been convincingly shown by Carol P. Christ: 'The simple act of telling a woman's story from a woman's point of view is a revolutionary act: it has never been done before. A new language must be created to express women's experience and insight, new metaphors discovered, new themes considered. Women writers who name the gap between men's stories about women and women's own perceptions of self, and world are engaged in creating a new literary tradition.'[3]

The woman and seer, Cassandra, is rooted in mythology. She is also confined by her myth, which has been told by men: Homer, Aeschylus, Pindar. Traditional mythology has no central place for her. She plays secondary parts in the *Iliad*, in *Agamemnon*, and in Pindar's poetry. Dictionaries of mythology devote only a few paragraphs to her. The 1968 edition of the *New Larousse Encyclopedia of Mythology* provides only these lines: 'when Apollo fell in love with Cassandra, daughter of King Priam, he conferred upon her the gift of foretelling the future on her promising to yield herself to him. But Cassandra refused to fulfill her part of the bargain. Apollo then begged a single kiss. In this way he breathed into her mouth and, though he left her with the power of foretelling the future, he took from her the power of persuasion so that from then onwards no one would believe what Cassandra predicted.' Cassandra's myth was not her own story. Her story was told about her, not by her and not for her.

Christa Wolf presents Cassandra's story from Cassandra's own perspective, as Cassandra's monologue. But Cassandra's own perspective is not and cannot yet be established. Rather, her story is her story of longing and searching for her own perspective, for her 'own voice.'

Christa Wolf's short novel does not rest on a theory, nor do I attempt to generate a theory from it. Rather, I present it as a reconstruction of the Cassandra myth as Cassandra's own story.

Telling a woman's story from a woman's point of view is not established practice, either for Cassandra or for contemporary women.

It is a practice in the formative and experimental stages. To under-stand that feeling and thought must be unified is not sufficient for generating ways of articulating experience. There can be no viable method of philosophical enquiry that does not rest on self-determined articulations of experience.

It is by virtue of one's articulated experiences that a self can be interrelated with other selves. It is one of the basic tenets of feminist and some other philosophers (e.g., Hegel, Nietzsche, Heidegger) that for an individual to be a self is to be interrelated with other selves, in mutual recognition and receptivity.

In traditional mythology Apollo takes from Cassandra the power of persuasion. In the myth according to Christa Wolf, Cassandra is condemned to be incapable of *communication*: of articulating her experiences of 'seeing' in such a way that she can reach other people through them. Only when facing death is she at last freed of the guiding and steering forces in her life. Neither human nor divine oppressors have power over her any more. Thus freed also from Apollo she now does speak in her own voice, but, paradoxically, in complete isolation from the human community.

A woman's own perspective on the basis of the unity of concrete experiences and thought engenders the attitude of pacifism as a necessary consequence. *Cassandra* is a novel about war and against war. Cassandra convinces us that war is based on the dichotomization of feeling and thought and this is grounded on men's perspectives. However, this aspect will not enter into my case study. I will focus only on Cassandra's search for her own voice.

Cassandra has the gift of veridical intuition. For her, as a seer, to intuit is to know. But she alone sees and is not able to communicate what she sees. In the view of others this amounts to blindness. However, this view is due to their blindness against Cassandra's visions. Cassandra's intuition is knowledge even though it cannot be brought under concepts for others to understand.

Kant, as I said, starts the tradition of founding epistemology on the unity of concrete experiences ('appearances' as immediately given in intuition) and concepts. But according to him intuition without concepts is blind. Cassandra is a counter-example.

Elsewhere I have argued at length that an artwork represents non-referentially and non-conceptually the complete pattern of an experience, i.e., a kind of experience, in all its essential respects, including the non-discursive component of subjectivity.[4] Further, I have shown that 'artistic insight' is a necessary component of artistic creativity. Artistic insight consists in immediate non-propositional understanding of a kind of experience: the complete pattern of an experience is given in the artist's consciousness. But this does not mean that the artist *has* the experience. Artistic insight is therefore not necessarily tied to the author's own perspective.

Hence one is more likely to find *artistic* representations of women's experiences from women's perspectives, rather than appropriate conceptual accounts. It is essential to my enterprise to choose a work whose protagonist is a woman who seeks self-determination through her own perspective. Given the nature of artistic insight it is not essential that the author of my chosen work is a woman. A male artist can create an artwork, literary or otherwise, in which women's experiences are articulated through woman's perspectives. I believe that this claim can be confirmed; however, this is not at issue in the present context. None the less, I deliberately chose a woman's work rather than a man's, on the highly plausible assumption that a woman is much more likely to be open to insights into the complete pattern of women's experiences. But in a work of art the protagonist's perspective, not the author's, is constitutive of the experience represented. Strictly speaking, the characters in a novel must be self-determined rather than determined by their author. The Czech novelist Milan Kundera holds this view and exemplifies it as follows:

Now, not only is the novelist nobody's spokesman, but I would go so far as to say he is not even the spokesman of his own ideas. When Tolstoy sketched the first draft of *Anna Karenina*, Anna was a most unsympathetic woman, and her tragic end was merely deserved and justified. The final version of the novel is very different, but I do not believe that Tolstoy had revised his moral ideas in the meantime; I would say, rather, that in the course of writing, he was listening to another voice than that of his personal moral conviction. He was listening to what I would like to call the wisdom of the novel. Every true novelist listens for that suprapersonal wisdom, which explains why great novels are always a little more intelligent than their authors. Novelists who are more intelligent than their works should change jobs.[5]

II

Traditional epistemology has in general favoured propositional knowledge over knowledge by acquaintance. Seldom do we find the view that there can be immediate knowledge not determined by concepts. In the history of philosophy immediate acquaintance with something is often held to be a condition of knowledge or translatable into propositions. But as mere presentation in my consciousness immediate acquaintance is rejected as a possible bearer of truth values. In the analytic tradition it may even be considered as irrelevant to the constitution of truth-values – by contrast with the Kantian tradition as critically continued by Hegel, Husserl, and Heidegger, among others. In this tradition philosophers offer varieties of the view that immediate concrete experience is a necessary constituent of knowledge and, therefore, a determinant of a feasible theory of knowledge.

Kant says: 'In whatever manner and by whatever means a mode of knowledge may relate to objects, intuition is that through which it is in *immediate* relation to them, and to which all thought as a means [of knowledge] is directed' (A 19).[6] Kant, by contrast with, for example, Husserl, thinks of such intuition as passive. According to him, inner representations of objects, i.e., appearances, as immediately given and inner, are constituted by sensation, the 'matter of perception.' Appearances are ordered multitudes of sensations; it is not single sensations or a disordered multitude of sensations that is given to us. In other words, what Kant insisted is passive intuition entails the presence of unity and diversity, of relatedness, in one's mind.

Kant could not see a way of establishing the unity of intuition, nor could he conceive of it as integral to the unity of understanding, i.e, the transcendental unity of apperception. He comes closest with the 'Schematism' in which he claims to establish homogeneity between intuition (immediately given 'appearances' that are strictly unique) and understanding (the categories that are strictly universal). Hegel subsequently proposes that both sensuous presentation *and* concepts are immediately and *inseparably* given and that without reflection they are fixed and both blind.

According to Kant, immediate appearances, as merely given, are multitudes of sensations, ordered and unified prior to being subsumed under concepts. Kant leads us to conclude that it is appearances as unified that we actively determine by concepts and that such determination presupposes non-conceptual or preconceptual recognition. If intuition, perception as *insight*, entails recognition, can it be right to speak of *mere* intuition as blind? Can it be right, for that matter, to speak of it as passive, as Kant does?

Merely to intuit, according to Kant, is not to have an experience. A perceptual experience entails determination of what is given by means of concepts; a perceptual experience entails description. Those aspects of experience that elude concepts are not received into phenomenal reality even though they may necessarily underlie it. In effect we are said to be necessarily ignorant of the strictly human, inner features of perceptual experience and thus *forced* to ignore them: Merely, immediately, to see is thus to be blind, on Kant's account. This conclusion is not acceptable.

In mere sense-perception without concepts what is given is present *in* consciousness. If what is given and recognized as a whole is determined by concepts what is given is an object *of* consciousness. I want to show with *Cassandra* in mind that an object *of* consciousness is necessarily a restricted version of an object *in* consciousness and, further, that it is possible to isolate an object of consciousness from any object in consciousness and thus blindly to use concepts and make statements that are open to truth-value conditions. The voice with which one would speak in such a case would not be one's own because it would not be based on one's own experience. It would be a voice determined by established concepts, governed by rules that have an exclusively external basis. With such a voice I would not speak for myself.

Of course, concepts are necessary. I *must* speak for it to be possible for others to see what I see. I *must* restrict what I see. But immediate intuition as thus necessarily restricted would make room for new questions and reconstructions of the concepts used because they *must* stem from pre-judgments, prejudice; without new questions leading to reconstructions of concepts we may run the danger of deadening our disposition for immediate intuition and closing our consciousness to anything that is not foreseeable in terms of the concepts we already have. Our descriptions would have to be clichés. They would correspond to common and fixed ways of seeing, not to the newly seen, so far unforeseen, and unfamiliar. They may even be closed against the possibility of the unfamiliar.

To speak in my voice, that is, from experience by what is given in my consciousness, I must use concepts in order to question and reconstruct them. This is not to say that conceptual meaning can ever reach the meaning of experience.

> ... There is, it seems to us,
> At best, only a limited value
> In the knowledge derived from experience.
> The knowledge imposes a pattern, and falsifies,
> For the pattern is new in every moment

And every moment is a new and shocking
Valuation of all we have been.[7]

I have, by now, pointed in the direction of Cassandra's message. Cassandra 'wollte die Sehergabe, unbedingt'[8] (43; 6, 11) (E: 36. 'I wanted the gift of prophecy, come what may'). *Unbedingt*: i.e., not for the sake of playing the *role* of priest at the court of Troy. When she did get captivated by the role she turned blind: 'Getragen von der Achtung der Troer, lebte ich scheinhaft wie nie. Ich weiss noch, wie mein Leben mir entwich ... Ich sah nichts. Mit der Sehergabe überfordert, war ich blind' (33) (E: 27. 'Upheld by the respect of the Trojans, I lived in semblance more than ever. I still remember how my life drained out of me ... I saw nothing. Overtaxed by the gift of sight, I was blind').

It is 'scheinhaft leben' that she wanted to make impossible for herself: 'Warum wollte ich die Sehergabe unbedingt? – Mit meiner Stimme sprechen: das Äusserste' (6) (E: 4. 'Why did I want the gift of prophecy, come what may? To speak with my voice: the ultimate)'. And even this extreme cannot reach what she may see if the gift is granted to her: 'Das Letzte wird ein Bild sein, kein Wort. Vor den Bildern sterben die Wörter' (26) (E: 21. 'The last thing in my life will be a picture, not a word. Words die before pictures'). Even her own voice will stop short of what she sees, i.e., experiences.

Cassandra, as presented in Wolf's novel, receives the gift of seeing from Apollo, in a dream. Because Cassandra refuses him sexually Apollo attaches a curse to the gift: no one is to believe what her visions lead her to say.

Until she is imprisoned, condemned to death, seeing her death and, knowingly, very close to it, she is to be unable to speak with her own voice, i.e., to find language as it would newly arise from her seeing-experiences. For her, merely to see, to intuit, is to experience. 'Ich fühlte. Erfuhr – ja, das ist das Wort, denn eine Erfahrung war es, ist es, wenn ich "sehe", "sah"' (68) (E: 59. 'I felt. Experienced – yes, that's the word. For it was, it is, an experience when I "see", when I "saw"'). Her goal, to speak with her own voice, is the goal to achieve unity of her own inner experience with its expression, to know her experience and make it known, to close the gap between her immediate experience and concepts. Thus she must aim to speak from the foundation of her immediate unrestricted experience; she must aim to free herself from any form of direction and guidance in order to be guided only by her own experience. Of course this is impossible for human consciousness. Strictly, she aims at severing herself from the realm of human consciousness and its limits, in order to know and make known. Such a sequence amounts to insanity, as she is aware; insanity precludes any voice by which one can relate to others. Only close to her own death does she succeed in overcoming the logical impossibility of being severed from human community *and* speaking in her own voice. She is herself and free, but free by virtue of being severed from human community.

This freedom entails her liberation also from belief in the gods, thereby from Apollo. To be free in and for her *own* humanity she must sever herself from humanity: Cassandra's paradox of freedom. Her own voice, at last found, cannot possibly reach humanity, even if others were open to seeing what she sees, and willing to believe. Her own voice is completely within herself. Because it cannot be for others it cannot be for herself. Thus having attained the utmost of her own humanity she lacks humanity and is forced into solipsism. Until the moment close to her death Cassandra is not free even to the extent of finding 'une voix, presque mienne'[9] – the most she could hope for within the universal realm of human consciousness. She is a member of a human community in which individuals as selves have no voice. There is only the common voice governed by exclusively external rules of language and behaviour. Thus this human community is dehumanized and anti-human. In this community Cassandra must lose herself as a self to relate, to be received and understood. Attaining her own voice, the utmost, just before her own death, she finds herself, but only to be lost within herself. Again, her own voice cannot be for others and, therefore, not for herself. Thus she is condemned to one kind of self-loss, while being submitted to Apollo's curse, steered, guided, and driven; and to another, that of the impossibility of being for herself, in freedom from Apollo's curse the day before her death.

Apollo's curse is effective within the human community, not outside it. 'Das Äusserste': 'mit meiner Stimme sprechen' is not within the reach of his influence. But Cassandra can't know this until she is free from him as well as severed from humanity. One result of Apollo's curse is that, because she is a seer, she must long for the impossible freedom of expressing her experiences without restriction. The common language she is condemned to cannot even touch her experiences; it is totally alien to them, to herself. For her experiences to remain merely inner and unformulated means for her to be severed from humanity and to fall to insanity. My own voice, if I speak as a member of the human community, can only be 'une voix, presque mienne'; my freedom of self-expression is necessarily limited. But she is condemned to be even less free than we must be: '... frei, ach, frei. In Wirklichkeit: gefesselt. Gelenkt, geleitet und zum Ziel gestossen, das andere setzen' (28) (E: 23. 'Free; oh, free. In reality: captive. Steered, guided, and driven to the goal others set'). In her actions and communication she is steered and guided by the court, her father, the Trojan people – just those people she is supposed to bring to see what she sees. It is the other side of the curse that these people who are 'blind' must remain blind: because Cassandra is cursed to speak in their lanquage, and not at all her own.

Two phases ensue in consequence of being condemned to lacking her own voice: total introversion and insanity. She first disappears within herself and thereby gives up on her relatedness within the world that surrounds her. Such relatedness is, however, essential to being a self. 'Sie hinderten mich nicht, dass ich vollkommen in mir selbst verschwand. Nicht sprach. Kaum ass. Mich beinahe nicht bewegte. Zuerst nicht schlief. Mich den Bildern überliess, die sich in meinem Kopf eingefressen hatten' (139) (E: 123. 'They did not stop me from disappearing inside myself completely. I did not speak. Hardly ate. Barely moved. Did not sleep, to begin with. Gave myself up to the pictures that had eaten their way into my head'). Such withdrawal is not yet insanity, *Wahnsinn*. She could be brought back to herself, in her world, by the lively restfulness of love: 'Ruhe, die nicht Grabesruhe war. Lebendige Ruhe. Liebesruhe' (139) (E: 123. 'Peace that was not the peace of the grave. Living peace. Love's peace'). Without such solace the next phase is indeed *Wahnsinn*, as protection from unbearable pain: 'Wahnsinn als Ende der Verstellungsqual. O, ich genoss ihn fürchterlich, umgab mich mit ihm wie mit einem schweren Tuch, ich liess mich Schicht für Schicht von ihm durchdringen. Er war mir Speise und Trank. Dunkle Milch, bitteres Wasser, saures Brot. Ich war auf mich zurückgefallen. Doch es gab mich nicht' (69) (E: 60. 'Lunacy: an end to the torture of pretense. Oh, I enjoyed it deadfully, I wrapped it around me like a heavy cloak, I let it penetrate me layer by layer. It was meat and drink to me. Dark milk, bitter water, sour bread. I had gone back to being myself. But my self did not exist'). Her self could not exist any longer because its essential feature of relatedness was lacking. 'Nur der Wannsinn schützte mich vor dem unerträglichen Schmerz, [...]' (70). (E: 60. 'Only madness stood between me and intolerable pain'). However, a self's freedom to acquire one's own voice consists in being open to the extreme pain that splits one's skull: 'Wer wird, und wann, die Sprache wiederfinden. Einer, dem ein Schmerz den Schädel spaltet, wird es sein' (10). (E: 8. 'Who will find a voice again, and when? It will be one whose skull is split by a pain'). Obviously, *Wahnsinn* is no salvation from the curse of merely seeing, and not being seen as seeing.

Apollo's curse upon Cassandra is a mythological occurrence, which presents an archetype as well as a logical feature of human experience. It is necessarily true that my language cannot be *exclusively* based on my experience, on what is given in my consciousness. But it is not necessary that I completely adhere to descriptive conventions that must precede any of my experiences and refrain from questioning and modifying them in the light of every new experience. Every concrete inner experience gives direction towards 'une voix, presque mienne.' I must be free to follow this direction, free to give (external) form to my inner experience to the utmost extent that this is possible.

Cassandra lacks this freedom, by Apollo's curse. What is the archetype that is presented by this mythological occurrence? What is it that deprives me or you of such freedom? Cassandra has a name for it: 'Übereinstimmungssucht.' Literally, agreement-addiction: the weakness that leads to losing oneself, to conducting oneself according to rules in which the dimension of one's own experiences, the dimension of feeling, is lost. I play at being someone; I am not myself: 'Ich spielte die Priesterin. Ich dachte: Erwachsensein bestehe aus diesem Spiel: sich selbst verlieren' (32) (E: 27. 'I played the priestess. I thought: To be grown up consists in this game: to lose oneself'). And of Paris she says: 'Schwach, Bruder, schwach. Ein Schwächling. Übereinstimmungs-süchtig. Sieh dich bloss im Spiegel an' (144). (E: 127. 'Weak, Brother, weak. A weakling. Hungry to conform. Just look at yourself in the mirror'). The archetype is characterized by the dichotomy between my experiences as mine and the voice in which I speak as well as the behaviour I display in relation to others: 'gelenkt, geleitet und zum Ziel gestossen, das andere setzen' (28) (E: 23. 'Steered, guided, and driven to the goal others set'). My self-awareness may at last be deadened, cut off from my comportment, so that I become 'fühllos': 'Mit Genugtuung fühlte ich die Kälte, die sich in mir ausbreitete. Ich wusste noch nicht, das Fühllosigkeit niemals ein Fortschritt ist, kaum eine Hilfe' (59) (E: 51. 'With satisfaction I felt the coldness spreading through me. I did not yet know that not to feel is never a step forward, scarcely a relief'). The consequence of 'Fühllosigkeit' prevents *Angst*, which in accordance with Cassandra's story arises from the split between feeling (experience, insight) and words; from the difficulty or impossibility of being present to others complete with one's present feelings and insights, of *being* through oneself with and for others, and thus for oneself. The *Angst* may be directed fear, more or less conscious: I may fear to rouse the animosity or even aggression of others ('others' may be lovers, friends, parents, students, colleagues). If I speak from the ground of my own experiences (in Cassandra's sense of 'experience') in a voice close to my own I am necessarily bound to break, abandon, or expand some of the rules that govern our common language and behaviour. This fear could be fought down without loss of the self's life ('Lebendigsein') if it were only fear of others, and not tied to fear of my own presence. Experience of Angst is a secondary experience; it presupposes other experiences, on one side of a split between myself and others.

To be able to give my inner picture of our world to others (to make others see what I see) is to make myself present, to let myself be given in others' consciousness. I am altered with every new experience, every picture in me. To make others see what I see is therefore to alter the picture of myself that others may have of me; to alter the way I am given in their experience; to let myself be given differently with every experience. This is what Cassandra calls 'being alive': 'Was ich lebendig nenne? Was nenne ich lebendig. Das schwierigste nicht scheuen, das Bild von sich selbst ändern. Worte, sagte Panthoos ... Nichts als Worte, Kassandra. Der Mensch ändert nichts, warum ausgerechnet sich selbst, warum ausgerechnet das Bild von sich' (25) (E: 21. 'What do I mean by alive? What I mean by alive – not to shrink from what is most difficult. To change one's image of oneself. "Words", said Panthous ... "Nothing but words, Cassandra. A human being changes nothing, so why himself of all things, why of all things his image of himself?"'). It is not, to respond to Panthous, that I can perform alterations upon myself; my alteration is given inseparably with anything given in my experience. This is what Panthous misunderstood.

If I alter the picture of myself I run the risk of being exposed to hostility from the steering, guiding, and driving voices that are nobody's own; they are voices arising from rules for games, power games, not from anyone's own experiences. The bearers of such voices do not look for me as I may be given in their experiences, but they look for me as they want me for their purposes: 'Zum ersten Mal kam mir der Gedanke, die Vertraulichkeit beruhe, wie so oft zwischen Männern und Frauen darauf, das ich ihn kannte und er mich nicht. Er kannte sein Wunschbild von mir, das hatte still zu halten' (58) (E: 50. 'For the first time it occurred to me that the intimacy between us was based, as is so often the case between men and women, on the fact that I knew him and he did not know me. He knew his ideal of me; that was supposed to hold still'). Thus Cassandra, about her relationship with her father, Priamos. But the real picture of me, alive with my experiences, my stream of consciousness, cannot hold still. If others are blind to such a picture of me, I cannot be present to them even if I present myself alive with my experiences. Then I am a likely object of their power, made to hold still. Despite this likelihood I may continue to be present, in the face of their blindness, or their picture of me which did not originate in me; then I will have to live in *Angst*. Cassandra's story is the story of her *Angst* because she was condemned to be alive in the face of blindness, of disbelief. She could not choose not to 'see'; she could only choose to fall into the speech of others' voices, which she did, especially in the early days of her priesthood. She could not be 'fühllos' without being aware that she was; thus 'Fühllosigkeit' could not free her of Angst. Being 'fühllos' was a felt experience for her. Being 'fühllos' she remained alive, and therefore continued to 'see'.:

Wer lebt, wird sehen. Mir kommt der Gedanke, insgeheim verfolge ich die Geschichte meiner Angst. Oder richtiger, die Geschichte ihrer Entzügelung, noch genauer: ihrer Befreiung. Ja, tatsächlich, auch Angst kann befreit werden, und dabei zeigt sich, sie gehört mit allem und allen Unterdrückten zusammen. Die Tochter des Königs hat keine Angst, denn Angst ist Schwäche, und gegen Schwäche hilft ein eisernes Training. Die Wahnsinnige hat Angst, sie ist wahnsinning vor Angst. Die Gefangene soll Angst haben. Die Freie lernt es, ihre unwichtigen Angste abzutun und die eine grosse wichtige Angst nicht zu fürchten, weil sie nicht mehr zu stolz ist, sie mit anderen zu teilen. – Formeln, nun ja (41)

(E: 35. Who lives will see. It occurs to me that secretly I am tracking the story of my fear. Or more precisely, the story of its unbridling, more precisely still: of its setting free. Yes, it's true, fear too can be set free, and that shows that it belongs with everything and everyone who is oppressed. The king's daughter is not afraid, for fear is weakness and weakness can be amended by iron discipline. The madwoman is afraid, she is mad with fear. The captive is supposed to be afraid. The free woman learns to lay aside her unimportant fears and not to fear the one big important fear because she is no longer too proud to share it with others. – Formulas. granted.)

Panthous was one who roused and kept vivid in her the temptation to rid herself of Angst by giving up on herself, on her visions and the longing for her own voice. But trying to overcome Angst with 'Übereinstimmunssucht' is to forgo freedom, not to gain it; the sacrifice would be herself; to live in Angst is a way of keeping alive, towards living as oneself: 'Ich mochte ihn zuletzt nicht mehr, Panthoos. Ich mochte nicht in mir, was durch ihn verführbar gewesen war' (41) (E: 35. 'In the end I no longer liked Panthous. I did not like the thing in me which he had been able to seduce'). According to the myth Apollo is responsible for Cassandra's lack of her own voice. According to Cassandra she herself is. The belief in Apollo and his power is hers; she, by virtue of this belief, accepts both his gift and his curse. Her ultimate freedom is freedom also from this belief. But thereby she does not lose the gift of 'seeing'; to see, to be alive in experience, is to be oneself and potentially free. To free herself from her belief in Apollo is to realize that the gift of seeing cannot be endowed, but must originate in herself: 'Aber der Glaube wich allmächlich von mir, so wie manchmal eine Krankheit weicht, und eines Tages sagst du dir, du bist gesund. Die Krankheit findet keinen Boden mehr in dir' (112) (E: 98. 'But faith ebbed away from me gradually, the way illnesses sometimes ebb away, and one day you tell yourself that you are well. The illness no longer finds any foothold in you').

Cassandra's gain of her ultimate freedom, very close to her death, paradoxically, severs her from humanity: 'Hier spricht keiner meine Sprache, der nicht mit mir stirbt' (8) (E: 6. 'Of those here who speak my language, there is none who will not die with me'). [I would prefer the translation: 'Here no-one speaks my language who does not die with me.'] But, of course, she dies her own death, necessarily alone.[10] People who die at the same time do not die with each other. 'Wozu leb ich noch, wenn nicht, um zu erfahren, was man nur vor dem Tod erfährt' (111) (E: 97. 'Why do I go on living if not to learn the things one learns only before death?'). Ultimate freedom – 'mit meiner Stimme sprechen: das Äusserste' – entails her severance from humanity as it entails liberation from self-reflection. Ultimate freedom consists in experience *as* cognition, unrestricted by concepts based on pre-judgment. In ultimate freedom, to perceive is to know. Ultimate freedom is not human freedom.

'For, nearing death, one doesn't see death; but stares / beyond, perhaps with an animal's vast gaze.'[11] Like Cassandra, Rilke sees the possibility of unrestricted human freedom, at least of perception, only in closeness to death. Non-human animals, by contrast, are seen as capable of free, knowing perception:

With all its eyes the natural world looks out
into the Open. Only our eyes are turned
backward, and surround plant, animal, child
like traps, as they emerge into their freedom.
...
... Free from death.
We, only, can see death.[12]

'Staring ahead' while nearing death one perceives, accordingly, without self-reflection, without questioning one's own being or the being of anything. Everything is now unrestrictedly open to one's perception. If I have a voice then it must be completely my own. My language would be a private language. Therefore, with this voice I could not possibly make others see what I see.

Cassandra's human voice, as a seer's, cannot possibly be completely her own. Accordingly her vision is to be restricted: '... immer habe ich mir diese Zeiten von Teilblindheit gegönnt. Auf einmal sehend werden, das hätte mich zerstört' (47) (E: 40. 'I have always granted myself these times of partial blindness. To become seeing all of a sudden – that would have destroyed me'). As we have seen: 'auf einmal sehend werden' is to be severed from humanity while nearing death.

But every human experience or vision, restricted by language based on pre-judgment, must lead to questioning this language and keeping it in flux. To make others see what I see is to urge new questions on them. In a world split by *Angst* and smoothed by 'Übereinstimmungssucht' the freedom to pose new questions is refused. Panthous says to Cassandra: 'Und wer bist du, ihnen Fragen aufzudrängen. Lass alles, wie es ist, Kassandra, ich rate dir gut' (35) (E: 29. 'And who are you to force other questions on them? Leave everything as it is, Cassandra, I'm giving you good advice').

We can leave everything as it is only if all seeing is *seeing – as*, that is, if there is seeing only under descriptions and no original seeing. For Cassandra, however, to 'see' is to 'know the place for the first time.'[13] Therefore there must be a split between what I see and what I know propositionally. Unity of perception and knowing can, in the durational world, obtain only for non-human animals, according to Rilke's poetic vision, and for humans nearing death. According to Kant's philosophical vision, 'intellectual intuition,' in a non–spatio-temporal world, would unite experience and knowledge: objects would be given to intellectual intuition as they are in themselves, unrestricted.

We do not need Cassandra to get the message that there is no knowledge without experience. Her message is that there cannot be human knowledge without individual experience, intensely felt; that every new experience dissociates us, me, from past and common knowledge. I am my experiences. My experiences are completely my own, my voice cannot be. It can necessarily be only 'presque mienne.' A voice completely my own entails the unintelligibility of my language: it would be a private language. A voice completely my own entails my severance from human community. Cassandra's possession of her own voice, ultimately, is her death. Her own voice can be heard only through poetic articulation, as through Christa Wolf's *Cassandra*, not through discourse. An individual self can be complete and unified only in death, not in life.

I must live with the split between my experiences of the world and the world, between the certainty of immediate knowledge in experience, and the uncertainty of propositional knowledge derived from experience. If I don't give myself up, lose myself to preconceived patterns of being in the world, playing at being according to rules, rather than being myself, my story must be a story of Angst, generated by the difficulty or impossibility of being present to the world with my experiences, and of seeing myself, and of taking the necessary step from 'I' to 'we.'

Du meinst, Arisbe, der Mensch kann sich selbst nicht sehen.
– So ist es. Er erträgt es nicht. Er braucht das fremde Abbild.
– Und darin wird sich nie was ändern? Immer nur die Wiederkehr des gleichen? Selbstfremdheit, Götzenbilder, Hass? – Ich weiss es nicht. Soviel weiss ich: Es gibt Zeitenlöcher. Dies ist so eines, hier und jetzt. Wir dürfen es nicht ungenutzt vergehen lassen.
Da, endlich, hatte ich mein 'wir'. (141)

(E: 124 'You think that man cannot see himself, Arisbe?' [I prefer: 'You think that a person cannot see herself or himself, Arisbe?'] 'That's right. He cannot stand it. He needs the alien image.' 'And will that never change? Will the same thing always come again? Self-estrangment, idols, hatred?' 'I don't know. This much I do know. We cannot let it pass without taking advantage of it.' There at last I had my 'we.')

It is part of the myth that Cassandra 'saw' alone: 'Ich allein sah' (68) (E: 59. 'But I, I alone saw'). Here again, the myth presents an archetype and a necessary truth. For my experiences *must* be mine. In this sense each of us sees alone. As one of 'wir' I am restricted by language. In myself, in my own inner experiences, I am free. But I need 'wir' to have a voice. With every experience I must forgo freedom, and be freed again if only for new questions, visions, and revisions.

Empiricism, according to Cassandra, entails constant additions to the real world: additions of inner pictures that alter the picture of each of us. She would not accept Wittgenstein's view that philosophy leaves everything as it is, that it does not add anything to the world: 'Ich aber. Ich allein sah. Oder "sah" ich denn? Wie war das doch. Ich fühlte.

Erfuhr – ja, das ist das Wort; denn eine Erfahrung war es, ist es, wenn ich "sehe", "sah"' (68) (E: 59. 'But I. I alone saw. Or did I really "see"? What was it, then? I felt. Experienced – yes, that's the word. For it was, it is, an experience when I "see", when I "saw"'). And what is an experience? An inner picture corresponding to something in the outer world: 'Noch alles, was mir widerfahren ist, hat in mir seine Entsprechung gefunden. Es ist das Geheimnis, das mich umklammert und zusammenhält, mit keinem Menschen habe ich darüber reden können. Hier erst, am äussersten Rand meines Lebens, kann ich es bei mir selber benennen: Da von jedem etwas in mir ist, habe ich zu keinem ganz gehört, und noch ihren Hass auf mich habe ich verstanden' (6) (E: 4. 'So far, everything that has befallen me has struck an answering chord. This is the secret that encircles and holds me together; I have never been able to talk of it with anyone. Only here, at the uttermost rim of my life, can I name it to myself: There is something of everyone in me, so I have belonged completely to no one, and I have even understood their hatred for me').

I have tried to outline Cassandra's empiricism: Knowledge must be based on individual, felt, experience, which it is impossible to convey. The only chance I have to convey unrestricted and unrestricting immediate knowledge is by 'lebendig sein': letting myself be altered by every experience and thus letting the picture of me, in me and others, be altered; being present in the world with my inner pictures of it. 'Lebendig sein' is the indivisible unity of concrete inner experience and reason.

Another aspect of the message I have hardly touched: that 'lebendig sein' requires extreme pain as the most intense kind of experience; the 'lebendige Ruhe' of love, and dreams. They, according to Cassandra, constitute the foundation of our individual humanity.

NOTES

1 For instance, F. Nietzsche, *The Will to Power*, trans. W. Kaufmann and R.J. Hollingdale (New York: Vintage, 1967), especially par. 481
2 Cf. M. Merleau-Ponty, *Phenomenology of Perception*, trans. Colin Smith (London: Routledge and Kegan Paul, 1962), passim
3 Carol P. Christ, *Diving Deep and Surfacing* (Boston: Beacon, 1980), p. 7
4 Petra von Morstein, *On Understanding Works of Art* (New York and Toronto: Mellen Press, 1986)
5 Milan Kundera, 'Man Thinks, God Laughs,' in *New York Review of Books*, 13 June 1985, pp. 11–12

6 References to Kant are based on *Immanuel Kant's Critique of Pure Reason*, trans. Norman Kemp Smith (London, New York: Macmillan, 1964)

7 T.S. Eliot, *Collected Poems: 1909–1962* (London: Faber and Faber, 1963); 'East Coker,' II, p. 199

8 Quotations marked with page numbers are from Christa Wolf, *Kassandra* (Darmstadt: Luchterhand Verlag, 1984). The translations marked with 'E' and page numbers are from *Cassandra* by Christa Wolf, trans. Jan van Heurck (New York: Farrar, Straus and Giroux, 1984)

9 Rainer Maria Rilke, *Vergers* (Paris: Gallimard, 1978), p. 17:
Ce soir mon coeur fait chanter
des anges qui se souviennent ...
Une voix, presque mienne,
par trop de silence tentée,

monte et se décide
à ne plus revenir;
tendre et intrépide,
à quoi va-t-elle s'unir?

10 The notion of one's own death, of death, as one's own innermost experience, is to be found in Rilke's poetry and his *Malte Laurids Brigge*, and in Heidegger's *Being and Time*. For instance: 'O Herr,gieb jedem seinen eignen Tod. / Das Sterben, das aus jenem Leben geht, / darin er Liebe hatte, Sinn und Not!' ['Oh Lord, give each his own death. / The dying, which comes from that life / in which he had love, sensed, and suffering' (my trans.)] from R.M. Rilke, 'Das Buch von der Armut und vom Tode,' in *Gesammelte Gedichte* (Frankfurt: Insell-Verlag, 1962)
   Heidegger thinks of death as 'this ownmost potentiality-for-Being, which is non-rational and not to be outstripped, is constantly an issue for Dasein' and says: 'No-one can take the other's dying away from him.' In M. Heidegger, *Being and Time*, trans. J. Macquarrie and E. Robinson (New York: Harper and Row, 1962), especially sects. 46–53

11 R.M. Rilke, *The Selected Poetry of Rainer Maria Rilke*, ed. and trans. Stephen Mitchell, (New York: Vintage Books, Random House, 1984), from 'The Eighth Elegy,' p. 193

12 Ibid.

13 T.S. Eliot, *Collected Poems: 1909–1962*, from 'Little Gidding,' v, p. 222

Credibility:
A Double Standard

LORRAINE CODE

The Double Standard

The outstanding features of the 'double standard' whose political and epistemological effects I shall explore here are vividly illustrated in the conduct of the 1984 Grange Inquiry into a number of infant deaths from cardiac arrest at Toronto's Hospital for Sick Children. Calling the inquiry 'the highest-priced, tax-supported sexual harassment exercise that we've ever witnessed,' Alice Baumgart observes: 'When lawyers, who were mostly men, questioned doctors, the questions were phrased in terms of what they *knew*. When nurses were on the stand, the question was, "Based on your *experience* ..." Experience in our society is considered second-class compared to knowledge. Nurses should not know.'[1] Now this occurrence is neither a unique nor an isolated one in the politics of knowledge. Baumgart's observation points to the fact that, even today, women enjoy a severely limited cognitive authority. It suggests that there is a double standard at work, within the medical profession at least, which manifests itself in a hierarchical organization of male and female practitioners. Its structure reflects a distinction between knowledge and experience, in terms of which knowledge is more highly valued than experience and is able to confer authority where experience cannot. More broadly viewed, this sort of hierarchical distinction is visible throughout 'public' or would-be public knowledge. It is one of the shaping forces of a political situation in which women are, in general, confined within narrowly circumscribed private spheres of knowledge and expertise.

Two complex epistemological/political patterns converge to maintain this lesser mode of cognitive being, for women, and to thwart their efforts to gain recognition as authoritative members of an epistemic community. First is the persistence of stereotypes according to which women are variously labelled as scatter-brained, illogical, highly emotional, incapable of abstract or purely intellectual thought, their judgments constantly vitiated by an unpredictable subjectivity. The influence of such stereotyping is so tenacious that, even as contradictory evidence accumulates, the view remains astonishingly widespread that this is how women *are*. By 'applying' stereotypes, people still claim to *know* what women are like, what they can do, and how they should be treated. Such stereotype-governed 'knowledge' often derives support from seemingly well-accredited experimental findings about female nature. Hence it is only by unmasking stereotypes for the crude epistemological tools that they are that one can begin to counter them and weaken their potential for damage, a potential that the Grange Inquiry has highlighted.

Interwoven with this pernicious epistemological pattern is the equally curious distinction between knowledge and experience. This distinction acts to discredit any putative claims to knowledge that do not fall within the purview of a carefully, but arguably unjustifiably, stipulated scope of the term. There results a designation of what it is permissible to *count* as knowledge, which creates an awkward double bind for certain potential knowers (in this case women) with regard both to the raw materials of which knowledge is to be constructed and to the knowing process itself. Perceived through stereotypes, women are declared capable of attaining access only to experience, and hence not to the proper stuff of which knowledge is made. In consequence of the same misperception, is it assumed that women lack the capacity to acquire the methodological tools held to be prerequisites for all potential knowers. All of these considerations raise epistemological questions about how, when, and why it is permissible to confer the honorific label 'knowledge' upon products of human cognitive endeavour. When one notes what it is that currently predominant methodological strictures render unworthy of the label, one must wonder whether female experience really is at fault, or whether epistemological assumptions themselves are in need of closer scrutiny.

Questions about objectivity are central to what is at issue here. With regard to stereotypes, it is noteworthy and problematic that evidence confirming their aptness is often adduced by methods and from sources that appear to comply with acceptable standards of objective inquiry. Yet with regard to methodological assumptions, the ideal of objectivity upheld as that which must be respected if one is to qualify as a knower is one whose stringency disqualifies a good deal of what our pre-philosophical institutions tell us must surely count as knowledge. In view of the significance of these points, a reconsideration of the implications of regarding *objectivity* as an overarching epistemological ideal will be an important part of this discussion of credibility.

In the next section of this paper I shall examine the tenacity of stereotype-based claims to knowledge and their epistemological/political implications. In the following section, I shall elaborate the central points of some recent feminist challenges voiced against prevalent epistemological methodologies. And in the final section, I shall offer some tentative suggestions as to how the situation created by the interaction of these two factors might be circumvented through a re-vision of some presuppositions about objectivity. Before considering these questions more closely, however, I shall outline some of the epistemological assumptions that lead me to present the enquiry in the form of an investigation of credibility and cognitive authority.[2]

It is a primary human concern to be good at knowing what the world is like: to know how best to respond to and interact with the physical environment, and with other animate, intelligent, and sensitive creatures. Within a knowledge-acquisition process, it is as important to develop a sense of whom one can trust, and about how one can know that someone else knows, as it is to be able to give evidence, oneself, of knowing certain facts, and knowing how to do certain things. This is so because knowledge is an interpersonal product that requires communal standards of affirmation, correction, and denial for its existence. Concentration upon individual, putatively autonomous knowledge claims, derived from 'direct' contact with the world, loses sight of the role of these credibility-discerning and -establishing activities. Often, epistemologists seem to forget just how small a portion of one's knowledge is gained by straightforwardly observational, empirical means. Yet, to a much greater extent than examples commonly taken to illustrate epistemological points might lead one to believe, people are dependent, at a fundamental level, upon other people – parents, teachers, friends, reporters, authorities, and experts – for what they, often rightly, claim to know.

My point is that a study of the workings of epistemic community is as important a focus of epistemological enquiry as is an analysis of individual perception- and memory-based knowledge claims that aims to discern conditions of their possibility and reasons for their justification. In fact, some of the workings of that community and some of the effects of the status enjoyed both by cognitive authorities and by 'state of the art' knowledge *count* among the conditions that make knowledge possible.[3] More often than not, with respect to something one wants or needs to know, one simply has no choice but to consult 'experts,' either in person or in their writings. And the results of such investigation can only be as good as is one's judgment about which experts are worthy of consultation. So learning whose pronouncements are properly authoritative and justly deserving of credence is crucial to establishing one's own status as a responsible member of an epistemic community.

But such properly authoritative knowers are not always straightforwardly discernible as such, for 'high-ranking' status within epistemic communties is achieved as much on the basis of ideologically coloured, third-person, status-conferring judgments as in consequence of good cognitive endeavour. For similar reasons, 'low(er)-ranking' status sometimes cannot, unequivocally, be taken as a sign of ignorance or lesser reliability. (The case of the nurses at the Hospital for Sick Children illustrates this point well.) Yet, it is a complex epistemological task to untangle the factors that go into the creation of authorities and experts, upon whose alleged expertise most people are so fundamentally dependent. Because of the complexity of the issues, in a paper such as this one can only hope to offer a preliminary exploration of some of them and some tentative suggestions as to how they might be approached.

The Stereotype

Baumgart's point about the authority knowledge can confer but experience cannot reflects a pattern embedded in what passes for knowledge about woman's nature. Yet, should one think that the number of women entering the medical profession as *doctors* shows the stereotype not to be as tenacious as I suggest, it is instructive to consider historical evidence indicating that women were not entirely welcome there, and recent intimations that history might be on the point of repeating itself. For it is no coincidence that even as numbers of female doctors are increasing, there are suggestions in the press that there are too many doctors and that medical schools will have to admit fewer students. There are historical parallels which may well give cause for alarm.

To cite one such historical example, in the late nineteenth century, women's attempts to enter medical school began to meet with success just when doctors were beginning to worry about the depressed state of the profession. They feared that a steady increase in the number of women in the profession would exacerbate this depression, both by creating still more doctors than the society could support and by leading female patients to desert already economically threatened male practitioners to support their struggling, newly qualified sisters. What, then, was to be done? Mary Roth Walsh observes: 'One solution was to prove that a woman's nature, far from being an asset in a medical career, was an insurmountable liability. Nowhere in the profession was there a greater urgency to promote this idea than among those men who specialized in gynecology and obstetrics, the areas where women physicians posed the greatest threat.'[4] The question was discussed in all seriousness as to whether 'the quirks of a woman's brain have any peculiarities which necessarily unfit her from profiting from the most advanced medical instruction.'[5] And the efforts of highly trained scientists, whose expertise confers authority upon their findings, were directed towards providing an answer. This move parallels one taken by nineteenth-century doctors to disqualify female lay healers and midwives by producing "scientific" evidence that woman's essential nature was not to be a strong, competent help-giver, but to be a *patient*.'[6] In short, when women approached medical science with a view to becoming knowledgeable, authoritative practitioners within it, they found medical science itself working to establish an imposing body of knowledge to show that they could not, in fact, *be* effective practitioners. Their nature precluded it.

Historically, too, the exclusion of women from authoritative positions as practising scientists has been supported on grounds of propriety, with such claims as 'It [is] unseemly for a woman to expose her talents outside the home, especially to a male audience, or to acknowledge, let alone enjoy, any compliments or recognition she might receive':[7] or 'members of the stereotypically delicate female sex might either be embarrassed at the scientific discussion of biological facts or divert stouthearted men from the serious pursuit of science.'[8] Alternatively, it is stated as obvious that female minds cannot cope with science; and that if they try to, their possessors will become unfeminine.[9] Lest one think that these are merely antiquated historical postures, evidence shows that, while there may be apparent shifts in overt behaviour, within the scientific establishment women continue to meet similar obstacles, and those who persist and succeed are the exceptions who prove the rule.[10]

These examples illustrate women's double-edged relation to knowledge as such. Not only is it difficult for women to establish authoritative modes of being recognized as knowers; there is also a problem about the way 'received' knowledge itself exacerbates that difficulty. There is an impressive accumulation of 'expert' knowledge that purports to show that women simply cannot know and do certain kinds of things. Recent right- and left-hemisphere brain research is open to being used to support these same conclusions. And the point is that it is not easy to establish the credibility necessary to challenge the validity of such alleged knowledge when the mere posing of the challenge can be read as further evidence of one's unfitness. Many of the central cognitive domains in which women seek to participate have a history of producing (allegedly objective) 'knowledge' demonstrating their natural incapacity to do so.

A range of evidence, both recent and historical, reinforcing the stereotype and justifying belief in natural differences that dictate appropriate male and (inferior) female activity is adduced from animal behaviour, in particular that of the higher primates. It is curious that such evidence should be granted credence, since it is neither self-evident that primate and other animal behaviour reflects the kind of behaviour – and division of labour – that is natural, and/or desirable, for human beings, nor is it clear that the selection of primates for study is conducted in as theory-neutral a manner as one might hope. Naomi Weisstein notes that the primates studied are often those that behave just as the proponents of biological determinism would wish. Thus, she writes: 'baboons and rhesus monkeys are generally cited: males in these groups exhibit some of the most irritable and aggressive behaviour found in primates, and if one wishes to argue that females are naturally passive and submissive, these groups provide vivid examples ... *The presence of counterexamples has not stopped florid and overarching theories of the natural or biological basis of male privilege from proliferating*'[11] (emphasis added). Confirming evidence is selected out from observational data in such a way that the stereotype is reinforced; and the possibility that human gender differences thus taken to be confirmed might be constructed rather than natural is simply suppressed.

Nor does the development of Darwinian theory mark the end of anthropocentrism or of androcentrism in biology. Indeed, as Ruth Hubbard notes, Darwin's results reinforce the Victorian stereotype of the active male and the passive female reflected in the structure of Victorian patriarchy. She cites the example of Wickler's observations about bighorn sheep, a species in which the sexes cannot be distinguished on sight. Wickler finds it curious that 'between the extremes of rams over eight years old and lambs less than a year old one finds every possible transition in age, but no other differences whatever; the bodily form, the structure of the horns, and the color of the coat are the same for both sexes.' Hubbard continues: 'Now note: "... the typical female behaviour is absent from this pattern." Typical of what? Obviously not of Bighorn sheep. In fact we are told that "even the males often cannot recognize a female," indeed, "the female are only of interest to the males during rutting season." How does he know that the males do *not* recognize the females? Maybe these sheep are so weird that most of the time they relate to a female as though she were just another sheep.'[12] The point is that if research is begun from the assumption that active behaviour on the part of an organism exemplifies the male principle, passive behaviour the female, then it is not surprising (given the way people tend to observe what they are prepared to observe) that the conclusion should emerge that the Victorian stereotype is bioligically determined. Even algae, Hubbard remarks, can be seen to exhibit this behaviour; and apparent exceptions tend to be regarded as aberrant, rather than as indications of inadequacy in the theory.[13] Hence Janet Sayers is able to trace a long history of writing about woman's nature in which there is a pattern of 'falsely project[ing] human sex roles onto animal behaviours in order to claim the biological determination of these roles.'[14]

The epistemological-political consequences of the tenacity of stereotypes in determining woman's place in an epistemic community are manifold. If, for example, in the face of such scientific 'knowledge' about her nature, a woman should try to establish a level of credibility that the reinforced stereotype judges impossible, she will meet with resistance, both subtle and more blatant. This point is well illustrated in Baumgart's example. It is borne out in Charlotte Perkins Gilman's attempts to speak from her experience against the knowledge and authority of the experts, documented in her autobiographical novel *The Yellow Wallpaper*. Here the heroine tries to convince her (doctor) husband that she needs work and stimulation rather than a 'rest cure' of the sort designed by Dr S. Weir Mitchell, to treat her for what has been diagnosed as a serious nervous disorder.

In preparation for her own treatment by Dr Mitchell, Gilman prepared a history of her experiences which Dr Mitchell dismissed 'as evidence of "self-conceit".' He did not want information from his patients; he wanted 'complete obedience.'[15] The example is analogous to the case Baumgart cites: women are dismissed as having only experience to go on, men are judged to have knowledge. By comparison with the latter, the former is deemed worthless. Investigations to determine whether this state of affairs arises by chance, or in consequence of women's nature, tend to opt for the second of these possibilities and to support their findings with evidence, expertise, and authority.

Women's efforts to defy stereotypes in the wider scientific world mirror the situation in medicine. As late as 1968, women graduate students in science at Yale were *told* that they were being trained to be the wives and research associates of their male fellow-students.[16] It is difficult to see this as any improvement over the situation of women astronomers in the Harvard College Observatory in the 1880s and 1890s, where the alleged champion of women's right to higher education and to employment in the sciences, Edward Pickering, hired innumerable patient, and *grateful* women for the painstaking (but publicly invisible) task of observing and classifying stellar spectra. This incident serves as a microcosmic illustration of woman's place in professional science per se.

Circumstances such as these are designed to ensure that women's cognitive authority remains as limited as it has been throughout the history of science, where outstanding, authoritative, paradigm-creating achievement rarely bears the name of a woman. We have Boyle's law, Lavoisier's theorem, Einsteinian physics, Darwinian and Freudian theory. Yet there are few noteworthy theorems, laws, or theories that bear women's names.[17] When one considers the authoritative role of a paradigm in designating what counts as valid cognitive endeavour, it is small wonder that the absence of female-created paradigms might suggest the conclusion that such high-quality research is beyond woman's capacity. Yet it is equally reasonable to suppose that an explanation for this absence of women might lie in the subtle effect of what persistently poses as knowledge about how women's nature renders them unfit for high-profile intellectual activity of any sort. The Victorian stereotype is plainly as hard at work here as it is in Darwin's research.

Such illustrations of how alleged knowledge about female 'nature' determines women's place within an epistemic community suggests that research into gender differences is not to be accepted acritically as objective, theory-neutral research, however apparently respectable its methodological procedures. Now, this claim, in itself, is neither startling nor particularly damning at a time when most epistemologists and philosophers of science are conversant with Thomas Kuhn's work.[18] Even those who do not endorse Kuhn's conclusions will be familiar with his contention that innumerable social, historical, cultural, and personal factors influence the shape and content of scientific research. In consequence, the unlikelihood of pure objectivity, perfect theory-neutrality, either in science of in knowledge-seeking more generally, is widely acknowledged. Our concept of what it is to know has expanded to accommodate this recognition, partially as a result of Kuhn's work.

In fact, there are noteworthy points of functional similarity between stereotypes and Kuhnian paradigms. Most striking is the way in which, in stereotype-governed perceptions and claims to know, exceptions tend to be discounted as aberrant. This similarity is one implication of Weisstein's remark, emphasized in the passage quoted above, to the effect that counter-examples fail to prevent theories of natural male privilege from proliferating, and of Hubbard's demonstration of how the unquestioned assumption that active behaviour on the part of an organism exemplifies the male principle, and passive behaviour the female, leads biologists to *see* in certain theory-determined ways. Like Kuhnian paradigms, stereotypes filter out counter-evidence so as not to be significantly weakened by it, although they also tend to be strengthened by confirming instances. These similarities indicate something of why it is so difficult to make progress against the tenacity of the stereotype.[19]

It would be a mistake, though, to see parallels with Kuhnian scientific practice to be too close, for there are several points of disanalogy. The most significant of these is in the fact that, on Kuhn's theory, it is not possible for practitioners to engage in normal science without paradigms to guide their recognition of problems, and their problem-solving endeavours. Stereotype-governed thinking is different in this respect, for it is both possible and indeed desirable to think and to know in a manner *not* governed by stereotypes.

A still more important point of disanalogy, for the purposes of this discussion, is in the fact that paradigms governing research in the physical sciences are, in the main (whether rightly or wrongly is another question), regarded as morally neutral. And this could not be so in the human sciences.[20] This point requires some clarification. I commented above upon the importance, for human beings, of knowing well, and gave some indication of how this capacity is connected with having a good intellectual character. Good intellectual character is manifested in responsible cognitive endeavour, some of whose features are: a just degree of open-mindedness; a recognition of how far an enquiry should be taken before one can rightfully claim knowledge; a self-critical stance to be wary of undue prejudice and bias; an educated imagination, attuned to the implications of what one is doing; and a willingness to assume responsibility for the consequences of the enquiry.

Undue bias might be detected from having results come out *too well* in confirmation of one's starting hypotheses, just as it might be evident in an inability to account for persistently troubling aspects of a situation. It requires a combination of the right degree of integrity and a well-developed imagination to detect such shortcomings in one's own intellectual efforts. More often it requires persistent questioning and criticism from other persons before one is prepared to relinquish cherished theoretical assumptions. But knowing well is a matter as much of *moral* as of epistemological concern. So, it is not just because of how the results, for example, of gender research are *used* that one can declare the stereotype often governing it to be morally dubious, but because the conduct of the research itself is not responsible.

In psychology and anthropology it is by now well known that the presence of an observer affects the nature of what is observed,[21] and is bound to affect that nature differently according to the preconceptions an observer brings to the project. Even in carefully controlled experiments, where there is no outward, conscious difference in behaviour, the hypotheses that provide the impetus for research projects may influence the behaviour of subjects tested.[22] The importance of this point in evaluating studies of women is obvious, for social expectation has a deep influence upon how people literally *can* be.[23] It is not difficult to imagine that stereotypical expectations on the part of an experimenter might act as self-fulfilling prophecies, influencing the performance of female subjects or leading to an implicitly wished-for interpretation of their responses. This matter is by no means a morally neutral one with regard either to the way research is conducted or to the use to which its results are put.

An awareness of these factors puts a considerable onus upon putative knowers to be circumspect, so that inevitable subjective factors (i.e., factors arising out of the cognitive 'location' of knowers) are recognized and controlled. These factors act as a constant constraint upon the very possibility of objectivity. Yet, when science – or social science – looks at women, it seems that observers are no longer as neutral as they could be, even taking into account the unattainability of pure theory-neutrality. Findings that purport to show certain traits to be inherent in female nature reveal so persistent an observer bias that one must conclude that an intolerable degree of closed-mindedness is at work in the processes that produce them.

Such findings are often articulated so as to obscure the symmetry of the relation of difference, and hence to point to unjustified evaluative conclusions. If woman's nature could be shown to be essentially different *from* man's nature, then it would also be true that man's nature is different from woman's. Yet, from the demonstration that a difference exists, no evaluative conclusions can legitimately be taken to follow as a matter of course. More often than not, however, the results of research into male and female 'natures' are interpreted so as to show that it is *female* nature alone that is different. The implication, of course, is that male nature *is* human nature, and that female nature is aberrant. This conclusion is taken to support the 'complementarity' thesis, which designates separate male and female domains, alleging that it is natural for the female of the human species to behave in a certain way and hence to remain at home with the children, engaged in passive, submissive, nurturing activities. (The view that it is more appropriate for women to be nurses than doctors is a variation on this theme.)

These remarks about the epistemological rigidity of stereotypes may seem to indicate that women are trapped without hope of escape. But this is not the only possible conclusion. In fact, there seem to be two routes to be taken to undermine the stereotype, both implicit in what has been said so far. To take these routes with any hope of success, one must learn to recognize the extent to which stereotypical perceptions of what women *are* sustain the obstacle women face in trying to bring an end to patriarchy. I have given some indication of how widespread these perceptions are.

One such route is to show repeatedly that women can *do* all of the things the stereotype takes to be beyond their capacities. Without begging the question as to whether there are inherent differences between women's and men's capacities, one can propose that women show what they think, know, and feel *as themselves*, with whatever positive sense of self they know to be their own. To do this, they have to defy the stereotype sufficiently to stand up for the validity of that sense of self. But this need not be a solitary task: the women's movement constantly demonstrates the effectiveness of collective realization and action.

The second complementary task is to maintain vigilance for manifestations of stereotypical perceptions, and to demonstrate their falsity. Its performance requires an awakened feminist consciousness, with the altered awareness of self, of others, and of 'social reality' that constitutes that consciousness. The 'apprehension of possibility' implicit in feminist consciousness,[24] together with a differently illuminated meaning of hitherto-unnoticed practices, attitudes, and nuances, can make it possible for feminists to discern the subtler effects of stereotyping and to respond to its manifestations appropriately. Appropriate response will be finely tuned to avoid simply, and irresponsibly, countering ideology with ideology. For such a confrontation could only result in a stand-off, rather than significant change.

Neither practical measures nor theoretical challenge alone will do. The former will have no lasting effects until they come to reflect a loosening of the stranglehold of entrenched theory; and that theoretical stranglehold will not be broken without practical measures to show its inadequacy. But Kuhnian paradigms do, ultimately, yield to excessive strains upon their explanatory and action-directing capacities. There is every reason to suppose that stereotypes are like them in this respect, particularly when political efforts to demonstrate their inadequacy are sustained.

Epistemology

The distinction between knowledge and experience, upon which so much of the credibility of participants in the Grange Inquiry is taken to rest, is puzzling. From a theoretical point of view, the assumption that there is a sharp break between experience and knowledge, such that accumulated experience can neither be equated with knowledge nor taken to be its source, is curious, if not paradoxical, given the persistent high esteem enjoyed by empiricist methodology both in philosophy of science and in knowledge more generally. Empirical investigation, i.e., investigation based in sensory observation, which is surely a form of experience, is commonly regarded as the surest and most reliable source of knowledge. So, it is odd that persons whose *experience* is clearly recognized should not, on the basis of it, be regarded as rightful knowers.

Part of the explanation seems to lie in the long-standing epistemological assumption that *knowledge* properly deserving of the name will in fact transcend or prescind from experience. Although it may begin there, it must soon leave experience behind, with the particularity and seductiveness of its sensory and affective components, if it is to approach an ideal of objectivity, perfect rationality, and impartiality. Knowledge properly so called is untainted by the subjectivity of experience.[25]

This knowledge/experience dichotomy is of a piece with several other dichotomies standardly taken to mark crucial philosophical distinctions, all of which have epistemological implications: namely, the mind/body, reason/emotion, theory/practice, and public/private dichotomies, among others. Feminists are now well aware that the male/female dichotomy runs parallel to those just cited, and that, as with the other dichotomies, the distinction between male and female is marked evaluatively, and not just descriptively. In each dichotomy cited, the left-hand term marks that which is the more highly valued; and in most cases, the right-hand term marks that which is not only devalued, but is often outrightly denigrated.[26]

It is a philosophical commonplace that mind and its activities are superior to body and its experiences. From Plato's insistence that knowledge can be achieved only when one has liberated oneself from the deceptiveness of the senses, through Descartes's conception of the soul as pure intellect, to Kant's critique of pure reason, this philosophical theme is a persistent and common one. The alignment of reason with matters of the mind, and emotion with bodily experience, is a related line of thought. Emotion, it is believed, clutters and constrains the efforts of reason in the performance of its essential task: that of arriving at certainty in knowledge. The theory/practice dichotomy reflects these same assumptions. Theoretical knowledge is held to be the highest achievement of reason working to its fullest capacity. Such knowledge is characterized as abstract, universal, timeless, and true. To attain this status it must transcend the particularity of practical knowledge – clearly a lesser breed – with its preoccupation with the contingent, the concrete, and the here and now.

The parallel between the public/private dichotomy and those dichotomies I have just mentioned is less close, but none the less evident. Throughout the history of philosophy it is assumed that reason is alike in all *men*, and that results of intellectual endeavour that follows the dictates of reason have the best chance of being true. Although these assumptions alone do not warrant aligning reason with the 'public' side of the public/private dichotomy, the alignment looks more plausible when one considers characterizations of emotion, as it is construed in opposition to reason. Emotions belong to individuals, and are thus associated with the particular, whimsical (that is, not subject to rule or regulation) aspect of what it is to be human. Human beings are often believed to be passive with respect to emotion, and emotion is to be suppressed when one is engaged in deliberation and ratiocination. It is the products of these latter processes that are appropriately placed before the public eye, and used as the bases of policy and action by authoritative public figures. It is not that one may not care about the everyday affairs of practical life and, in particular, about one's personal associations with other human beings. But these belong to the private aspect of life, which theoretical reasoning must leave behind in its efforts to attain universally valid, public knowledge.[27]

All of this connects with the familiar view that men live their lives, in the main, in the public realm and women in the private realm. This historical-sociological fact (or belief) is related to, and may indeed derive from, the dichotomies I have mentioned. The association of woman with the material, the bodily, the seductive, that which diverts the (male) mind from its highest pursuits, runs through the history of philosophy, in various guises, from Aristotle through Descartes, Rousseau, Kant, and Hegel, to Sartre and even de Beauvoir. Equally persistently, women are taken to be emotional beings (often pejoratively so), whereas it is men who are attracted to, and excel in, the life of reason. Indeed, it is from the *Man of Reason*, as Genevieve Lloyd shows us, that the common Western understanding of reason as an intellectual character ideal is derived. And conceptions of reason have, throughout a long history, been articulated through more or less conscious 'exclusions of the feminine.'[28] Because of their essentially emotional, and more purely physical nature, women are assumed to be best suited to take care of practical matters, whereas the theoretical realm has been largely a male preserve, often jealously guarded. Since rationality, a sound grasp of theoretical principles, and highly developed mental capabilities have long been touted as the prerequisites for entry into the public domain, it follows that those more preoccupied with particularity and the practical should occupy themselves with private matters.

These, then, are some of the factors shaping the hierarchical confrontation between women and men that Baumgart describes, where it is the men who know, and the women who have only (individual, practical) experience to call upon. Within the experiential domain itself, a hierarchical division is inferred, and in consequence these nurses are 'privatized' even with respect to their work in the public domain. Their 'experience' is regarded quite differently from the experience that supports empirical knowledge claims and is regarded as universal, generalizable, publicly accessible, and experimentally testable. Caught in a complex social power structure generated out of stereotyped assumptions and false dichotomies, the nurses are credited only with practical experience, individually lived and felt, inchoate and unsystematic.

It is instructive to consider what it means, for a cognitive agent, to have her experience denigrated and the expertise it might be supposed to confer denied the status of knowledge. Established credibility determines a person's status in an epistemic community; status (authority) within that community determines the extent to which one's experience can influence knowledge; and a capacity to contribute knowledgeably goes unnoticed if one is prevented from presenting one's knowledge in acceptable form. Taken together with indications of the extent to which social expectation structures possibilities of *being*,[29] the implication is that women indeed cannot (barring a few exceptions) be accredited members of an epistemic community; their knowledge cannot become part of that community's received knowledge; and, one might venture, received knowledge, as a product, is thus impoverished by contrast with what it might be.

Some of these points are, admittedly, open to challenge of a methodological nature. But I do not include the apparent circularity of the argument leading up to them, for it reflects the viciousness of the circle created by this situation. However, I have based these observations upon contingent, empirical facts about (female) human existence, and have presented them as though there were in fact a discernibly different female way of knowing, thus apparently buying into the feminine stereotype and ignoring the symmetry of difference. These points require further comment.

The observations are based in contingent empirical facts out of the conviction that this is where philosophical reflection should begin. It may be logically possible for every human mind both female and male, to know exactly the same things in exactly the same ways. Much epistemological theory is written on the assumption that there is just such a standard human mind capable, logically at least, of attaining knowledge defined as the ideal product of a closely specified reasoning process. Such assumptions underlie and sustain the dichotomies I have discussed. But reference to logical possibilities is irrelevant when practical possibilities so clearly structure the situation upon which reflection is needed. It is difficult to see how philosophical reflection can serve human beings well if, in its preoccupation with theoretical perfection, it loses sight of the practical concerns it is meant to illumine.[30]

In suggesting that knowledge is impoverished by the extrusion of all that is *traditionally feminine*, my point is to say that knowledge is a lesser product than it might be in consequence of having drawn its methodological boundaries so as to exclude experiential, emotional, practical, and subjective elements. Given that, in its public presentation, it has also excluded women, and that women have long been associated with these aspects of human existence, it is not too preposterous to surmise that the inclusion of aspects of the traditionally feminine into the product might change the nature of that product.

Feminists working in theory of knowledge have begun to offer some suggestions as to how this inclusion of the feminine might be effected. And this is a task that can responsibly be undertaken without first taking a stand with respect to the question of natural differences either way, except to recognize that human beings are creatures whose nature is, to a great extent, constructed by nurture. The results of these investigations are such as to render plausible the suggestion that epistemology might look quite different from the way it standardly looks, had women (traditionally socially constituted) been creators of epistemic standards, only later to have 'male' characteristics taken into account. So, too, the introduction of 'female' characteristics might bring quite a different perspective to reflection upon the product historically created by (traditionally socially constituted) men.

The epistemological situation is analogous to the one in the moral domain that prompted Carole Gilligan to challenge the basic premises of Lawrence Kohlberg's theory of moral development, where women's moral experience has fallen into a shadowy realm of the not properly moral.[31] Gilligan contends that the apparent failure of women to achieve autonomy and moral maturity as measured on Kohlberg's scale is more plausibly interpreted as evidence of inadequacy in the scale itself than as a demonstration of natural *female* inadequacy. The tendency of female subjects to 'contextualize' their moral responses by drawing upon a cluster of experiential considerations can be read, on a different standard of interpretation, as evidence of moral strength and sophistication.

Gilligan's work, despite its flaws,[32] has given valuable impetus to a radical philosophical questioning of assumptions embedded in standard ethical theory. And here there are epistemological parallels. I have given some examples of how women fail to qualify as fully fledged members of the epistemic community, in certain cognitive domains, just as they fail to qualify as mature, properly autonomous members of the moral community. Woman's place in the epistemic community per se and her place in the moral community alike block access to the authoritative public being that knowledge and/or moral maturity confer(s) upon its possessors.

Some epistemologists, pursuing a type of enquiry analogous to Gilligan's into the moral domain, suggest that the very notion of objectivity is an essentially masculine one. They are not accusing philosophers, scientists, and 'experts' of *intentionally* taking a masculine point of view into cognitive endeavour, distorting theories, experiments, and findings so as to sustain and reinforce that bias. What is at issue is more subtle. The fact that experiments are set up, designed, and carried out 'objectively' is not denied. It is the governing conception of objectivity itself that is considered dubious, though often at an unconscious level. Nor is the point simply that it is men who have been the philosophers, scientists, and authoritative knowers, and hence have created both the prevailing methodology and the criteria of truth and rationality. Rather, it is that, at least in Western societies, there is something about the way male human beings are nurtured, moulded, and *created* as adult human beings that contributes to the structure of the knowledge they create and the science they practice. So, they approach all that they do – and hence all cognitive activity – with an orientation created by a culturally transmitted, internalized 'sex/gender system.'[33]

Gilligan, for example, shows that in moral discourse male subjects exhibit an orientation towards maximum autonomy and objectivity, and an adherence to universal principles, while female subjects, in general, produce more contextual responses. Standard male responses mirror the high value placed upon objectivity, abstraction, generality, and theory-neutrality in (masculine) scientific methodology. Feminists working in ethics and in epistemology are alike tracing the roots of this way of thinking to the (Western) developmental process, where male human beings are nurtured towards separate, self-sufficient, maximally autonomous adult being. Female human beings, by contrast, are nurtured towards connected and caring adulthood.[34] In these developmental processes, it is suggested, we can see some explanations for the way scientific and moral thought and action are structured, and for the intellectual postures deemed essential to their proper conduct.

Arguing that concepts of 'rationality and objectivity, and the will to dominate nature,' have supported both the growth of a particular vision of science and the institutionalization of a definition of manhood, Evelyn Fox Keller points to the elusive problem that faces thinkers who would re-examine science – and, by extension, knowledge per se. She claims that 'Because science as we know it developed only once in history, the notion of a "different" science is to a considerable degree a contradiction in terms.'[35] Keller does not query the 'maleness' of science as it is practised. She denies neither the efficacy of its methodology nor the impressiveness of its accomplishments. So, the differences she envisages would not entail a rejection of scientific method as we know it. Rather, her project is to bring critical reflection to bear on the presumptions that sustain its hegemony, to locate science within human life, and to draw attention to the importance of what it *excludes*, at least in its dominant ideology.[36]

Space permits only the sketchiest account of the re-vision of scientific thinking Keller urges. She suggests that a science that would approach nature on the assumption that it is orderly, but not law-bound, hence neither unruly nor fixed, could accommodate the generativity and resourcefulness of nature within an enquiry 'premised on respect rather than domination' (p. 135). Out of such an approach might arise an attitude to difference, not unlike a view Keller has discerned in Barbara McClintock's methodological beliefs.[37] Because of McClintock's respect for difference in the specimens she studies she avoids dismissing difference as aberrant, and turns, rather, to study it with the aim of showing how it can assist her in interpreting conformity. Rather than positing a sharp rift between observer and observed (between subject and object), Keller points to the possibility of working in terms of a reciprocal subject-object relation, premised *not* on the belief that objects will be better known insofar as knowers achieve an 'objective' distance from them, but rather on the belief that it is possible to weaken presumed boundaries between subject and object. The primary goal of the activity is understanding, rather than manipulation, prediction, and control.[38] That Keller is not proposing a search for methodological pie in the sky is evident in her examples from scientific practice, which show that the hegemony of received methodology is a matter of history and politics, rather than of scientific and/or cognitive necessity, and hence it is inherently open to change.[39]

In fact, Keller suggests that standard scientific practice has tended to attract practitioners for whom an objectivist ideology, 'the promise of a cool and objective remove from the object of study,' provides emotional comfort.[40] In promising power and control over nature it selects individuals for whom these are worthwhile goals. In short, science draws to itself those who adhere strongly, in their character development, to the values implicit in the left-hand terms of the dichotomies I have discussed.

The solution as I see it is not to institute a celebration of feminine values, to be followed by a program that pastes these values on to already existing assumptions about good scientific practice, in order to arrive at an androgynous amalgam.[41] Unclear as the notion of an optimal solution may be, it might start from an exploration of two possibilities.

First, the divisiveness at the core of traditional epistemological thinking, manifested in dichotomies such as those I have discussed, has to be overcome. A first step towards achieving this might be to start thinking in terms of *differences* rather than dichotomies. Differences need not be construed as bipolar opposites, nor as pairs of terms pulling against each other, on a quasi-conflictual model, as is almost inevitable in dichotomous thinking. Rather, one might recognize a plethora of differences, shading into one another and reciprocally influencing each other. Thus one might avoid the construction both of sharply oppositional modes and of illegitimate evaluative assumptions. This approach might open a way towards developing that respect for difference manifested in McClintock's work; and towards seeing 'sameness' and 'difference' as knower-selected points of comparison in the objects of experience, rather than as (quasi-Heraclitean) metaphysical entities, in permanent tension one with another.

Second, one could draw a distinction between what scientific (and other) results enable human beings to *understand*, both about themselves and the world, and about science and knowledge and their place in human lives – and what they enable 'man' to *do*, by virtue of progress in scientific technique. Writing of technology, Ursula Franklin wisely cautions that it is 'as important to know what cannot be done any more because a certain technology is put in place as what the technology actually achieves,'[42] Technology, she says (and here she could be referring to the Grange inquirers!), has 'little use for experience.'[43] These thoughts indicate some of the conclusions that could be drawn from learning what it means to live on the negative side of certain dichotomies. Questions about meaning and appropriate response are central to the rethinking process. Franklin herself shows by example that this can be done, even by one well trained and immersed in 'malestream' science.

Conclusion

It is increasingly apparent that simple changes in surface social structures will not bring about the desired restructuring of thought and action that feminists recognize as necessary. It cannot simply be proposed, as though it were a solution, that more women be encouraged to enter science, and other masculine preserves, within currently dominant thought structures. The mere admission of a few women to a few carefully chosen and controlled places within scientific (or any other) practice, with the allegation that they will serve their successors as 'role-models' – those cardboard and superficial constructs – can serve no revolutionary purpose whatsoever. The problem exists at a much less ephemeral and transitory level, not captured in the notion of a role, to be put on and taken off at whim. It is a problem about who and what we are as human beings. Genuinely to change the status quo demands nothing less than a radical critique of entrenched thought structures. Yet, to follow the routes I have proposed seems to involve relinquishing some of the props that have long kept (or have appeared to keep) epistemic endeavours manageable. So, it might be insisted that the development of pure theory, following the dictates of reason, adhering to strict canons of objectivity, according to a publicly agreed-upon procedure, is the only way to promote a clarity and certainty in knowledge unassailed by the darker forces that are part of our 'lower' natures. To abandon that route is to admit ambiguity and tentativeness into both process and product. This move may well appear to be a reckless, dizzying, and even regressive one.

It can be made steadier, I suggest, through the development of a concept of responsible epistemic activity, where the notion of responsibility itself is amenable to spelling out. Epistemic responsibility can regulate cognitive activity in much the way virtues, such as kindness or justice, regulate moral activity: not absolutely, but often well. Among its other attributes, good intellectual character, shaped by a concern for responsible epistemic practice, can enable one to preserve the open-mindedness crucial to the development of a refocused cognitive vision, and can serve as a guard against the reductivism hitherto characteristic of much scientific – and other – knowledge. Such reductivism has manifested itself in stereotype-based knowledge claims, in the reduction of human behaviour to primate behaviour, in 'reducing the complexity of the real world by the construction of a model that represents an isolated, small part of that reality,'[44] and, to end where we began, in dismissing or discarding (female) experience in favour of granting authority only to knowledge obtained by a specific, often quantitative (masculine) methodology.[45]

NOTES

1 Alice Baumgart, 'Women, Nursing and Feminism,' in *The Canadian Nurse*, January 1985. Baumgart continues: 'In the health care system, doctors have been regarded as the only "rightful knowers". What the doctor-nurse game is really all about is that nurses know, but can't let the world know that they know' (p. 21).
2 The epistemological position in which this discussion is based is developed in my *Epistemic Responsibility* (Hanover, NH: University Press of New England/Brown University Press, 1987).

3 In my 'The Importance of Historicism for a Theory of Knowledge,' *International Philosophical Quarterly* 22, no. 2 (June 1982), I discuss some of the ways in which 'state of the art' knowledge counts as such a condition.

4 Mary Roth Walsh, 'The Quirks of a Woman's Brain,' in *Biological Woman: The Convenient Myth*, ed. R. Hubbard, M.S. Henifin, and B. Fried (New York: Schenkman, 1982), p. 245

5 Ibid., p. 244

6 The process, with many similar ones, is well documented in Barbara Ehrenreich and Deirdre English, *For Her Own Good: 150 Years of the Experts' Advice to Women* (New York: Doubleday Anchor Books, 1979). Here I quote from pp. 102–3.

7 Margaret Rossiter, *Women Scientists in America: Struggles and Strategies to 1940* (Baltimore: Johns Hopkins University Press, 1981), p. 74

8 Ibid., p. 76

9 It is awareness of these misconceptions, no doubt, that prompts Katherine Hilbery, in Virginia Woolf's novel *Night and Day*, to conceal her secret passion for mathematics; and such fears must trouble Ann Veronica's father, in H.G. Wells's novel of that title, when he tries to protect Ann from the potentially harmful effects of going up to London to study chemistry.

10 The continuing need to struggle against such obstacles is well documented, for example, in Anne Sayre, *Rosalind Franklin and D.N.A.: A Vivid View of What It Is Like to Be a Gifted Woman in an Especially Male Profession* (New York: W.W. Norton & Co., 1975); and in Evelyn Fox Keller, 'The Anomaly of a Woman in Physics,' and Naomi Weisstein, 'Adventures of a Woman in Science,' both in *Working It Out: 23 Women Writers, Scientists and Scholars Talk about Their Lives*, eds. S. Ruddick and P. Daniels (New York: Pantheon Books, 1977).

11 Naomi Weisstein, 'Psychology Constructs the Female,' in *Woman in Sexist Society*, ed. V. Gornick and B. Moran (New York: 1974), p. 219

12 Ruth Hubbard, 'Have Only Men Evolved?' in *Biological Woman*, pp. 31–2

13 Ibid., p. 27

14 Janet Sayers, *Biological Politics* (London: Tavistock Publications, 1982), p. 79

15 Ehrenreich and English, *For Her Own Good*, pp. 101–2. Mitchell's 'rest cure,' with its requisite complete obedience, was prescribed to countless intelligent middle- and upper-class women who were unable to cope with woman's lot in late-nineteenth-century society, defined, as it was, by the prevalent conception of woman's nature as 'weak, dependent, and diseased.'

16 Vivian Gornick, *Women in Science* (New York: Simon & Schuster, 1983), p. 78

17 The Cauchy-Kovalevskaia theorem in mathematics is an important, if obscure, exception here. But Sofia Kovalevskaia's struggles to gain recognition do not give us much cause to see her situation as a genuine challenge to the stereotype. (Her story is told by Ann H. Koblitz in *A Convergence of Lives: Sofia Kovalevskaia: Scientist, Writer, Revolutionary* [Boston: Birkhauser, 1983].) Perhaps Barbara McClintock could be seen as a genuine exception, in view of her having been awarded the Nobel Prize for genetics. But the story of her long obscurity does not inspire confidence that change is occurring rapidly, or significantly. (See Evelyn Fox Keller, *A Feeling for the Organism: The Life and Work of Barbara McClintock* [New York: W.H. Freeman & Co., 1983].) In her paper 'The Man of Professional Wisdom,' in *Discovering Reality: Feminist Perspectives on Epistemology, Metaphysics, Methodology, and Philosophy of Science*, ed. S. Harding and M. Hintikka (Boston: D. Reidel Publishing Co., 1983), Kathryn Addelson has a useful discussion of the role of cognitive authority in the growth of knowledge.

18 See Thomas Kuhn, *The Structure of Scientific Revolutions* (Chicago: University of Chicago Press, 1970).

19 I examine other aspects of the epistemological workings of stereotypes in my article, 'The Tyranny of Stereotypes,' in *Women: Isolation and Bonding: The Ecology of Gender*, ed.K. Storrie (Toronto: Methuen, 1987).

20 Kuhn, of course, does not think that there are paradigms in the human and social sciences, though many practitioners in these fields cite his work as though it were straightforwardly applicable to their discipline. But this is aside from the point at issue here.

21 In consequence of Heisenberg's having demonstrated that an observer has an effect upon the behaviour of the observed in particle physics, one must reserve judgment as to whether there could be any validity in a claim that physical sciences differ from human sciences in this regard.

22 Weisstein, 'Psychology Constructs the Female.' She cites an example of IQ testing where students whose teachers had been told that they were 'promising' showed remarkable improvement in later tests; and suggests that something in the conduct of the teachers towards those they believed to be the bright students worked to 'make' those students brighter.

23 I discuss the influence of social expectation on how women can be in my 'Responsibility and the Epistemic Community: Woman's Place,' in *Social Research*, vol. 50, no. 3 (October 1983).

24 I owe this characterization of feminist consciousness to Sandra Lee Bartky, in her 'Toward a Phenomenology of Feminist Consciousness,' in *Feminism and Philosophy*, ed. M. Vetterling-Braggin, F. Elliston, and J. English (Totowa, NJ: Littlefield, Adams & Co., 1977), pp. 23–5.

25 Notable recent exceptions to this attempt to consider knowledge in ab-

straction from the human experiences that produce it are Richard Rorty's *Philosophy and the Mirror of Nature* (Princeton, NJ: Princeton University Press, 1980) and Richard Bernstein's *Beyond Objectivism and Relativism* (Philadelphia: University of Pennsylvania Press, 1984). Both Rorty and Bernstein take some of their inspiration from Heidegger, and from the American pragmatist tradition; and it is fair to say that Heidegger and the pragmatists are alike in expressing unease about philosophical attempts to separate discussions of knowledge and truth from their sources in, and implications for, human practical affairs.

26 Both Mary O'Brien, in *The Politics of Reproduction* (London: Routledge & Kegan Paul, 1981), and Genevieve Lloyd, in *The Man of Reason* (London: Methuen, 1984), show how these dichotomies, with their attendant evaluative associations, have arisen historically out of the Pythagorean table of opposites.

27 As Genevieve Lloyd observes: 'From their earliest origins in Greek thought, our ideals of Reason have been associated ... with the idea of a public space removed from the domestic domain. Reason is the prerequisite for, and point of access to, not just the public domain of political life but also a public realm of thought – a realm of universal principles and necessary orderings of ideas' (in 'Reason, Gender, and Morality in the History of Philosophy,' *Social Research* 50, no. 3 [October 1983]).

28 Lloyd, *The Man of Reason*, p. 109. My discussion here owes much to Lloyd's subtle account of the history of our ideals of reason.

29 In addition to Weisstein, 'Psychology Constructs the Female,' the influence of expectations upon women's possibilities is discussed in Matina Horner's work. See especially her 'Toward an Understanding of Achievement-related Conflicts in Women,' *Journal of Social Issues* 29 (1972).

30 This separation of theory from practice is one principal source of feminist disenchantment with traditional epistemology. Genevieve Lloyd observes, 'In the perception of many contemporary women, Philosophy is identified with theoretical thought in its most aberrant form – distanced from concern with human goods, distanced from the realities of life' (in 'History of Philosophy and the Critique of Reason,' *Critical Philosophy*, vol. 1, no. 1 [1984], p. 22).

31 See Carol Gilligan, *In a Different Voice: Psychological Theory and Women's Development* (Cambridge, Mass: Harvard University Press, 1982).

32 Some of these flaws are discussed in the articles in *Social Research* 50, no. 3 (1983).

33 This is Gayle Rubin's phrase, introduced in her article, 'The Traffic in Women: Notes on the "Political Economy of Sex",' in *Toward an Anthro-*

pology of Women, ed. R. Reiter (New York: Monthly Review Press, 1975). Sandra Harding examines the epistemological implications of this 'system' in her paper, 'Why Has the Sex/Gender System Become Visible Only Now?' in *Discovering Reality*. She develops an extensive account of feminist epistemological concerns in *The Science Question in Feminism* (Ithaca, NY: Cornell University Press, 1986). Both Jane Flax's and Nancy Hartsock's papers in the Harding and Hintikka volume are important contributions to the growing feminist epistemological literature.

34 An instructive account of this developmental process is elaborated in Nancy Chodorow, 'Gender, Relation, and Difference in Psychoanalytic Perspective,' in *The Future of Difference*, ed. H. Eisenstein and A. Jardine (New Brunswick, NJ: Rutgers University Press, 1985).

35 Evelyn Fox Keller, *Gender and Science* (New Haven and London: Yale University Press, 1985), p. 64

36 Keller maintains that 'the practice of science is in fact quite different from its ideological prescriptions ... [and that] actual science is more faithfully described by the multiplicity of styles and approaches that constitute its practice than by its dominant rhetoric or ideology,' (ibid., p. 25).

37 Idem. See her biography of McClintock, *A Feeling for the Organism*.

38 In like vein, Hilary Rose writes of feminist-informed biological research: 'A preeminent characteristic of these investigations lies in their fusing of subjective and objective knowledge in such a way as to make new knowledge [where] Cartesian dualism, biological determinism, and social construction fade' in 'Hand, Brain, and Heart: A Feminist Epistemology for the Natural Sciences,' *Signs: Journal of Women in Culture and Society* 9, no. 1 (1983).

39 Compare Keller, *Gender and Science*, chaps. 7, 8, and 9.

40 Ibid., p. 124

41 Thus, in her Marxist analysis of the same problem, Rose argues that it is 'not enough merely to add a female dimension to a basically productionist argument by bringing in the caring contribution of women. Such an additive process runs the danger of denying the social genesis of women's caring skill ... it moves toward the essentialist thought that women are "naturally" more caring' (*Signs*, p. 84).

42 Ursula Franklin, 'Will Women Change Technology or Will Technology Change Women?' (Ottawa: CRIAW papers, 1985), p. 5

43 Ibid., p. 7

44 From Ruth Benston, 'Feminism and the Critique of Scientific Method,' in *Feminism in Canada*, ed. G. Finn and A. Miles (Montreal: Black Rose Press, 1982),p. 62

45 The writing of this paper was made possible by a Strategic Grant from the
Social Sciences and Humanities Research Council of Canada. Earlier
versions were read to the Research Seminar at Queen Elizabeth House
Centre for Cross-Cultural Research on Women in Oxford; at the Work
in Progress Seminar at the Humanities Research Centre in Canberra; and
at the Department of Philosophy at Macquarrie University in Sydney,
where I benefited greatly from the discussions. I am indebted to Murray
Code for extensive comments on a previous draft.

Feminism, Ontology, and 'Other Minds'

CHRISTINE OVERALL

This paper begins with a quotation and an anecdote.

'It is not easy to make clear an ontological proposal when basic concepts are involved. The difficulty is that the terminology in which the new ontology is to be articulated is automatically interpreted in terms of the accepted ontology, so that one is always at the risk of having one's statements construed either as nonsense, or as a quaint phrasing of what are familiar truths according to the old ontology.'[1]

Some years ago I was enrolled, with two other students, in an undergraduate seminar course in metaphysics. One of the topics we examined was the notorious 'problem of other minds.' After examining a variety of proferred solutions to the problem, I felt very puzzled. There seemed to be something wrong with the problem itself. But what was wrong was unclear to me, and I was not successful in conveying to the professor and my fellow students the nature of my doubts. In response to my ill-expressed worries, one of the students – now a successful Canadian philosopher – remarked, in jocular fashion, 'Ms Overall must be an existentialist.' And at that time, and in that place, he was not paying me a compliment.

A number of years have passed, and in the mean time we have witnessed the development of a feminist voice within contemporary philosophy. This feminist voice has offered a critique of some of our most cherished political, moral, and even epistemological tenets. Gradually, too, we are seeing the development of what Mary Daly calls a critique of ontology. But many of the ontological issues of Western philosophy have not yet been fully discussed by feminist philosophers. Such issues persist – even those one would expect to have died a quiet death. One example is my old friend, the problem of other minds, resurrected in born-again fashion in recent articles appearing in mainstream journals.

In this paper I want to grapple once more with those doubts that I felt years ago about the problem of other minds. This time, however, I shall do so from my perspective as a feminist. My discussion has been enormously aided by several papers by Caroline Whitbeck, who is in the process of developing what she calls 'a feminist ontology or metaphysics.'[2]

The paper has four sections. First I discuss the nature of the problem of other minds; that is, why it is and has been a problem, and the assumptions on the basis of which it is traditionally formulated. I next raise some questions about three features of the problem: its focus on *minds*, on the *otherness* of minds, and on *belief* in the otherness of minds. I then suggest, tentatively, a feminist re-vision of the problem, involving an alternative understanding of the self/other relationship, which is such that there is no genuine problem of other minds. And I conclude by exploring some more general questions about the sources of feminist ontology. Both in my critique of the traditional problem and in my re-vision, my primary resource is our experiences of human relationships: I argue that the problem of other minds has been false to those experiences, and that a genuine re-vision of the problem must take account of them.

Before proceeding farther, let me confess the limitations of my discussion. Although, of necessity, I talk a great deal about minds, I advance no explicit theory of the nature of the mind, or of the nature of the relationship of mind to body. Of course, these philosophical problems and the solutions offered to them are not irrelevant to the problem that I discuss here. For example, P.M.S. Hacker once made the helpful remark that there is nothing about a person that is inherently concealed, although we can, if we choose to, conceal (or reveal) our thoughts, hopes, etc. The mind is at least not the sort of thing that, like a wallet, one can somehow conceal about one's person. This point seems to be a particularly significant one in view of the usual approach to the problem of other minds which assumes that '"a mind" is something like an unobservable component or possession, and that what *is* observable is a (mindless) body or, at most, behavior.'[3] An example of this approach is the work of Alec Hyslop, who describes one proffered solution to the problem of other minds in the following terms: '[W]hat is seen as requiring explanation is the behaviour of other human figures, and the best explanation is the hypothesis that other human figures behave as they do because they are minded.'[4]

Nevertheless, despite the promising nature of suggestions like Hacker's, I believe that some important aspects of the problem of other minds can also profitably be discussed independently of a theory of the mind or an answer to the mind-body problem.

In addition, I confine my analysis of the problem to versions of it presented very recently – that is, since about 1970. I do this partly because I could not hope to deal with all of the voluminous literature on the topic accumulated during this century, but mainly because I want to show that, perhaps surprisingly, the problem is still, among a certain group of philosophers at least, very much a current one. I emphasize that I do not assume that all philosophers deal with the issue of other minds in just the way that this group does; nevertheless, what is criticized here is a remarkably consistent, long-lasting, and popular approach to the topic.

Finally, I acknowledge that the analysis offered in this paper is not the only possible way of criticizing the problem of other minds, and that feminists are by no means the sole theorists to be troubled by the problem. Nevertheless, the feminist approach is, I believe, a particularly fruitful one, and it provides a backdrop for more general speculations about ontology.

The Nature of the Problem

By treating other minds as constituting a *problem*, philosophers make certain assumptions about where the burden of proof rests – or, to be more exact, about what exactly is problematic in our relationships with other people. The other-minds theorist is puzzled as to how he can know that other minds exist and are something like his own.[5] He assumes that his most plausible pre-philosophical premise for this topic is that other minds do not exist, or that if they do, they are not like his. Then the burden of proof rests on the person who wishes to argue that there are other minds, and that they are (somewhat) like her own.[6] The problem is set up in such a way that there is an onus on the person who wishes to demonstrate likeness and similarity. The challenge becomes the epistemological one of justifying a belief whose foundation is, apparently, precarious.

Now why should this be? Must we accept this assumption as to where the burden of proof rests? I can imagine that one might instead start from an entirely different pre-philosophical assumption: that other persons exist and are very much like oneself. Then the burden of proof would rest upon the philosopher who wishes to demonstrate difference and dissimilarity, or maybe even the non-existence of other minds. If I were a mystic, I might assume a fundamental oneness of all living things; the burden of proof would rest with those who claim diversity and difference. Now, I do not suppose that most of us are mystics, or have had the sort of unitary experience on which mystics' convictions seem to be founded. But I mention the idea only to show that there is another possible approach, and that the assumption about where the burden of proof lies is not self-evident.

Both the manner in which the problem of other minds is set up and the various solutions that have so far been offered to it exemplify very well what Janice Moulton has called the 'adversary method' in philosophical thought.[7] Moulton remarks: 'With the Adversary Paradigm we do not try to assess positions or theories on their plausibility or worthiness or even popularity. Instead we are expected to consider, and therefore honor, positions that are most *un*like our own in order to show that we can meet their objections.'[8] Thus, having placed the burden of proof on the person who believes that there are other minds – on almost all of us, in other words, in our non-philosophical moments – traditional philosophers then advance various candidates that purport to solve the problem. The most frequently encountered of these, to which I shall refer briefly in my discussion, are the analogical argument; the criteriological argument; the theoretical-entities argument; the *verstehen* ('intuitive understanding') argument; and, most recently, the evolutionary argument.[9] Proponents of each of these fire off volleys of words at one another to defend their own view and demolish those of the competition.

What all of them have in common is not only the adversarial method of philosophizing, but, more generally, an adversarial view of human relationships, according to which establishing the existence of other minds and their partial similarity to one's own involves overcoming the fundamental alienation inherent in the human condition. Each of us must travel from what we think to be true of ourselves to what we surmise to be true of others. Thus, Alec Hyslop describes us as being 'confronted with' other human bodies.[10] The assumption is that we interact not with other persons but with bodies. We then somehow 'connect' these bodies with feelings. But no very great certainty is thereby attained: R.I. Sikora finds that we can conclude only that it is 'very highly probable that other bodies have experiences.'[11] Michael Levin describes this process as follows: 'When I see you writhing after banging your thumb with a hammer, I believe this behavior is contingently connected with pain."[2] Even more bizarrely, Robert Pargetter says the following:

Suppose I were to see a man with a deep cut in his hand. The cut is bleeding. The man is clutching the cut hand with his other hand. He looks pale and tense, and he has beads of perspiration on his brow. He wrings his hands up and down, and utters sentences such as 'My hand is hurting', 'I am in pain', and also groans and grunts.

One explanation of this man's behaviour is that he is in pain, his pain being much the same as mine in similar circumstances. Of course it is not the only explanation. He could be behaving like this for some other reason altogether. His behaviour may be caused by (or associated with) a very different kind of mental state from the kind I have had when I have behaved similarly. It is even possible that there is no mental state associated with this man's behaviour at all. However *one* explanation is that he is in pain, and that his pain is qualitatively similar to pains that I have experienced.[3]

From the alienated standpoint of the other-minds theorist, prior to offering a solution to the problem he has generated, my situation when I am spoken to by another human body is apparently no less puzzling than it would be if I were spoken to by my heretofore inanimate teapot. Hyslop says, 'The attempt to get directly from the known cause of my behaviour to the cause of the behaviour of others falls foul of [the] claim ... that faced only with others' behaviour the most likely explanation is that it has a purely physical cause.'[4] Similarly, Don Locke says, 'the fact that ... my feeling the blow was what made me cry out does not warrant the inductive inference that the behaviour of others is similarly related to mental states of their's [*sic*], not until we have established that in other cases there are not other sources of behaviour, e.g., the brute, mindless workings of an electo-chemical mechanism.'[5] And, in the end, according to these theorists, the big advantage in finally coming to know that human bodies are probably connected with minds is just that one can then predict what these bodies are likely to do. Says Levin, 'It is useful to know about the minds of others because what is on someone's mind is a good guide to what he will do, in particular if he will attack you.'[6]

Furthermore, both the problem of other minds and the solutions offered to it are founded upon a view of the person according to which each individual is alienated not only from others, as I have just shown, but even from himself. Other-minds theorists assume that I survey myself as if from the outside, and notice what kind of being I am: 'My mental states are characteristically accompanied by certain physical states and behavior patterns of my body, and characteristically occur in certain situations,' says Philip Ostien.[17] Levin says that an individual tends to 'read [his own] impulses to behave off [his] mental states.'[18] Pargetter says, 'I explain much of my own behaviour in terms of causation by mental events.'[19] Sikora says each of us forms the hypothesis that at least one person is associated with our body throughout its active existence.[20] Hyslop describes all of us as opting for the hypothesis that our mental states have a causal role in the production of our behaviour,[21] and he speaks of individuals as observing that their own 'manifestations of pain-behaviour are accompanied by pain.'[22] Thus the other-minds theorists appear to assume that we routinely observe ourselves from the outside in this apparently objective manner, and that each of us predicts her own behaviour and aligns it with her mental events.

Questionable Features of the Problem

According to the classic formulations of the problem, we must seek to justify our belief in the existence of other minds. As Ostien expresses it, 'We have good rational evidence for our belief in other minds but cannot state clearly and precisely what that evidence is.'[23] The challenge then is to discover the evidence on which our belief rests.

But do we in fact *believe* in the existence of other minds? In posing this question, I do not want to suggest that we do not believe in other minds. I am not saying that the belief is one which we just happen not to have. Nor am I saying, of course, that we disbelieve in other minds: that all or most of us consciously or unconsciously believe that other individuals do not have minds. So I am not saying that we entertain the belief that the statement 'Other minds exist' is false.

Instead, what I want to suggest is that the concept of belief is not appropriate here. We do not believe in other minds, and it is not even correct to say that we act as if we believe in them.[24] And it is not a matter of simply substituting another propositional attitude – such as the forming of a hypothesis – in the place of belief.[25] It would be a little more accurate (although problems remain with the other terms) to say that we accept the existence of other minds; we assume their existence. As Ostien says, their existence is a central tenet of our explanatory framework.[26] Yet even this redescription is, surely, inaccurate, for it suggests a cognitive approach to other persons which utterly fails, through inadequacy, to capture the lived experience of relating to the people one encounters. As T. Michael McNulty expresses it, 'I ... have no need to infer the existence of other minds; I *encounter* them.'[27] Wittgenstein also hints at this point when he writes, '"I believe that he is suffering." – Do I also *believe* that he isn't an automaton? It would go against the grain to use the word in both connexions ... My attitude towards him is an attitude towards a soul. I am not of the *opinion* that he has a soul.'[28]

A second feature of this problem is that it is formulated in terms of questions about a relationship to other *minds*. Here, for example, is how Ostien describes the data which we supposedly all possess: 'Other human beings appear to think and reason, sense and feel; in short, it appears that they too are minded beings.'[29] Similarly, Pargetter refers to 'the clearly justified belief that each of us has, namely that other people are minded, and that their minds are qualitatively similar to our own.'[30]

I would argue that this feature, too, of the problem is an error. Let us consider what really happens when I confront other persons. A variety of problems and questions may puzzle me. I may ask myself: What is he feeling or thinking? Can she remember the incident I am referring to? What do they know about this topic? What were his plans at that time? And so on. As a human being, I have specific doubts, problems, puzzles, and questions about other human beings, and they are genuine and, often, significant. I am helped to deal with my doubts and to answer my questions by a gradual accumulation of experience of human relationships; I am aided, sometimes, by reading literature, seeing plays, perhaps by studying psychology, or by undergoing a course of therapy. I thereby gradually come to understand and, it is to be hoped, to empathize with other people. But, as a human being, I am not grappling with any general problem. I do not ask myself whether another individual has a mind or whether, in general, there are other minds. And all of my concern about people's thoughts, beliefs, feelings, intentions, hopes, etc., does not add up to any belief that they have *minds*.

This is not to deny that a remotely related version of this philosophical problem crops up, on rare occasions. If, for example, a person is seriously ill, or apparently comatose, or severely injured, one might find oneself asking, in a sense, whether that person has a mind – that is, whether the individual is conscious, or is capable of rational thought, or is experiencing sensations and feelings. But notice that what is important about these cases is, first, their rarity; we seldom have to confront them, since in the great majority of cases it is entirely evident that the persons around us are conscious, capable of rational thought, and having sensations and feelings. Second, when doubts arise, they are not formulated in terms of asking whether a given individual has a *mind*; rather they are formulated as queries about what the person can or cannot do, and does or does not experience.

But the philosophical problem I am examining here is not just a problem about minds; it is a problem about *other* minds: How do we know that there are other minds? Notice what this formulation assumes: that there is a fundamental difference between my mind and others' minds; that there is a distance between us to be overcome. This emphasis on the *otherness* of other minds is connected to the adversarial nature of the problem which was discussed earlier. The problem of other minds rests upon solipsistic underpinnings, which are themselves founded upon feelings of isolation and remoteness. Hyslop, for example, asks, 'How do I know that I am not alone?'[31] Pargetter exclaims, 'there is a possibility that I am unique,' and he adds, 'Any argument to other minds is an attempt to justify the belief that I am not unique.'[32]

These are extraordinary claims. Admittedly, each of us is unique in the sense that no one else has exactly the same concerns, dreams, memories, ideas. But Pargetter's worry about uniqueness is a different one. It is that solipsistic, 'dark night of the soul' feeling that one is completely alone and entirely misunderstood.[33] The problem of *other* minds is founded upon suspicions of utter uniqueness that perhaps we all entertain from time to time. But these suspicions are entirely inadequate for founding an ontological problem. For of course, although I may at times be alone and ignored and misunderstood, at other times I am understood and loved and known − known well. In other words, there are other significant sorts of human experience that are just incompatible with the stance taken in the other-minds problem.

Now, those who take seriously the problem of other minds might make the following objection to my critique of its three features: Your error, they might say, is that you have entirely misconstrued the nature of the problem. You take it to be a sort of quasi-historical or perhaps psychological account of the origins of the belief in other minds. But it is not that at all; it is a conceptual account of our justification for this belief. Naturally, there is no real doubt in our ordinary lives about whether there are other minds; but as philosophers our concern is to know on what basis we have this 'clearly justified belief.'[34]

To this sort of objection I have three responses. First, I would point out that part of the issue here is whether the so-called problem of other minds should be seen at all, as its proponents claim, as a matter of philosophical justification for a belief. I contend that it should not; that it is conceptually inappropriate, for the reasons I have described, to construe our relationships to *other* people as involving a *belief* that they have *minds*. So the objection does no more than insist on the very point I am attacking.

Second, it should be observed that several of the traditional solutions to the problem of other minds may themselves be similar in some respects to a historical or psychological account of the development of our relationships to other persons. The analogical, theoretical entities, and *verstehen* arguments all involve discussions of the processes by which we gradually come to an understanding of 'what goes on in other people's heads.' The existence of these processes is not at issue. There can be no doubt that infants only gradually come to a realization and a growing understanding of the fact that the people in their lives have feelings. Certainly my children, when very small, seemed to operate from within an unverbalized yet clearly demonstrated assumption that mothers have no nerve endings, for they used me as a climbing frame and landing mat, with no apparent awareness that jumping on their mother might cause pain. One must teach a child not only to respect the feelings of other people, but, more fundamentally, to understand that other people *have* feelings. In making references to these sorts of processes, then, proponents of some of the traditional solutions to the other-minds problem themselves adopt a sort of psychological approach to trying to solve the problem; they could hardly then complain when a critic of the problem does the same.

But third, I would claim that any attempt to deal with philosophical problems about our relationships to and interactions with other people ought to have some connections to what people actually feel and do. I believe that it is entirely appropriate and relevant for me to talk about the kinds of questions we often do have about other people's thoughts and feelings. And it is an error to worry about such a problem in the absence of any connection to what our relationships with other people are really like. In short, I am insisting here on the fundamental importance of taking into account our actual experience of human relationships.

A Feminist Re-Vision of the Problem

Adrienne Rich defines 're-vision' as 'the act of looking back, of seeing

with fresh eyes, of entering an old text from a new critical direction.'[35]
A feminist re-vision of the problem of other minds would begin by
rejecting the alienated view of the self and its connection with others
which is implicit in the problem. It would observe that the very
condition of seeing oneself as a self is the recognition of other selves. As
I remarked earlier, a very young child clearly does not recognize its
mother (or anyone else) as being an 'other mind' – but then it does not
see itself that way either, for it is not yet a developed person. The
recognition, or more fundamentally the constitution, of oneself as a
self requires the presence of other selves. Thus the relationship to
other persons provides a context for the development of oneself;[36] and
each of us comes to recognize others as persons as we come to recognize
ourselves as separate beings. This means much more than the mere
acknowledgment of an adversary or the admission of the existence of
an object to be subordinated. As Whitbeck puts it, '[R]elationships
between people ... develop[ ] through identification and differentiation, through listening and speaking, with *each other*, rather than
through struggles to dominate or annihilate the other.'[37]

Some specific relationships seem to be particularly illuminating of
this developmental process. But they have not often been discussed by
philosophers. As Whitbeck remarks,

Bodily experience, like human vulnerability and mortality, are subjects
that modern philosophy has shunned describing except in the most abstract
terms. The fantasy that the philosopher is a 'pure' intellect, or even that
philosophy is the paradigm activity of 'pure intellects', runs through much of
the history of western philosophy, and influences both the choice of problems and the mode of discussion and argument ... That our bodies are (an
aspect of) ourselves, that human experience is the experience of an embodied being is still often unthinkable for many men and women, and the
aspects of bodies and bodily experience that are peculiar to women are still
often regarded as unspeakable, even among academics.[38]

What is being proposed is that we must widen our understanding of
what constitutes evidence for philosophical theorizing. In particular,
feminists draw attention to the relationships of a pregnant woman to
her foetus, and of a parent to her child.

The relationship of a pregnant woman to the foetus growing within
her is unique within human experience. When seen from the (predominantly male) medical point of view, it is often misunderstood; the
medical model sees mother and foetus as separate individuals, adver-

saries with often incompatible needs.[39] By contrast, Whitbeck suggests that pregnancy might most fruitfully be compared to the experiences of being possessed or inspired.[40] To the woman, the foetus is both self and not-self; most intimately a part of her and also an intrusive stranger. At least in the case of wanted and accepted pregnancies, the foetus is not experienced as an adversary; but neither is it experienced as just another body part.[41] The relationship to it is a concrete and immediate experience of identity in difference. And this simultaneous relationship to what both is and is not oneself continues in a transformed fashion after the birth, when the woman breast-feeds her infant,[42] and even beyond that stage, as the child grows through the initial stages of dependence and vulnerability. In those early stages the well-being of mother and child are inextricably linked.[43]

I suggest that, for the woman involved, all of these interactions constitute immediate lived experience that she is not unique, not a solipsistic self in an indifferent universe inhabited by programmed robots. As Whitbeck expresses it, 'bringing another person into full social being requires continual renegotiation of the self-other boundaries.'[44]

And this suggestion is in no way diminished by the claim that some mothering may be oppressive or involve domination of the child. For the nature of successful mothering is that it is non-adversarial, and involves the acceptance and fostering of the child who is cherished for her own sake, recognizing her as a vital and genuine person in her own right. To cherish a child without binding or constraining her to one's own vision, to enfold her in one's love without smothering her in one's anxieties, to respond to her needs without fostering her dependence, is to fully mother that child.

Hence, there is not a problem, in this context at least, of how to construe the mothering experience.[45] For I am not suggesting merely that those who mother have special and unique experiences on the basis of which they then feel qualified to make claims about the existence of other selves. I am suggesting that certain sorts of experiences are, in themselves, incompatible with the cognitive stance inherent in the problem of other minds. '[T]o start with a being that is not a relational being, and to call her or him forth into human relationship'[46] is to *know*, to fully live the realization, that one is a human self among other human selves, both developed and developing. This recognition, I would suggest, *constituted* as it is in experience, must cause us to regard the problem of other minds as illegitimate, a pseudo-problem.

Concluding Remarks

This discussion has offered a specifically feminist re-vision of the other-minds problem. In saying this, I do not merely mean that the re-vision is proposed by feminists. Rather, it is feminist because it is derived at least in part from an awareness of the experiences and practices of women.

Here it might be asked whether those practices and experiences inevitably belong to women only. Are they contingent upon the special socialization and training of women, or are they somehow inherent in women's very nature? If they are inherent then there is an unavoidable incommensurability in women's and men's perspectives on these issues. But if they are merely contingent, then a change in socialization will mean a change in women's (and men's) perspectives.[47] From this latter point of view, then, there is nothing specifically feminist about the ontological view offered here. For it is just an accident of history that women are an oppressed group and therefore advance criticisms, based on their experience, of the dominant ontology; but in a matriarchy, where women rule, it would be men whose perspectives and interests would offer important insights into ontological problems.[48]

In response, I hasten to say that although I believe that the experiences I have cited are particularly significant to this feminist re-vision of the problem of other minds, I am claiming neither that all women inevitably are subject to them, nor that only women are subject to them. Moreover, such experiences may not be the only possible source of insight into an alternative understanding of the self/other relationship. Of course, human biology being what it is, only women (so far) can gestate, give birth, and suckle infants. But the ongoing experience of 'calling forth' a child into full human relatedness is one which men may share. One need not be a mother in the biological sense to engage in mothering. Furthermore, I suspect that other close relationships of human caring, including, but not limited to, some friendships and some sexual/romantic relationships, may also involve that state of engrossment[49] and personal concern which characterizes mothering at its best. In other words, I am calling attention to a range of similar experiences, only some of which are unique to (some) women. For my purposes, what is primarily important in mothering is, therefore, not the sex of the person who mothers, or the immaturity of those who are usually mothered, but rather the nature of the regard expressed for them. So these experiences are not exclusive to women who have procreated, or even to women in general. Although I am criticizing the cognitive privilege which has traditionally been appropriated by the alienated world-view of the other-minds theorist, my argument is not a claim of cognitive privilege[50] for (some groups of) women; it is a plea for inclusion, for taking seriously certain experiences often overlooked within philosophy.

Nevertheless, women may be more likely than men to have had these sorts of experiences. And there are important reasons for this. The foremost is that membership in a disadvantaged group has meant that we are, by custom and tradition, allotted the mothering function. As Marilyn Frye remarks, 'There is a women's place, a sector, which is inhabited by women of all classes and races, and it is not defined by geographical boundaries but by function. The function is the service of men and men's interests as men define them, which includes the bearing and rearing of children.'[51] To the extent that most women, at some time in their lives, share in some aspects of caring for developing beings, this process of 'calling forth' may fairly be called a pervasive aspect of female experience.

Now, this fact appears to suggest that changes in role allotments and socialization practices (enormous though these would have to be) would suffice to permit most men to have the same sorts of experiences. In this respect, then, the proposal by women of ontological re-visions is an 'accident of history' in the sense that it is partly contingent upon existing child-rearing and perhaps other socialization arrangements that might (though with great difficulty, I fear) be changed. Thus male and female perspectives would not be necessarily and permanently incommensurable.

Furthermore, it is not in general impossible for people to learn in an indirect way about experiences and world-views which they do not themselves share. Women, for example, have long been expected to be, so to speak, bilingual and bicultural when we aspire to the male realms of business, science, education, and politics. We learn to adopt a perspective in many ways foreign to much of our socialization. And this fact seems to suggest that men of goodwill may be able to acquire a perspective foreign to their experience.

Nevertheless, it would be most unwise to conclude that a reversal of the roles allotted to the sexes, as they have developed historically, could have occurred, resulting in men's being the dominated group and having the appropriate experiences to equip them to make various critiques of the dominant culture.[52] In this respect, it is a mistake to see the sort of re-vision described here as only contingently feminist. For the patriarchal system is no mere accident of history: it is profoundly related to the appropriation by men of women's unique sexual capacities and reproductive labour, and therefore the reversal of that power inequity would not have occurred merely by virtue of different socialization practices. It is no mere historical accident that it is men, not women, who rule; that we live in a patriarchy, not a matriarchy. There are significant social and historical connections between the political and cultural position of women and women's biology, including most especially our reproductive and sexual capacities. I am certainly not positing here a simplistic linear causal relationship between female biology and male oppression; but I am claiming that the arrogation of women's sexuality and procreative capacities plays more than an incidental role in the maintenance of patriarchy.

The latter claim does not mean that the feminist re-vision offered in this paper must therefore be rooted simply in female 'nature' or biology. Feminist theory is founded upon female experience, and that experience includes but of course is not limited to experiences such as pregnancy, labour, childbirth, and breast-feeding. As Whitbeck remarks, 'these experiences do not readily fall into either the nature category or the nurture category.'[53] They are shaped but not entirely constituted by our nurture as women. And they are founded upon but not reducible to our biological nature as women. So, it is a mistake to see nature and nurture as entirely distinct, or to suppose that experiences must fall into one or the other of these two categories. Just as our sexuality is socially constructed, so also our experiences as beings with reproductive capacities, which are founded in biology, are nevertheless socially constructed. Furthermore, these experiences are not divorced from all of the other experiences in a woman's life. It is false to assume that a woman's experiences of pregnancy and giving birth, for example, have no connections with the other facets of her life. They both influence and are influenced by her other life experiences. Moreover, even if she never procreates (and a sizeable minority do not), she lives her life as a woman, with an awareness of all the strengths and vulnerabilities attendant upon being a woman. Human beings are embodied beings. No woman is a woman, a female, only when pregnant or in labour: the fact of being female permeates her sense of self and her ways of relating to the world. (The fact of being male, I would contend, likewise permeates a man's sense of self. But it may be harder for him to recognize that fact, since in a patriarchal culture to be a person is, pre-eminently, to be male. Hence, men may tend to take their awareness of themselves as male to be simply an awareness of themselves as persons.)

There is, therefore, something which is inherently feminist in the ontological re-vision presented in this paper, because it is at least partly founded upon experiences of women that are not mere accidents of history. The kinds of experiences cited here do have a heuristic value for the formation of a new ontology, and part of the general significance of feminist theory lies in what it draws our attention to. But the value of these experiences for the formation of theory is also more than heuristic. These experiences do not just *happen* to lead feminists like Whitbeck to new insights, in such a way that other, quite different experiences would do just as well. The point is that the very nature of these experiences is such that they constitute and are constituted by an ontological stance different from that inherent in the traditional construction of the problem of other minds.

An examination of the problem of other minds reminds us that philosophical problems have a history and that they need not be permanent features of our intellectual landscape. The fact that this particular problem has been perennially popular may partly be due to the Adversary Paradigm in philosophy, which, as Moulton points out, 'affects the kinds of questions asked and determines the answers that are thought to be acceptable ... The only problems recognized are those between opponents.'[54] Of course, we do have very real problems about our relationships and interactions with other persons; some of those problems are ethical ones, and some are epistemological or ontological. But we need not regard human differences as oppositions or as threats, and it is not necessary to seek some unachievable guarantee that our differences are not insuperable. To worry about the foundations for our supposed belief in the existence of other minds is, then, to entertain a non-existent problem.

NOTES

For helpful comments on this paper my thanks are due to the participants in the 1985 conference of the Canadian Society for Women in Philosophy and the members of the Queen's University Philosophy Department Colloquium. I am particularly indebted to Carlos Prado for his detailed commentaries on earlier versions of this paper.
1 Caroline Whitbeck, 'A Different Reality: Feminist Ontology,' in *Beyond*

Domination: New Perspectives on Women and Philosophy, ed. Carol C. Gould (Totowa, NJ: Rowman & Allanheld, 1984), p. 74

2 Ibid., p. 64

3 Caroline Whitbeck, 'Afterword to "The Maternal Instinct" (1982),' in *Mothering: Essays in Feminist Theory*, ed. Joyce Trebilcot (Totowa, NJ: Rowman & Allanheld, 1984), p. 194, Whitbeck's emphasis

4 Alec Hyslop, 'Other Minds as Theoretical Entities,' *Australasian Journal of Philosophy* 54, no. 2 (August 1976): 158

5 I use 'he' for two reasons: first, because, as a matter of fact, it has been almost exclusively male philosophers who have dealt with the problem; and second, because I believe that the issue itself, and the usual approaches taken to it, are representative of a masculist approach to philosophical thought.

6 Whitbeck, 'A Different Reality,' p. 75. Whitbeck attributes the placing of the burden of proof in this way to the underlying assumption that 'self and other are fundamentally *opposed*' ('Afterword,' p. 194, Whitbeck's emphasis).

7 Janice Moulton, 'A Paradigm of Philosophy: The Adversary Method,' in *Discovering Reality*, ed. Sandra Harding and Merill B. Hintikka (Dordrecht: D. Reidel Publishing Company, 1983), pp. 149–64

8 Ibid., p. 158, Moulton's emphasis

9 For example, Alec Hyslop attacks the theoretical-entities argument and defends a version of the analogical argument in 'Other Minds as Theoretical Entities,' pp. 158–61. Philip A. Ostien attacks the analogical argument and defends the theoretical-entities argument in 'God, Other Minds, and the Inference to the Best Explanation,' *Canadian Journal of Philosophy* 4, no. 1 (September 1974): 149–62, and Robert Pargetter does so also in 'The Scientific Inference to Other Minds,' *Australasian Journal of Philosophy* 62, no. 2 (June 1984): 158–63. Despite his title, R.I. Sikora defends the analogical argument in 'The Argument from Analogy Is *Not* an Argument for Other Minds,' *American Philosophical Quarterly* 14, no. 2 (April 1977): 137–41. So do A. Hyslop and F.C. Jackson, 'The Analogical Inference to Other Minds,' *American Philosophical Quarterly* 9, no. 2 (April 1972): 168–76, and in 'A Reply to Don Locke,' *Australasian Journal of Philosophy* 53, no. 1 (May 1975): 68–9. Don Locke attacks the analogical argument in 'Just What Is Wrong with the Argument from Analogy?' *Australasian Journal of Philosophy* 51, no. 2 (August 1973): 153–6; his attack is attacked by Barry Maund in 'What Is Wrong with Locke's Objection?' *Australasian Journal of Philosophy* 52, no. 3 (December 1974): 240–2. Michael E. Levin defends the evolutionary argument in 'Why We Believe in Other Minds,' *Philosophy and Phenomenological Research* 44, no. 3

(March 1984): 343–59; Roderick M.Chisholm defends the verstehen argument in 'Verstehen: The Epistemological Question,' *Dialectica* 33 nos. 3–4 (1979): 233–46.

10 Alec Hyslop, 'A Multiple Case Inference and Other Minds,' *Australasian Journal of Philosophy* 57, no. 4 (December 1979): 332

11 Sikora, 'The Argument from Analogy,' p. 137

12 Levin, 'Why We Believe in Other Minds,' p. 346

13 Pargetter, 'The Scientific Inference to Other Minds,' p. 158, Pargetter's emphasis

14 Hyslop, 'Other Minds as Theoretical Entities,' p. 160

15 Locke, 'Just What Is Wrong with the Argument from Analogy?' p. 154

16 Levin, 'Why We Believe in Other Minds,' pp. 347 and 349

17 Ostien, 'God, Other Minds, and the Inference to the Best Explanation,' p. 153

18 Levin, 'Why We Believe in Other Minds,' p. 354

19 Pargetter, 'The Scientific Inference to Other Minds,' p. 162

20 Sikora, 'The Argument from Analogy,' p. 137

21 Hyslop, 'Other Minds as Theoretical Entities,' p. 160

22 Hyslop, 'A Multiple Case Inference and Other Minds,' p. 331. Compare Sikora, 'The Argument from Analogy,' p. 140

23 Ostien, 'God, Other Minds, and the Inference to the Best Explanation,' p. 150

24 Levin, 'Why We Believe in Other Minds,' pp. 350–1

25 Here Levin is partly right when he says that we do not *infer* the existence of other minds (pp. 343–5), but still wrong in insisting that we nevertheless *believe* in their existence.

26 Ostien, 'God, Other Minds, and the Inference to the Best Explanation,' p. 151

27 T. Michael McNulty, 'James, Mach, and the Problem of Other Minds,' *Transactions of the Charles S. Peirce Society* XVIII, no. 3 (Summer 1982): 252–3

28 Ludwig Wittgenstein, *Philosophical Investigations*, trans. G.E.M. Anscombe (Oxford: Basil Blackwell, 1968), p. 178e; Wittgenstein's emphasis

29 Ostien, 'God, Other Minds, and the Inference to the Best Explanation,' p. 153

30 Pargetter, 'The Scientific Inference to Other Minds,' p. 159

31 Hyslop, 'A Multiple Case Inference and Other Minds,' p. 330

32 Pargetter, 'The Scientific Inference to Other Minds,' pp. 162, 160

33 Compare Whitbeck, 'A Different Reality,' p. 69

34 Pargetter, 'The Scientific Inference to Other Minds,' p. 159

35 Rich, 'When We Dead Awaken,' p. 35

36 Whitbeck, 'A Different Reality,' p. 77; Whitbeck, 'The Moral Implications of Regarding Women as People,' p. 256
37 Whitbeck, 'A Different Reality,' p. 76; Whitbeck's emphasis
38 Whitbeck, 'Afterword,' p. 195, 198. Compare Moulton, 'A Paradigm of Philosophy,' p. 162.
39 Rothman, *Giving Birth*, p. 276
40 Whitbeck, 'The Moral Implications of Regarding Women as People,' p. 264
41 For this reason I reject Rothman's supposedly 'woman-centred' view of the mother-foetus relationship as involving 'an organic whole, the fetus being part of the mother's body' (Rothman, *Giving Birth*, p. 276).
42 Caroline Whitbeck, 'The Maternal Instinct (1972),' in *Mothering*, pp. 190–1
43 Whitbeck, 'A Different Reality,' p. 78
44 Whitbeck, 'The Moral Implications of Regarding Women as People,' p. 264
45 Prado, 'Gender and Objectivity,' p. 7
46 Whitbeck, 'The Neonate,' p. 120
47 Prado, 'Gender and Objectivity,' p. 5
48 Ibid., pp. 4 and 8
49 Noddings, *Caring*, p. 17
50 Carlos Prado drew my attention to this criticism.
51 Marilyn Frye, 'Oppression,' in *The Politics of Reality: Essays in Feminist Theory* (Trumansburg, NY: The Crossing Press, 1983), p. 9
52 Prado, 'Gender and Objectivity,' p. 8
53 Whitbeck, 'The Maternal Instinct,' p. 186
54 Moulton, 'A Paradigm of Philosophy,' p. 157

MORALS

Shifting Perspective:
A New Approach to Ethics

SHEILA MULLETT

'What threatens us is indifference, affective dissociation, progressive attenuation of concern with our fellows.'[1]

Most of us know what it is like to try to describe an experience that meant a lot to us to someone who is quite unimpressed or indifferent. It is frustrating, and our feelings about the experience are dampened in the telling. If we found the experience amusing or exciting, it seems less so. If we found it terrifying or aggravating, we feel foolish. Strangely, it seems that somehow our access to our own experience is mediated by the response of our hearers. If we are not heard at all, or the hearer distorts the message, we, the speakers, are affected. In this paper I shall describe some of the characteristics of feminist ethics that result from the fact that feminist moral philosophers are attempting to communicate views about moral life within a dominant culture that is essentially hostile, or at least unreceptive to those views. When feminists talk and write about moral values they do so within a public sphere of shared meaning and value, insofar as they use the language of the culture in which they live.

Feminist ethics attempts to produce a shift in perspective away from systems of knowledge and valuation that render women's suffering invisible or simply irrelevant. It documents the failure of these interpretations and the social arrangements associated with them to allow women the full life of a self-interpreting subject of experience. But feminist ethicists, living in this culture, are continually having to shift back and forth between the old and the emerging perspective. For as long as we are operating within the mainstream our meanings will be misunderstood and taken to be something else. Thus we are constantly shifting perspectives, under the magnetic pull of ordinary interpretations and the lure of liberated and empowered discourse.

There are many who feel that contemporary Anglo-American ethics has become overly academic and quite irrelevant to experience.[2] Two such philosophers, Iris Murdoch and Nel Noddings, have made innovative and rich contributions to our understanding of moral life. It is the purpose of this paper to show that although these writers have opened up new perspectives, and have moved the discussion well out of the cul-de-sac of the contemporary debates, generating valuable insights in the process, nevertheless a *further* shift in perspective is necessary to characterize the kind of awareness involved in moral life today. Feminist moral philosophers have made a crucial shift in perspective to disclose a kind of understanding not available in the Anglo-American tradition. Some features of this major change of viewpoint can be found in the innovative approaches to moral theory in the work of Iris Murdoch and Nel Noddings, both of whom turn away from the dominant view of the moral agent as either a calculator of utility or a rational agent making moral choices on the basis of a hypothetical contractarian relation with the members of society. But a satisfactory description of the shift of perspective needed in moral life today requires additional insights lacking in these authors.

Iris Murdoch

Iris Murdoch has proposed that the task in moral life is to 'move away from the self.' The kind of awareness that Murdoch describes as central to moral life is to be found by shifting our attention away from the self to an external and objective reality.

Murdoch begins with a Freudian picture of the psyche as a fragile system of energy continually striving to protect itself from reality by means of fantasy and self-pity. To counteract this 'proliferation of blinding self-centered aims and images'[3] we need to shift our attention to some inspiring or energizing aspect of reality. The flaw in contemporary moral philosophy, in Murdoch's view, is that it has 'lost a vision of a reality separate from ourselves.'[4] Moral philosophy should depict this independent reality and suggest techniques for reorienting this naturally selfish energy, for the defeat of 'the fat relentless ego.' Looking inward will not provide the source of inspiration necessary for moral life.

Murdoch compares moral experience to aesthetic experience. We often find our energies renewed when our attention is turned to beauty in art or nature: 'it is a psychological fact ... that we can all receive moral help by focusing our attention upon things which are valuable ... Our ability to act well ... depends partly ... upon the quality of our habitual objects of attention.'[5]

She illustrates this moral experience with an example. A person might be sitting at the window consumed with a sense of hurt pride and wrapped in self-pity, when she notices a hovering kestrel. Her attention is shifted from her self-preoccupation and fantasies to the kestrel. She sees the kestrel in all its magnificence, and returns to her thoughts, freed from the narrowness, perhaps released from their paralysing effect. Similarly, in moral life we can turn our attention to goodness and be liberated from harmful self-preoccupation: 'The chief enemy of excellence in morality (and also in art) is personal fantasy: the tissue of self-aggrandizing and consoling wishes and dreams which prevents one from seeing what there is outside one.'[6]

The crucial feature of goodness, however, is its transcendence. We cannot see goodness itself the way we see beauty. Our awareness of goodness is an awareness of something that cannot be experienced the way we can experience 'things of this world.'[7] This 'transcendent object' is, in some ways, according to Murdoch, 'mysterious.'[8] Thus, a moral agent should strive to focus her attention on the idea of uncorrupted good while really seeing clearly the evil and suffering of this world.[9]

There are obvious difficulties with Murdoch's Realism in ethics. But one of the merits of Murdoch's perspective is that it puts the spotlight on a dimension of experience that is almost entirely ignored in contemporary Anglo-American ethics, namely, the experience of narcissism and self-obsession so typical of members of an affluent consumer society.[10]

'Much of contemporary moral philosophy appears both unambitious and optimistic. Unambitious optimism is of course part of the Anglo-Saxon tradition; and it is also not surprising that a philosophy which analyses moral concepts on the basis of ordinary language should present a relaxed picture of a mediocre achievement ... Yet modern psychology has provided us with what might be called a doctrine of original sin, a doctrine which most philosophers either deny (Sartre), ignore (Oxford and Cambridge), or attempt to render innocuous (Hampshire).'[11]

It is crucial to moral life that we face evil. To ignore it or downplay it, as is our wont, prevents us from achieving an accurate perspective. I will return to this point later in this paper and argue that the evil that Murdoch describes, excessive fantasy, and narcissism are located in a social context that invalidates the experience of women and encourages fantasy and self-deception.

Although it is a positive feature of this account that it describes the moral agent as having to shift perspective, or focus her attention on something other than herself to acquire moral awareness or understanding, nevertheless the difficulty is that the object to which the moral agent is supposed to shift her attention, in this theory, is hopelessly abstract and obscure. Another difficulty is that the moral agent is depicted in isolation from others. The shift of perspective recommended does not take place in a shared dialogue with others seeking to understand and change the world. Furthermore, this kind of Realism not only ignores the social dimension but tends to work against social change. Sabina Lovibond makes a similar point in her criticism of objectivist moral philosophy. There is a reifying tendency, Lovibond says, 'which serves to obscure the theorist's (and the reader's) complicity in a form of life that happens to be antagonistic to moral experiment. It seems ... to be characteristic of objectivist moral philosophy to attribute any rejection of the demands of consensual morality to the dissidents' assertion of their own private claims at the expense of the common good.'[12]

This would appear question-begging to the Realist whose point is, of course, precisely to deny that morality is a consensual matter. It may not be possible to present conclusive arguments for either view; however, it should be noted that in Murdoch's Realism, power relations, relations of dominance, recede to the background. The merit of the feminist perspective that I shall present is that the power structure remains in the foreground of moral theory and of the moral agent's consciousness. The feminist shift in perspective in moral theory corresponds to a shift in perspective on the part of moral agents collectively seeking to transform society, or, at least exercise some control over the context of our duty.[13]

What is missing in Murdoch's view, from the feminist point of view, is the realization that the chief enemy is fantasy, indeed, but fantasy that results from loss of power and opportunity and fantasy that is derived from the images forced upon women by definitions of them as sexual objects. Fantasy is the habitual mode of those who are cut off from effective interaction with the world. So, Murdoch is right to say that moral life requires a shift of attention, and right to note that fantasy is a sign that all is not well. But the reality she describes as the appropriate focus of one's attention is an abstract concept of goodness utterly removed from social and political understanding.

A further difference between Murdoch's approach to ethics and the feminist approach is that Murdoch's moral agent is described, in traditional Anglo-American style, in isolation from others. Moral life is a private matter of getting your attention on to the right thing, whereas in feminist ethics moral life is a matter of elaborating shared categories of experience and of collective disentanglement from a disabling perspective.

Nel Noddings

Like Murdoch, Noddings wishes to shift the perspective of moral theory from its traditional preoccupation with the formulation of rules and principles. It is a mistake, she claims, to 'suppose that ethics is necessarily a subject that must be cast in the language of principle and demonstration.'[14] Noddings shares with Murdoch the view that morality involves turning away from self. But the reality which energizes the moral agent is not the abstract and mysterious notion of 'goodness' we find in Murdoch, but the very specific and concrete individuals for whom we care. Moral life, in this view, is based upon our 'innate desire' to care for others. When we turn our attention to the 'ones cared-for' we are engrossed with them. What we come to know, as moral agents, are the specific, particular details of the life of the one cared-for and what actions on our part will contribute to his flourishing: 'When my caring is directed to living things, I must consider their natures, ways of life, needs and desires. And, although I can never accomplish it entirely, I try to apprehend the reality of the other ... [There is] a displacement of interest from my own reality to the reality of the other.'[15]

This caring is often filled with joy, but when it is not, when we do not feel like caring for the other, we must have recourse to our commitment to the ethical ideal of caring. We must, in order to maintain this ideal ethical self, be sure to take heed of our own condition, take rest, seek congenial companionship, etc., so as to be able to be as receptive as possible to the cared-for and have this person 'fill the firmament': 'the test of my caring is not wholly in how things turn out; the primary test lies in an examination of *what I considered*, how fully I received the other, and whether the free pursuit of his projects is partly a result of the completion of my caring in him' (emphasis added).[16]

Although Noddings concedes that we must maintain the self, and sees that caring is often accompanied by joy, and finally, that in caring for another a person maintains her 'ethical self,' nevertheless, the picture in this ethical theory is of a person pouring her energy and directing her attention away from self towards others. The consciousness of the moral agent, in this picture of moral life, is filled with the concerns and the reality of the other. In her chapter on 'the cared-for' we find under the heading 'reciprocity' that the responsibility of the one cared-for is, surprisingly, not to return the favour by caring for the one-caring but to continue on with 'his' projects and be 'himself' [sic]: 'The cared-for is free to be more fully himself in the caring relation. Indeed, this being himself, this willing and unselfconscious revealing of self, is his major contribution to the relation. This is his tribute to the one-caring.'[17]

The main problem with this vision of moral life, this picture of the moral agent filling her consciousness with the needs and desires of the other, is that it is presented as an abstract ideal with no reference to the social conditions under which people have aspired to that ideal.[18] The ideal of turning away from the self and becoming engrossed in the other has proved to be the ideal of the powerless. For women the qualities associated with this ideal have also been associated with gross oppression, exploitation, and victimization. This is what has been called 'the compassion trap.'[19]

Despite this difficulty Noddings is right in her attempt to give a new perspective to moral theory and in her recognition that moral life involves a shift in perspective on the part of the moral agent. The limitation in her account comes from identifying the object of this new consciousness as the reality, the needs and wants of others, without concern for the powerlessness associated with such an ideal. We have to turn to feminist writing to find a satisfactory descripton of the perspective of moral agents who are in the subordinate position within society and social structures.

Feminist Ethics

Feminist ethical theory calls for a complex alteration of consciousness. There are three dimensions to this perspective, which might be labelled 1 / 'moral sensitivity'; 2 / 'ontological shock'; and 3 / 'praxis.'

1 / Moral sensitivity: Feminist moral consciousness begins with an anguished awareness of violence, victimization, and pain. The highly developed capacity of human beings to avoid painful experience, to ignore, suppress, deny, and forget the agonies of life, is shifted aside and they fill our consciousness. We lose our moral callousness and see the violence around us: 'It is astonishing to note the profound silence in

ethics regarding violence against women – rape, battering, child sexual abuse and incest. The exceptions are few, recent and feminist. This silence must be broken.'[20]

Until we acquire this painful awareness of suffering we inadvertently perpetuate it: 'good people, nice people, people of good will, whom I do not hestitate to call "moral" in the ordinary sense of that term, myself included, all participate in and perpetuate, even extend and legitimate, violence against women simply by going about our business in an ordinary way. We do so primarily by our quotidian participation in social patterns and institutions which make up the bulk of everyday life.'[21]

This significant feature of this consciousness of pain is that it is made possible, in part at least, by a new attitude towards the social arrangements which contribute to suffering.

2 / Ontological shock: This new attitude is not a passive acceptance of misery but a commitment to 'reformulating our actions and thought.'[22] It is not merely a lament, but a transformation of the way the social milieu is present in our experience: 'Women have long lamented their condition, but a lament, pure and simple, need not be an expression of feminist consciousness. As long as their situation is apprehended as natural, inevitable, and inescapable, women's consciousness of themselves, no matter how alive to insult and inferiority, is not yet feminist consciousness.'[23]

Feminist consciousness involves a double perspective: we see the situation as it is in the present, and as it is understood and interpreted within the existing social context, while, at the same time, viewing it in terms of a state of affairs not yet actual, in terms of possibility, 'in which what is given would be negated and radically transformed.' 'Feminists are not aware of different things than other people, they are aware of the same things differently.'[24] Bartky calls this a state of 'ontological shock' because it involves a displacement of the world we have taken for granted, it opens up whole new areas of ambiguity and uncertainty and requires continuous attempts to formulated new possibilities for action. In short it puts everything into question. It involves, 'first, the realization that what is really happening is quite different from what appears to be happening; and second, the frequent inability to tell what is really happening at all.'[25]

In this perspective thought and feeling are blended. We experience the suffering of women and our own suffering as intolerable, and we experience the shock of seeing the 'normal' categories of interpretation shift before a perception of almost inchoate possibilities of social transformation.

3 / Praxis: A collective understanding of the transformative possibilities within a given social context. The third characteristic of the feminist ethical perspective is that it is disclosed, however dimly and with however much shock, in a collective awareness. We shift from seeing the world as an individual moral agent to seeing it through the eyes of a 'we.' It is not my moral perspective that I come to understand better but the emerging moral perspective of countless others committed to changing the structures in which we live our lives. We struggle to delineate the conditions under which we can develop forms of attachment that also serve as avenues to self-affirmation.[26] We search for forms of collective action which can lead to the transformation of existing social structures. When people are: 'truly committed to liberation, their action and reflection cannot proceed without the action and reflection of others.'[27] 'Authentic thinking, thinking that is concerned about *reality*, does not take place in ivory tower isolation, but only in communication.'[28]

There are several ideas embedded in the notion of praxis. First, there is the idea that our perception of reality emerges in our efforts to transform it. We must perceive our state 'not as fated and unalterable, but merely as limiting.'[29] This might be expressed as the idea that thought and action are inseparably linked in ethics. Second, there is the idea that this transformative perception is a collective one, emerging out of shared attempts to understand what is going on and to discern possibilities. This might be expressed as the view that in the development of a moral perspective self and others are inseparably linked. And third, there is the idea that the reality which we wish to focus upon as moral agents is a socially constructed reality, one which has not yet emerged but which may emerge out of our efforts. This might be expressed as the view that imagination is a crucial component of a moral perspective: 'We need to imagine an alternative human world so as to act in the present as if it had already begun to emerge and its anticipated norms had begun to bind us.'[30]

We can now see how a feminist moral philosophy presents a radically altered picture of the moral agent, who is depicted as constructing a moral perspective within the context of a collective endeavour to transform existing social arrangements. The moral perspective is thus depicted as multi-dimensional and incomplete. It is not something that can be fully grasped as it is in the process of being discerned. The attempts to articulate the obscurely discerned possibilities contribute to the construction of the perspective. It is inchoate and affected by our articulations of it. And, it requires attention to one's deepest sense of what is worthwhile. But feminist ethics goes one step farther than this and sees this deep sense as something that emerges in a collective consciousness.

Some Examples

In an illuminating discussion of in vitro fertilization[31] Susan Sherwin presents an analysis which illustrates the shift of perspective involved in feminist ethics. The question of in vitro fertilization is usually treated along utilitarian or contractarian lines. In these approaches the anguish women suffer when they put themselves through the process is minimized and the issue is treated as a matter of fulfilling one's desire to have a child. The social arrangements and values which lead to women being so desperate are made invisible and hence not questioned. On Sherwin's analysis, however, the perspective of the women is put in the foreground. What emerges is that the very strong desire to have children can be seen to be connected with the absence of other ways of achieving fulfilment in life, and with the social norms which prevent most people from having close and intimate relations with children unless they have their own. Sherwin's analysis can be characterized by the three features of feminist ethics. It reveals moral sensitivity in that it focuses directly on the lack of power of the women involved in this process and the limitations of their alternatives and even of their understanding of the process itself in some cases. It emphasizes the anguished consciousness which results in these desperate attempts to become pregnant.

Second, the element of ontological shock is present in her analysis, for she is aware of the problem in terms of how things could be, not only of how they are. Thus her analysis illuminates possible values and social arrangements that do not yet exist. This double perspective is quite troubling to women for it means that they are continually misunderstood by those who cannot, or will not, see the possibilities and acknowledge the lack of power of women. Furthermore, she points out that this is the sort of moral dilemma for which a simple answer cannot be found. She is reluctant to advocate that the practice be stopped and that women who might be able to bear children this way be prevented, yet she shows how the practice arises out of social conditions that are adverse to women's well-being.

In her paper on philosophical methodology[32] Sherwin describes the frustration attendant upon a continuous and daily clash of views and repeated failure to be understood. The feminist scholar understands the viewpoint of her adversaries, and knows how and why they hold the views they do, but her adversaries systematically misunderstand her position. In this sense she has a double perspective, that of her adversaries and the feminist view. And, worse, she frequently falls back into the views of her adversaries and judges her feminist work and views to be worthless. The pressure is constantly there to relinquish the feminist view and deny the problem, or to simply resign oneself to a mere lament, and thereby relinquish the perspective from which change is possible.

Third, Sherwin's analysis of in vitro fertilization reveals the dimension of praxis, for her analysis is not a matter of an individual opinion or perspective on the question of IVF but rather represents the collective experience and wisdom of women who have struggled to actually alter the conditions of women's lives.

This emphasis on women's experience is clearly developed in Jacqueline Davies's paper on pornography.[33] In her analysis the problem with pornography which cannot be seen in the analyses of analytical philosophers is that women are treated as symbols of sexuality, and this symbolization has public power such that women's own interpretation of the meaning of their bodies is precluded, silenced.

The name feminists give to this process of limiting what a person can be, by predetermining how her or his behaviour or appearance is to be interpreted, is 'objectification.' It defines me from without, according to someone else's needs, desires, and intentions, before I have a chance to exert any control over how I am determined or defined as a subject, i.e., to have my own needs, desires, and intentions reflected in public interpretations of who or what I am. Significantly, what is most forgotten in cases of objectification is the 'interpretive perspective of the subject who has been made the object of attribution.'[34]

These examples illustrate the subtle ways in which women's experience is ignored in a philosophical tradition which has consistently ignored experience in favour of intellectualized abstractions, universal truths, and principles. It may be that one of the aspects of domination, having power over others, is this capacity to ignore experience and to convince others to ignore their own experience. It might be that openness to the self-interpretations of others is antithetical to political power.

Positive and Negative Forms of Caring

Many authors have pointed out the debilitating effects of caring within present social structures.[35] These authors all claim that satisfactory caring relations require social transformation: 'We are playing with fire when we accept our special historical identity with reproduction and caring, sharing, nurturing human values as an essential component of our specific political voice. For our specificity as women has in the past been inseparable from our oppression as women.'[36]

We cannot simply endorse the values associated with women's caring, nor do we want to reject these values and 'assimilate' ourselves to the dominant ethos of the culture. Miles envisages a social transformation that would include getting away from the privatization of domestic labour, which is largely invisible and unremunerated, and left, in large part, to women, and would include altering the present division between public and private life.[37] Elshtain argues that the public world must be transformed so as to preserve the private-familial sphere and the values associated with that sphere.[38] Kathy Ferguson has shown that the social transformation that is required is the elimination of 'all institutionalized dominance/subordinance relations' that involve the division of nurturing traits from instrumental traits and the allocation of these to people according to gender.[39]

But, of course, life continues in the present and the possibilities of radical social transformation of the sort required are not imminent. So what should women do about their 'specificity,' the values which have traditionally been allotted to them? These values are clearly of utmost worth and not to be forsaken.

The first task is to recognize the distortions of caring which result from the oppressive structures in which women live. There are at least three factors which adversely affect caring for another person with whom one has a relationship: 1 / the economic dependence of the person who is doing the main nurturing and emotional maintenance of her partner; 2 / the fact that it is understood to be part of one person's role to provide most of the emotional support; 3 / the restriction of women to caring roles, especially of wife and mother, with little occasion to develop other parts of their being, which results in a loss of sense of self outside these roles.[40]

There are several criteria for positive, or undistorted caring, which will, no doubt, be easier to fulfil when social structures are altered, but which are nevertheless worth striving for within present contexts.[41] 1 / Caring that fulfils the one caring. This form is to be contrasted with caring that is done out of fear, or in exchange for economic support, or out of duty or 'blind devotion.' One woman has described her experience of spending two weeks with her daughter in Israel prior to a separation during which the latter will go to medical school. The experience was one of great joy for the mother. The daughter was a delight to be with and the mother felt energized and replenished by the occasion. 2 / Caring that calls upon the unique and particular individuality of the one caring. Care-taking tasks that can be done by anyone and do not require the special relationship, and the unique character of the one-caring would not constitute caring in the sense in question here. Using the same example, the daughter might have had just as much caring had she enjoyed the caring of some other person with whom she had a close relationship, but whoever had been there, caring for her, would have been expressing a unique relationship. In this kind of caring it really makes a difference who is caring. While anyone can be hired to clean the floor or wash the diapers (i.e., engage in 'caretaking'), an act or moment of 'positive' caring is an expression of the unique personality of the individual caring, and of the uniqueness of the relationship. 3 / Caring that is not produced by a person in a role because of gender, with one gender engaging in nurturing behaviour and the other engaging in instrumental behaviour.[42] 4 / Caring that is reciprocated with caring, and not merely with the satisfaction of seeing the ones cared for flourishing and pursuing their projects. 5 / Caring that takes place within the framework of 'consciousness-raising' practice and conversation, which serves to remind us of possibilities of alternative forms of passionate and practical human connection 'by loosening the hold that predefined collective contingencies of role, rank and conventional expression exercise over our experience.'[43]

An Example of 'Positive' Caring in an Oppressive Context

A description by Helen Levine of her experience as a patient in a psychiatric hospital illustrates these criteria of 'positive' caring as well as the shift of perspective that constitutes the crucial dimension of morality.[44] She was hospitalized for severe depression in an institution in which all doctors and senior administrators were male. These were some of the experiences she recorded in her journal. During the initial interview there was no visible concern for what she might be experiencing. She was handed a typed set of rules and regulations with no explanations. Privileges, such as walking out in the grounds or playing badminton, had to be earned. Patients, all female in this ward, were told what to do in minute detail. She was administered two powerful anti-depressants, as well as muscle relaxants and sleeping pills, at the beginning in full dosage, even though she was totally unaccustomed to medication of any sort. She was dizzy, dazed, and trembling from the medication and her vision was blurred. She noted many instances in which other patients were treated with scorn, indifference, or outright insult. One older woman was left to wait and suffer alone so that 'she would not become dependent.' Another woman was forced to undergo shock treatment against her will. Only one nurse spent time talking with Helen. Others simply handed out the medication. At one point, when she was sobbing and planning to leave, members of the staff criticized her for being demanding and hysterical. The ward was run in an authoritarian way and the ward meeting of patients turned out to be an occasion for nurses to complain about small infractions of the rules (patients putting their feet on the coffee table, which is not 'ladylike'). No real grievances were aired by patients because of fear of repercussions. During her stay in this institution where patients were treated as passive recipients of orders and medication, she began to talk with some of the other patients. Talking with P she discovered a woman who had put her husband through college and could not concentrate now that it was her turn to study. She had been told there is too much 'child' in her, not enough 'adult.' After talking with C, laughing about the absurdity of their daily humiliations, she found her to be an interesting, observant, self-educated woman. They began to do yoga together. Other women began to talk and share their fear. Fear of shock treatments, fear of being sent to the large provincial hospital, fear of loss of privileges if they complained. They began to have sing songs.

In this demoralizing social context we can identify some of the features of 'positive' caring and many of the features of the emerging feminist perspective: 1 / 'Moral sensitivity.' She was aware of the suffering of her fellow patients as well as her own. She did not ignore the demoralizing social relations between staff and patients. She listened with sympathy to the accounts of all the other patients. 2 / She experienced 'ontological shock' not just lament, in her recognition of the oppressive domination of the patients and her understanding that this is not the only possible way the situation could be structured. She saw the situation through the double perspective of seeing the present as unacceptable in light of the possibilities which are repressed. 3 / Her perspective could be characterized as a form of praxis insofar as it emerged from shared experience and common efforts to help one another and to alter the social situation (educate the staff by giving her doctor *Women and Madness* by Phyllis Chesler, encourage more physical activity and fitness, engage in discussions and sing songs and yoga, etc.). In this sense she contributed to the development of a collective consciousness of possibility in the midst of appalling oppression and weakness.

Further, in this case we can see the emergent paradigm of caring. Her caring for her friends on the ward had several characteristics. 1 / It was fulfilling turning her away from self-pity and despair, and was not extracted in exchange for economic support or done out of guilt or desire to fill her 'role.' 2 / It was an expression of her particularity and could not have been done by a hired person. It was her sensitivity and her ability to understand the social context of the oppression of her friends as well as her interest in exercise, yoga, music, and humorous caricature of the situation that constituted her individual expression of herself in her caring. 3 / It was not the expression of a social division of roles in which expressive and nurturing behaviour is relegated to one social class while instrumental behaviour is reserved for another class of human beings. She was not acting in her role as psychiatric social worker at the time of this example. 4 / It was reciprocated. 5 / It emerged in the context of conversations and actions that loosened the restricting effect of the predefined roles of 'female psychiatric patient' on the experience of herself and her friends.

Conclusion

One of the concerns of feminists has been to figure out how we could maintain our traditional concern with caring without the powerlessness associated with that concern. We have seen that an ethics of caring can fail to address that issue. The anguished feminist consciousness can deal with this shortcoming by producing the double perspective that consists in seeing the ways in which caring relations are distorted by the existing power relations and superimposing upon that picture imaginative possibilities of transformation. The feminist is thus aware of the distortions of caring and at the same time aware of the possibility of change. But the imaginative search for possibilities of transformation is a dynamic project and not a completed vision. The feminist perspective that I am describing does not produce a set of moral paradigms but rather focuses on the process of generating such paradigms. It is an experimental consciousness, a method of paying attention to suffering, a toleration of ambiguities.

Our experience with caring has, of course, prepared us for this double consciousness, for part of caring is precisely the ability to apprehend the world through the eyes of the other. The double perspective of feminism is characterized by the ability to see and feel the limitations of the present while imagining alternatives to it. It also involves relinquishing the perspective of a solitary moral agent operating alone and contributing to the construction of a consensual perspective by a process of sharing experiences and seeking to articulate and explain these experiences so as to generate new categories of interpretation.

The feminist perspective is a double one in yet another way. It involves recognition and acknowledgment of one's own complicity with the destructive social arrangements, through exchanging caring for economic support, through the moral callousness of denying suffering, or through the excesses of rage and narcissism to which the psyche is prone, while at the same time balancing this consciousness with a view of the possibilities of increased moral sensitivity. It is easy to give in to rage and just as easy to give in to apathy. The double perspective I am describing is one in which one recognizes and experiences the inclination to withdraw into rage or apathy while at the same time seeing that what is required is continued presence of mind within the contexts of oppression. This presence of mind was evinced by Helen Levine when she held firm in the face of powerful incentives to rage and self-pity, while she was drugged and master-minded in a psychiatric hospital. Grimly clinging to the possibility that things could be different she survived powerful inner resistance as well as nearly overwhelming collusion by those who were determined to invalidate her perception of the situation.

Any act we perform is either a confirmation of the existing social arrangements or a move away from them. Helen Levine could have submitted to the therapy passively. What prevents us from seeking new social arrangements? First, failing to see the destructiveness of the social context, i.e., oblivion or ignorance; second, denying or suppressing the painful view of the context, i.e., 'moral callousness'; third, despairing because one feels entirely alone; fourth, being overwhelmed by rage, and the paralysis that ensues; fifth, experiencing self-pity, again a matter of feeling separated from others. It takes imagination to see our connection with others and to see how our social arrangements are continually reinforced by daily choices and actions. Because we imagine our situation to be unalterable we fail to undertake the experiments that might enable us to reconstruct our familiar settings.[45]

In every social situation there are many small deviations from the dominant institutional and imaginative order. Some of these aberrations result

from the historical superimposition of the residues of past schemes of
social life, others from the need constantly to adapt a given scheme to new
circumstances, others yet from the failure of any scheme fully to inform
our experience of direct practical collaboration or passionate attachment.
The art of persuasion that accompanies a transformative political practice
consists in seizing upon these deviations ... And it demonstrates, more by
practice than by teaching, that, once they are suitably revised, these locally
successful exceptions can become the new dominant principles in their own
right.[46]

This is the challenge of shifting perspectives in moral life and in moral
theory.

NOTES

1 Paul Hahn, 'Leisure,' *Leisure and Mental Health: A Psychiatric Viewpoint*
  (Washington: May 1967) American Psychiatric Association
2 Alisdair MacIntyre, *After Virtue* (Notre Dame, Ind: University of Notre
  Dame Press, 1980)
3 Iris Murdoch, 'On "God" and "Good",' *The Sovereignty of Good* (London:
  Routledge & Kegan Paul, 1970), pp. 83–4
4 Ibid.
5 Ibid., p. 76
6 Ibid., p. 78
7 Ibid.
8 Ibid., p. 79
9 Ibid.
10 See C.B. McPherson, *The Political Theory of Possessive Individualism: Hobbes
  to Locke* (Oxford: Oxford University Press, 1970).
11 Ibid., p 50
12 Sabina Lovibond, *Realism and Imagination in Ethics* (Minneapolis, Minn.:
  University of Minnesota Press, 1983), p. 186
13 Ibid., p. 190
14 Nel Noddings, *Caring: A Feminine Approach to Ethics and Moral Education*
  (Berkeley, Ca: University of California Press, 1984), p. 8
15 Ibid., p. 14
16 Ibid., p. 81
17 Ibid., p. 73
18 Noddings does make references to institutions that diminish the ethical
  ideal (ibid., pp. 116–17), but these references make it harder to see

the harmful effects of the institutions which nurture the ideal for women and remove them from power and from the possibility of imagining social change.

19 See Margaret Adams, 'The Compassion Trap,' in *Women in Sexist Society*, ed. V. Gormick and B. Moran, cited in 'Altruism and Women's Oppression,' Larry Blum, Judy Housman, and Naomi Scheman, in *Philosophy and Women* (Belmont, Ca: Wadsworth Publishing Co., 1979), p. 190.

20 Mary D. Pellauer, 'Moral Callousness and Moral Sensitivity,' in *Women's Consciousness, Women's Conscience*, ed. Barbara Hilkert Andolsen, Christine E. Gudorf, and Mary D. Pellauer (Minneapolis, Minn: Winston Press, 1985), p. 33.

21 Ibid., p. 36

22 Ibid., p.34

23 Sandra Lee Bartky, 'Toward a Phenomenology of Feminist Consciousness,' in *Feminism and Philosophy*, ed. Mary Vetterling-Braggin, Frederick A. Elliston, and Jane English (Totowa, NJ: Littlefield Adams, 1977) pp. 253–4

24 Ibid.

25 Ibid., p.256

26 Roberto Mangabeira Unger, *Passion: An Essay on Human Personality* (New York: Macmillan, 1984), p. 185

27 Paolo Freire, *The Pedagogy of the Oppressed* (New York: Continuum Press, 1983), p. 120

28 Ibid., p.64

29 Ibid., p.73

30 Ibid., p.247

31 Susan Sherwin, 'In Vitro Fertilization,' paper read at the Canadian Philosophical Association, Winnipeg, June 1986

32 Idem, 'Philosophical Methodology and Feminist Methodology: Are They Compatible?' in this volume

33 Jacqueline McGregor Davies, 'Pornographic Harms,' in this volume

34 Ibid., p. 137

35 See Angela Miles, 'Political Hegemony in Political Discourse: Women's Specificity and Equality,' in *Feminism in Canada*, ed. Geraldine Finn and Angela Miles (Montreal: Black Rose Press, 1982); Jean Baker Miller, *Toward a New Psychology for Women* (Boston: Beacon Press, 1973); Kathy Ferguson, *The Feminist Case against Bureaucracy* (Philadelphia: Temple University Press, 1984); Jean Bethke Elshtain, *Public Man, Private Woman: Woman in Social and Political Thought* (Princeton: Princeton University Press, 1981); Blum, Housman, and Scheman, *Philosophy and Women*; and Kathryn Morgan, 'Women and Moral Madness,' in this volume.

36 Angela R. Miles, 'Ideological Hegemony in Political Discourse: Women's Specificity and Equality.' in *Feminism in Canada*, pp. 217–18
37 Ibid., p.225
38 Elshtain, *Public Man, Private Woman*, p. 351
39 Ferguson, *The Feminist Case against Bureaucracy*, p. 122
40 Larry Blum, Marcia Homiak, Judy Housman, Naomi Scheman, 'Altruism and Women's Oppression,' in *Philosophy and Women*, p. 192
41 These criteria have emerged from discussions of our experience of caring during several meetings of the Canadian Association for Feminist Ethics (CAFE).
42 See Ferguson, *The Feminist Case against Bureaucracy*.
43 Unger, *Passion*, p. 38
44 Helen Levine, 'The Personal Is Political: Feminism and the Helping Professions,' in *Feminism in Canada*
45 Unger, *Passion*, p. 184
46 Ibid., p.189

Pornographic Harms

JACQUELINE MACGREGOR DAVIES

It is often the case in public political debates that opponents tend to oversimplify and caricature each other's positions. The meanings of the terms 'liberal' and feminist' have suffered this way in the pornography debate. Upon more careful examination one can discern a variety of feminist approaches, some of which are markedly liberal despite differences of opinion about what should be done about pornography. In addition, liberalism spans a wide spectrum. Accordingly, some liberals are less open than others to feminist charges that they are more committed to abstract principles than concerned about real harms to women.

A detailed analysis of the many varieties of liberalism is not appropriate here. Rather I shall simply define as liberal in the broadest sense those arguments that place highest priority on the liberty and equality of individual persons where social justice is a function of respect for liberty and equality. Conflicts between these values are to be mediated by the harm principle, which states that the liberty of the individual may legitimately be limited only when it causes direct harm to other individuals.

In what follows, I shall examine what could reasonably be called liberal arguments about the ethical and political status of pornography, some of which arguments could also be called feminist. I shall point out various difficulties with these arguments from both liberal and feminist perspectives and then offer an alternative approach.

I call this approach post-liberal feminist. It could arguably be called a liberal approach, given its commitment to liberty and equality. but I call it post-liberal because of its rejection of the expression/action distinction that has, along with essentialist conceptions of the self, privileged the value of free expression. That I call this approach feminist is not meant to imply that liberal feminists are not feminists, but simply that, I think, this approach better reflects the interests of women than do the others examined in this paper.

The structure of this framework is, admittedly, sketchily drawn, and no immediate suggestions about how to deal with pornography are suggested. That is not my project, however. I merely wish to provide an alternative conception of what it is that is vulnerable to pornographic harms in order to indicate directions for future research towards finding more adequate solutions than are generally offered.

Harms to Individuals

Mediated Harms

The harm principle is refined for application by the distinction between action and expression. Thomas I. Emerson provides a statement of the political consequences of this distinction: 'expression occupies an especially protected position. In this sector of human conduct, the social right of suppression or compulsion is at its lowest point, in most respects non-existent. A majority of one has a right to control action, but a minority of one has a right to talk.'[1]

The women's movement has had an important influence on research into the potentially harmful effects of pornography. Research thus motivated is not concerned with possibly harmful effects on the consumer (unlike many earlier conservative arguments, which worried about corruption of the consumer's character or the decay of sexual mores) but rather on other persons, particularly women, whose rights may be threatened by pornography. Such rights might include freedom from physical harm, freedom from coercion, the right to equal consideration before the law, and so on.

A straightforwardly liberal case, consistent with liberal privileging of expression, could be made against pornography if it could be demonstrated, for example, that pornography is not merely associated with sexual assault but causes it, or that pornography prejudices judges, lawyers, juries, etc., against women when they appear in court.

Such arguments do not claim that pornography is harmful in itself but rather evaluate it strictly in terms of the harmful acts it causes. They rely on empirical evidence to establish the causal relation, and generally advocate restrictions on pornography, as a necessary evil, if all other routes for preventing the harmful acts prove unworkable.[2]

The main differences between feminist and non-feminist liberals regarding this argument are based on how much evidence is required to count as proof that pornography results in harms to women, as well as on the assessment of the comparative worths of freedom of speech and freedom from the harms that allegedly result from pornography. Although all the evidence is not yet in, a substantial amount of research has already been conducted. Though at times suggestive, it has yet to show where exactly the causal link lies (e.g., in the violence of some pornography, in its sexism, in its objectification of women and/or sexuality) if indeed there is one to be found.

Nuisance and Threat

Despite the fact that the harms, according to the aforementioned approach, are mediated by the consumer, if sufficient empirical evidence supports a causal link between pornography and the consumers' harmful acts, then the relation is direct enough to satisfy the harm principle. However, there are other, arguably liberal, arguments that posit a more direct relationship between pornography and harms to individuals. These, in non-feminist and feminist forms, I shall refer to as the nuisance argument and the threat argument.

The nuisance argument counts something like a right to privacy as vulnerable to harm and therefore to be accorded protection. This argument gives a rather interesting account of just what this right consists in, namely the right to peaceful enjoyment of one's 'inner states.' Joel Feinberg explains:

Some actions, however, while harmless in themselves, are great nuisances to those who are affected by them, and the law from time immemorial has provided remedies, some civil and some criminal, for actions in this category. So a second kind of legitimate reason for prohibiting conduct is the need to protect others from certain sorts of offensive, irritating, or inconveniencing experiences ... The offending conduct produces unpleasant or uncomfortable experiences – affronts to sense or sensibility, disgust, shock, shame, embarrassment, annoyance, boredom, anger, or humiliation – from which one cannot escape without unreasonable inconvenience or even harm.[3]

Feinberg points out that applying laws concerning nuisance involves an 'unavoidable legal balancing act.'[4] To assist with this 'balancing act' he describes a set of factors to be taken into consideration, modified for application to the kind of nuisance that pornography might produce.

Among the considerations he proposes are: 'The intensity and durability of the repugnance the material produces, and the extent to which repugnance could be anticipated to be the general reaction of strangers to the conduct displayed or represented (conduct offensive to persons with an abnormal susceptibility to offense would not count as *very* offensive),'[5] versus the reasonableness of the pornographer's conduct' as measured by, among other things, 'its personal importance to the exhibitors themselves and its social value generally, remembering always the enormous social utility of unhampered expression.'[6]

Setting aside Feinberg's prejudicing of the question of the value of the expression versus the harmfulness of the 'nuisance,' and the potential invocation of a problematic utilitarian calculus, a greater problem lies in the issue of the predictability and normality of responses to expression.

Surely statistical normality won't do. It could as easily be the case that although most people might not actually be offended by certain things perhaps they ought to be, as it could be the case that people might be unreasonably offended. In either case the lack of a critical principle here could leave us with a situation analogous to the unjust enforcement of positive morality, argued against so persuasively by H.L.A. Hart on liberal grounds.[7]

Proponents of the nuisance argument seem to, or ought to, assume a distinction between the enforcement of an obligation not to offend and the enforcement of positive morality. The power of this distinction, however, is weakened by the emptiness of the concept of 'the reasonable person' (and his/her normal and predictable responses).

Interestingly, when the concept of 'the reasonable person' gets spelled out, there is considerable resemblance between what turns out to offend the reasonable person and the area that is of concern to conservative advocates of the enforcement of positive morality, e.g., 'violence, cruelty or horror, or sexual, or faecal or urinary functions, or genital organs,' with considerably more emphasis on the latter three categories.[8]

It turns out that the capacity of these things to offend the reasonable person is supposed to be a function of their relation to the reasonable person's sense of the location of the boundary between public and private and what exactly counts as a transgression of that boundary. There is considerable ambiguity, however, with respect to what constitutes a reasonable judgment about the location of that boundary.

The notion of the private/public boundary is generally taken to rest on that of deceny. Liberals have claimed that while it is unjust to legislate morality the law does have a legitimate say in matters of decency. Decency is to be distinguished from positive morality, or mores, in such a way that certain acts that are moral in private are indecent when performed in public.[9]

Not all acts are like this of course. Some acts are moral and decent no matter where they are performed. What then marks certain acts as being potentially indecent? If judgments about propriety and decency in the public sphere are not moral judments then what are they?

The Williams Committee on Obscenity and Film Censorship has suggested that the perspective of the participants is to be taken into consideration in determining that pornography is an act of the boundary-violating kind. Pornography, they point out, is 'itself a public thing, a picture, book or film show, it represents already the projection into the public of the private world – private that is to say to its participant – of sexual activity.'[10]

This approach seems odd in two respects. First, if we could say that feelings of grief, for example, are private 'to the participant,' then expression of grief would be a projection of the private into the public. Why it would therefore be objectionable is not clear.

Second, the phrase 'private, to its participants' begs the question of who is to be considered a participant in the act. The idea that the viewer is not supposed to be a participant and is intruding on the privacy of those represented in the pornographic image is especially incredible in the case of centrefold-type pornography where the model appears to be posing expressly for the viewer, whose presence and arousal is required for the pornography to 'work.' In any case, according to the nuisance argument, is it not the viewer's privacy about which we are supposed to be worried?

The relation between the nuisance argument and violations of privacy might be salvaged if it were argued simply that displayers of pornography seduce or coerce the unsuspecting viewer. This argument, however, apparently is not supposed to affect the claim that pornography, as an instance of indecency, violates the public/private boundary. 'The basic point that pornography involves by nature some violation of the lines between public and private is *compounded* when pornography not only exists for private consumption but is publicly displayed,' (emphasis added).[11]

These passages suggest that there is a socially, or naturally determined boundary between public and private *in addition* to the definition of the private sphere by the individual's right to make self-determining choices. Pornography apparently always violates the former but threatens the latter only in cases when a viewer of pornography has not chosen to be exposed to it. Thus, we are left with the problematic conclusion that violations of the public/private boundary are permissible so long as they are contained within the private sphere.

The nuisance argument still allows and, in principle, defends the individual's right to freedom in the private sphere. However, in the absence of proof of the existence of a natural boundary, specification of a critical principle to justify a socially determined boundary is necessary. But what could such a principle be?

It seems to me that the harm principle, generally offered by liberals to justify limits on action, will not do. It will not do because it is precisely the question of what should count as harm that is at issue. If offensiveness (unwillingly encountered) is described as harmful, and offensiveness is created by violation of the public/private boundary, and the location of that boundary is socially determined, then appeal to the harm principle to justify the location of that boundary is circular.

While the nuisance argument as it is deployed, for example, in the Williams Report is explicitly 'not directed against the advocacy of opinion,' it is related to the legitimation of certain opinions, namely those of the decent majority, if not the moral majority.[12] To be sure, the expression of opinion denying the validity of the socially determined private/public boundary would be permissible. However, acts which presuppose such minority opinions (e.g., that it is no more wrong to be naked in public than it is to wear funny hats in public) would not be permitted. Thus, social legitimacy is conferred upon those opinions that are the basis of legally respected interpretations of certain acts as private/public boundary-violating acts.

Conservative arguments against pornography have been charged by liberals and feminists alike as being *merely* moral arguments. (This charge usually translates into a concern about patriarchal sexual mores.) The force of this charge is that morals are a private matter, whereas justice is public and requires liberty in the private sphere.

This charge is a somewhat anachronistic one since the distinction does not, properly speaking, exist in pre-liberal social and political theory and practice. Furthermore it is a distinction feminists would do well to be wary of since the 'private sphere' has historically been a sphere of oppression for women. Patriarchal sexual mores are oppressive to women but it is of dubious benefit to privatize this oppression, and it is an oppression that a liberal defence of decency, in the name of privacy, may in practice protect. Caution in the use of 'nuisance'-like arguments by feminists is to be recommended.

There is, however, a particular feminist argument against pornography, the threat argument, which does bear some resemblance to the nuisance argument in that it deals with harms suffered as a direct result of exposure to pornography. But this argument considers the harm as something more than mere 'nuisance.'

Considering pornography as a threat is a useful way of focusing on how pornography is perceived by women. While this is an important step towards taking seriously women's concerns about the issue, it obscures the fact that pornography does not speak *to* women – at least not directly. It speaks to men (or at least to a male perspective) *about* women. If communicating with women is not part of the purpose of pornography it cannot be said to have an intention of threatening women.

However, while pornographers may not be charged with having intentions to threaten, they may be charged with reckless disregard for the effects of their action and with paying insufficient attention to the means by which they realize their intentions to make money, entertain, make artistic or political statements, or what have you.

The fact that pornography does not make a statement that is, strictly speaking, a threat made to women also does not mean that pornography is not *threatening* to women. It is perhaps more dangerous and threatening that a person expressing vicious sentiments about someone is not at all interested in communicating with that person. Indeed, in such a case one would probably not feel particularly reassured to overhear, or hear second hand, that certain people had such beliefs about one, but were interested only in expressing them in the company of like-minded people, or did not care who (including the targets of abuse) overheard them.

Arguments for the banning or restriction of pornography based on its 'threatening' nature share with the nuisance argument most of the problems of application. That is to say, the value of freedom of expression must be weighed against the harm of the distress it causes. This evaluative process includes the question of the 'reasonableness' of the distress, which is near to unanswerable without involving an even more problematic utilitarian calculus to evaluate the significance of kinds and degrees of distress. Moreover, it leaves the issue of the morality of 'private' exchanges of pornography untouched.

Discriminatory Harms

Defamation perhaps better captures the relation between pornographer, consumer, and women. Women need not be exposed to pornography, nor need the statements made by pornography be addressed directly to women, in order for them to have been defamed.

However, other problems are raised by the charge of defamation. Often the success of such a charge depends on an estimation of the likelihood of harm being caused through the action of other persons who take the defamatory statement seriously. Thus, we are brought back to the empirical requirements of the mediated-harm argument. Even without that problem, another is raised by the fact that the charge of defamation relies on the verifiability of the claim that the defamatory statement is indeed false.[13] Nevertheless, this argument has been used by feminists against pornography: 'Pornography lies explicitly about women's sexuality, and through such lies fosters more lies about our humanity, our dignity, and our personhood.'[14] 'Pornography is the vehicle for the dissemination of a deep and vicious lie about women. It is defamatory and libelous.'[15]

The feminist anti-pornography slogan 'Porn lies!' originates in such analysis. It has an almost intuitive appeal for many feminists, especially when we see that pornography presents women as enjoying rape and assault, as masochistic by nature, or as singularly driven by carnal desire. The problem with the denial of these misogynistic 'statements' is that their refutation requires appeal to either normative or empirical claims about what women *really* are.

'Anti-pornography feminists' actually have made such claims, charging that pornography does not adequately represent female sexuality. They complain that it focuses on anonymous, coercive, mechanistic sex, emphasizing breasts, genitals, and ejaculation, at the expense of consensual, intimate, affectionate, and generally sensual contact, which is what, they claim, women really want. This kind of contact has been disparagingly described by self-proclaimed 'pro-sex feminists' as 'vanilla sex' and criticized as yet another idealization and mystification of femininity, and ultimately as another form of objectification.[16]

A Post-Liberal Feminist Analysis of Pornographic Discourse

All of the preceding arguments are more or less inadequate from the feminist perspective. Either they are structured in such a way that it is extremely difficult, if not impossible, to prove that pornography harms women (e.g., the empirical argument for a causal link between pornography and subsequent commission of harmful actions, and the link between defamatory statements and harms suffered), or they perpetuate patriarchally oppressive sexual mores (through the decency component of the nuisance argument), or they risk putting into question the reasonableness of women who feel threatened by pornography (the threat argument), or they require women to objectify themselves (the defamation argument). A substantively different approach is required.

Expression and Action

Examination of the nature of 'pornographic discourse' demonstrates that the illusory private/public boundary, particularly as it is reflected in the distinction between speech and action, both of which are characteristic of liberal theory, leaves freedom and equality, especially that of members of historically subjugated classes, vulnerable to assault, given that many prejudices that reflect pre-liberal social relations are reified in the very language we speak.

Analyses of pornography that treat it as private fantasy or speech are deceptive. The pornographer *acts* upon, or perhaps with, the consumer. Arousing desire is an act, albeit a symbolically mediated act. As long as the consumer and the pornographer were the only persons involved or affected by this act, liberal ethical concerns about coercion and exploitation would be exhausted by determining how freely each individual had entered into the relationship. However, the fact of symbolic mediation brings other issues to the fore. Who exactly is involved in an act of symbolic exchange, and who can harm and be harmed by it?

Feminists, among others, have suggested that there can be no such thing as relationships that are private in the sense of being non-political. The personal is the political insofar as personal relations are mediated by publicly shared symbols of meaning and value. The 'private' use of symbols, it is argued, always involves the public sphere of shared meaning and value. Use of a symbol affirms its socially constructed meaning and value. In a sense, it legitimates or validates particular forces of social construction.

Here, the significance of this point is enhanced by recognition of the fact that pornography, existing within a generally sexist mainstream media, has a near monopoly on sex education and plays a major role in determining popular conceptions of what sexuality is. Furthermore, the mode of pornographic discourse reflects the structure of pre-liberal patriarchal social relations.

The relation between the pornographer and the consumer is one of exchange, but what is exchanged? Women are not themselves exchanged in the way in which they are exchanged in the maintenance of (patriarchal) kinship structures, for example.

Levi-Strauss has explained how women can be literally exchanged: 'The total relationship of exchange which constitutes marriage is not established between man and woman, but between two groups of men, and the woman figures only as one of the objects in the exchange, not as one of the partners ... This is true even when the girl's feelings are taken into consideration, as, moreover, is usually the case. In acquiescing to the proposed union, she precipitates or allows the union to take place, she cannot alter its nature.'[17]

The exchange of real objects (including persons) is, however, a practice not entirely unrelated to the exchange of symbols. Women are exchanged, in the process of establishing and maintaining kinship structures, not simply for their use value (e.g., as a means to sexual gratification, entertainment, reproduction, or production), but also as signs or symbols (e.g., as symbols of *rights* of sexual access or as symbols of status and wealth).

Levi-Strauss pursued this notion of the exchange of women as an exchange of symbols. He noted the kinship structure's regard of women 'as being like words which are misused when they are not "communicated" and exchanged.'[18]

In pornography it is images of women, and not women themselves, that are exchanged, and these images like the women in the kinship structures are exchanged as signifiers. But what do these images signify? They signify women symbolizing sexual desire.[19] Is this more or less objectifying than the exchange of actual women?

One might be inclined to say that it is less objectifying since it leaves actual women freer to move and make their own choices. However, it leaves women less free to be *women*, since being a woman has come to mean being a symbol. And how easily this is done! Only a signifier need be exchanged to reinforce the meaning of a history of women understood as symbols rather than subjects.

Levi-Strauss cautioned, in regard to analyses of the exchange of women in kinship system, that 'woman could never become just a sign and nothing more, since even in a man's world she is still a person, and since insofar as she is defined as a sign she must be recognised as a generator of signs ... In contrast to words which have wholly become signs, woman has remained at once both a sign and a value.'[30]

Perhaps the irony is that women can only be both signs and sign generators (most likely in a marginalized subculture) when they are directly, rather than indirectly, oppressed, and are actually materially exchanged. In pornography, where only images or signs of women are exchanged, and that exchange is made meaningful by reference to woman as symbol, women are no longer present as human subjects who can generate signs. Only signs and symbols are present and they do not speak. They are spoken through.

In this context, women – who are not partners in the pornographic exchange – have no opportunity to speak. The pornographic model is like the exchanged bride who merely acquiesces to, but does not determine the meaning of her exchange. Unlike the exchanged bride, however, she becomes simply a silent two-dimensional image of woman.

Sexual meanings, like all meanings, are necessarily social. Should someone, or some social force, be free to determine that a woman's body is to be considered the sexual stimulus par excellence, when I at the same time, as a person with a woman's body would not choose to define myself as a sexual stimulus? But, you are free not to think of yourself as a sexual stimulus might come the (liberal) reply.

How I choose to think of myself is not, however, the same as how I am *defined*. I can determine my appearance and behaviour to a considerable extent, within a range of appearances and behaviours available to me, from among which it is possible for me to choose. I cannot, however, determine how other people are going to interpret these appearances and behaviours. Thus, if someone, or some social force, successfully establishes a given way of interpreting certain appearances and behaviours, and those interpretations cover most of the appearances and behaviours possible for me to choose from, then my self-determination has been sharply limited.

The name feminists give to this process of limiting what a person can be by predetermining how her or his behaviour or appearance is to be interpreted is 'objectification.' It defines me from without, according to someone else's needs, desires, and intentions, before I have a chance to exert any control over how I am determined or defined as a subject, i.e., to have my own needs, desires, and intentions reflected in public interpretations of who or what I am.

The identification of something with a certain function suggests that attributes associated with that function exhaust both the possible class of characteristics it might have, as well as the possibilities for interpretation of the appearances that form the basis for the attribution. This identification is most easily accomplished with symbols, for a symbol cannot have its own perspective on the interpretation of its meaning.

It is doubtful whether as symbol-manipulating, language-using creatures we could ever wholly avoid objectification, i.e., such naming in terms of function. The issue of which of these language-users hold the power to name and have their perspectives reflected in the dominant, evaluative, ascriptions of function, in their turn reflects real social power. However, the unequal distribution of that power is not something that need be unavoidable.

Sexual objectification is only one of the various forms of objectification that have limited what women can be. There is a strong tradition in both high and popular art (Western art at least) of representing woman as aesthetic object, or sentimentalizing her as a symbol of motherhood or virginal purity. Nor are women the only class of persons who have historically been objectified. However, it is woman primarily who is objectified as a sexual symbol by pornography.

This process involves the transformation not only of individual women into signifiers of sexual desire, but also the objectification of an entire gender. The former is dehumanizing, as is also the objectification of a person into, say, an aesthetic object, but gender objectification (which could take on the specific forms of sexual, aesthetic, etc., objectification) is in addition discriminatory. It implies that this (apparent) person is not a subject but a sexual sign, and what makes this person a sexual sign is the fact that her gender is a sexual symbol. That is, all women, in a culture where pornography (which focuses on images of women) is an effective mediator of sexual arousal, are sexual objects.

Privacy and Essentialism

I do not claim here that pornography alone transforms women into sexual objects. Rather, pornographers have harnessed and exploited two pre-existing social forces: a visual, verbal, and conceptual symbol system that reflects its origins in patriarchal society within which women were literally objectified as private sexual property and the consequences of liberal revolutions on the narrowed scope of the private sphere that have facilitated the commodification of sexuality.

In pre-liberal society ownership rights were distributed unequally, so that certain classes of persons constituted the property of the property-owning class. Thus, children, wives, slaves, and subjects were the property of fathers, husbands, masters, and monarchs, respectively.

Liberal revolutions, driven by the principles of liberty and equality, undermined those oppressive social relations but none the less maintained the concept of the sphere of ownership, or private sphere.

A peculiar consequence of transplanting this concept of the private sphere into the liberal context is that the individual must be her/his own sovereign and subject at once. The identification of the liberty of equal individuals with the integrity of their separate private spheres created a tension, if not a contradiction, between the principles of autonomy and equality.

The final manifestation of this contradiction could be, and has been, postponed through the preservation of a limited private sphere that still included other persons, or the alienated products of someone else's labour. Capitalist economy and the nuclear family have been fulfilling this function since the demise of the patriarchal privilege in the public sphere, signalled as it was by popular liberal revolutions and the industrial revolution. However, the logic of liberalism has entailed an expanding notion of who belongs to the rights-bearing class.

Extension of this 'privilege' to former slave classes, women, and to some extent children has had a corrosive effect on the private sphere, and particularly on 'the family' as buffer between the contradictory premises of liberal ideology.[21] Ultimately, however, the private sphere must comprise nothing but the individual who is thus required to alienate her/his self from herself/himself in order to have something to own and control, to 'have,' and to exchange at will.

Interestingly, many of the characteristics and powers associated historically with subjugated classes, e.g., the labour power of slaves and the sexuality of women, have come to be projected onto the 'autonomous individual,' or at least onto alienated parts of him or her. Thus, sexuality has come to be seen as an essential individual characteristic or property, whereas in earlier times, consistent with material social relations, it was projected onto 'The Sex,' i.e., woman.

'Sexual essentialism,' the term for this latest moment in the history of sexuality, has been described by Gayle Rubin as:

... the idea that sex is a natural force that exists prior to social life and shapes institutions. Sexual essentialism is embedded in the folk wisdoms of Western societies, which consider sex to be eternally unchanging, asocial, and and ahistorical. Dominated for over a century by medicine, psychiatry, and psychology, the academic study of sex has reproduced essentialism. These fields classify sex as a property of individuals. It may reside in their hormones or in their psyches. It may be construed as physiological or psychological. But within these ethnoscientific categories, sexuality has no history and no significant social determinants.[22]

The essentialist view of sexuality also represents one of the ways in which the function of the private sphere has been re-created in microcosm. An individual's sexuality, under her or his sole purview, can be exchanged (expressed), controlled, shared, hidden away, and so forth. It is something about which s/he can make moral judgments without involving anyone else, and with respect to which ethical concerns are exhausted by obtaining the other person's consent should any others happen to be involved.

If liberty requires privacy then it is necessary to objectify sexuality like this. Otherwise individual moral judgments would be thoroughly meaningless given the nature of the model of patriarchal value, within which liberty meant control over objects or persons who (like objects) constituted private property.

Thus, images of woman, historically the most tangible sign of private sexual property, are still the most effective symbols of sexuality, even in a liberal society where sex has come to be regarded as a property of all individuals.

Conclusion

Undue focus on the sexual nature of pornography, either as a good (e.g., as a form of 'sexual expression' protected by the right to freedom of expression) or as an evil (where pornography is seen to represent a threat to conservative mores upholding a system of private sexual property), is both conceptually and ethically problematic.

If sexual essentialism is abandoned, then it makes no sense to speak of purely sexual exchanges, or intentions to 'have sex,' suggesting that sex is an object rather than a social process. To speak this way is to fetishize sexuality into a moral patient (reflected in the protection of conservative mores), or into a commodity (reflected by the value placed by liberals on freedom of sexual expression).[23]

The first view subordinates the human subject to an ideal that actually reflects the interests of a particular privileged group of persons, and thereby excludes certain other groups of persons from the community of full subjects. The second view alienates human subjects from an essential social process, thereby estranging them from one another and from themselves. They are robbed of the medium in which to communicate and articulate individual and collective identities. Ultimately, community is denied as a context for affirming subjecthood.

While the position I have outlined above is not opposed to pornography because it is sexual, that it is sexual is not irrelevant to the actual basis of its opposition. The post liberal position objects to assault, coercion, and exploitation, and maintains that gender objectification constitutes just this kind of action, whether it takes the form dictated by patriarchal conservative mores or the form dictated by the liberal free market.

Sexual representation can be used to legitimate an oppressive and alienating sexual ideology; and, as long as the sexual ideology reflected by pornography relies on gender objectification it will continue to be politically and ethically objectionable.

The post-liberal feminist framework affirms the value of freedom and equality, but is also informed by the knowledge that our culture carries with it a history of objectified womanhood – a history that is not recognized in a liberal ideology of ahistorical autonomous and freely choosing individuals. Liberal ideology recognizes women as persons, yet its values, based on its conception of individual and society, do not reflect our experience. Women are a new class of persons created by liberal revolutions, who none the less still feel as painful the old patriarchal values tolerated in the liberal private sphere and exploited in the free marketplace.[24]

Articulating the basic assumptions behind this alternative analysis of pornography may help to indicate the areas of further inquiry it is necessary to pursue if we are to prevent pornographic harms. These assumptions are the following: (a) gender and sexuality are socially constructed phenomena rather than predetermined essences; (b) social recognition of personhood is a function of recognized participation in social discourse, which is determined by our understanding of what constitutes this discourse and who is understood to be capable of participating in it; and (c) equal access to the medium, and the power of naming, through which socially determined 'knowledge' is generated, is necessary to overcome objectification, i.e., the exclusion of certain persons from the community of subjects (recognized participants in social discourse).

Understood within this framework, human beings are social animals in the fullest sense of the expression. They are equal with respect to human dignity and capacity to be a human subject, but are none the less dependent on a social medium in which to substantively determine, or articulate, what is to be understood as the being of a human subject, given that meaning is intersubjective and cannot be autonomously determined. According to this view, what is good must be assessed in terms of what allows for meaningful conceptions of what it is to be a 'human subject,' and is not radically at odds with the interests and experiences of particular subclasses of the class of human subjects.

The substantive concept of the human subject is, of course, only a regulative ideal. The process it regulates is hermeneutic and directed at consensus, or making commensurate perspectives, which may at the outset appear to be at odds with one another. The achievement of an understanding and appreciation of differences is not to be confused, however, with tolerance. Tolerance can be achieved without understanding, such that someone might be *permitted* to believe something which others regard as utterly false and pernicious so long as such beliefs, and associated practices, were expressed privately.

In order for an experience or perspective to become integrated into the common understanding of the human, dialogue is required. This dialogue cannot be one which separates beliefs, speech, and action. It must be one which implictly recognizes that they each make the others meaningful and together constitute a 'form of life.' The process of integration will probably also involve modification of the perspectives, or forms of life, of all concerned – including the otherwise merely 'tolerant.'

Assault, coercion, and exploitation would be understood from this position to threaten the consensual process of articulating what it is to be human, and would therefore be ethically and politically objectionable. Pornography is here understood to pose such a threat. Although assault, coercion, and exploitation are objectionable from the liberal perspective also, since they pose a threat to individual liberty. I think liberals and post-liberal feminists would disagree as to what would count as instances of such acts, based on differing conceptions of what is essential to the human person and therefore vulnerable to assault.

Both would say that rape occurring as a consequence of consumption of pornography, if such a causal link could be demonstrated, would be dangerous, but only the post-liberal feminist would say that pornography itself is assaultive (to the conditions of consensual discourse and therefore harmful to those who would otherwise articulate themselves in that discourse). Coercion, for both liberals and post-liberal feminists, amounts to making the victim a party to her or his own assault. Exploitation, from both perspectives, is a means of profiting from assault on another. But assault from the liberal perspective is an attack on another's liberty. From the post-liberal feminist perspective it is a denial of her or his personhood, a denial of her or his status as a member of the community of subjects.

If we take seriously the values of liberty and equality we must also recognize that the possibility of their realization depends on amenable conditions of social discourse. We need to examine more carefully how to foster those conditions and how to protect them from the kind of harm which I have suggested pornography represents.

NOTES

1 Thomas I. Emerson, *The System of Freedom of Expression* (New York: Vintage Books, 1970), p. 8
2 See, for example, Susan Wendell, 'Pornography and Freedom of Expression,' in *Pornography and Censorship*, ed. David Copp and Susan Wendell (Buffalo: Prometheus Books, 1983).
3 Joel Feinberg, 'Pornography and the Criminal Law,' *Pornography and Censorship*, pp. 105, 106.
4 Ibid., p. 107
5 Ibid., p. 108
6 Ibid.
7 H.L.A. Hart, *Law, Liberty, and Morality* (London and Oxford: Oxford University Press, 1968)
8 The Williams Committee on Obscenity and Film Censorship, *Report of the Committee on Obscenity and Film Censorship* as quoted by Bernard Williams in 'Offensiveness, Pornography and Art,' *Pornography and Censorship*, p. 186.
9 See, for example, John Stuart Mill, *On Liberty*, Norton Critical Edition, ed. David Spitz (New York: W.W. Norton & Co., 1975), p. 91; Hart, *Law, Liberty and Morality*, p. 45; Williams, *Pornography and Censorship*, p. 186; and Feinberg, *Pornography and Censorship*, p. 106.
10 Williams, *Pornography and Censorship*, p. 189
11 Ibid., p. 189
12 Ibid., p. 193
13 The recent prosecution of James Keegstra under the Hate Propaganda Law brought this problem to light in a dramatic way. Not only did it have to be proved that by making certain statements he *incited* hatred, but also these statements, e.g., that the Holocaust was a Jewish hoax, had to be shown in court to be false. Many regarded the judicial countenancing of such doubt as yet another slap in the face to Holocaust survivors and their families.

See RSC 1970, C.C-34 s.281.2 for the statement of and defences against a
charge of public incitement of and wilful promotion of hatred against
an identifiable group. Incidentally, gender is not (yet) included as a group
identifier.

14 Helen Longino, 'Pornography, Oppression, and Freedom: A Closer
Look,' *Take Back the Night*, ed. Laura Lederer (New York: Bantam
Books, 1982), p. 32

15 Ibid., p. 35

16 For 'pro-sex feminist' criticisms of the feminist anti-pornography move-
ment see *Women against Censorship*, ed. Varda Burstyn (Vancouver:
Douglas and McIntyre, 1985), and *Pleasure and Danger*, ed. Carol S. Vance
(Boston: Routledge & Kegan Paul, 1984).

17 Levi-Strauss, *The Elementary Structures of Kinship*, p. 115, as quoted by
Gayle Rubin in 'The Traffic in Women: Notes on the "Political Economy" of Sex,' in *Toward an Anthropology of Women*, ed. Rayna R. Reiter
(New York and London: Monthly Review Press, 1975), pp. 174–75.
That the structure of this sort of relationship persists outside of 'primitive'
cultures is illustrated by the following remarks about distinguishing
rape on the basis of presence or absence of consent: 'Desirability to men is
commonly supposed to be a woman's form of power. This echoes the
view that consent is a woman's form of control over intercourse, different
but equal to the custom of male initiative. Look at it: man initiates,
woman chooses. Even the idea is not mutual. Apart from the disparate
consequences of refusal, or openness of original options, this model
does not envision a situation a woman controls being placed in, or choices
she frames, yet the consequences are attributed to her as if the sexes
begin at arm's length, on equal terrain, as in the contract fiction. Ambigu-
ous cases of consent are often archtypically referred to as 'half won
arguments in parked cars.' Why not half lost? Why is it an argument? Why
do men feel entitled to 'it' when women don't want them? That sexual
expression is even framed as a matter of women's consent, without expos-
ing these presuppositions, is integral to gender inequality. Woman's
so-called power presupposes her more fundamental powerlessness.' Catherine A. MacKinnon, 'Feminism, Marxism, Method, and the State:
Toward a Feminist Jurisprudence,' *Signs: Journal of Women in Culture and
Society* 8, no. 4 (1983): 655.

18 Levi-Strauss cited by Rubin in *Toward an Anthropology of Women*, p. 201

19 In other contexts female images are signs of women as symbols of Beauty,
Purity, Justice, and all manner of abstract ideas. Perhaps they are traces
of metaphysical desire. See Mary O'Brien, *The Politics of Reproduction*

(Boston, London, and Henley: Routledge and Kegan Paul, 1981), for an examination of the meaning of masculine metaphysical desire.

20 Levi-Strauss as quoted by Rubin in *Toward an Anthropology of Women*, p. 201

21 Robert Paul Wolff has noted that, within the power politics of liberal pluralism, the preservation of ethnic, religious, and other 'interest groups' has also served the function of buffer between 'the ideals of justice and individual freedom on the one hand and the facts of the social origin and nature of personality on the other.' See Robert Paul Wolff, 'Beyond Tolerance,' in *A Critique of Pure Tolerance*, ed. Robert Paul Wolff, Barrington Moore Jr., and Herbert Marcuse (Boston: Beacon Press, 1980), p. 25 et passim.

22 Gayle Rubin, 'Thinking Sex: Notes for a Radical Theory of the Politics of Sexuality,' *Pleasure and Danger*, pp. 275–6. Discussions of sexual essentialism also figure in Michel Foucault's *The History of Sexuality*, vol. 1, trans. Robert Hurley (New York: Vintage Books, 1980).

23 The concern for harms to sex rather than to persons is reflected in the wording of s.159 of the Canadian Criminal Code, which reads: 'For the purposes of this act any publication a dominant characteristic of which is the undue exploitation of sex, or of sex and any one of the following subjects, namely, crime, horror, cruelty, and violence, shall be deemed to be obscene' (RSC 1970, C.C-34 s.159).

24 'A transvaluation of values can only be accomplished when there is a tension of new needs, and a new set of needy people who feel all the old values as painful – though they are not conscious of what is wrong.' Quote attributed to Friedrich Nietzsche by Mary Daly, *Beyond God the Father* (Boston: Beacon Press, 1973), p. 98.

That women are only newly recognized as persons is demonstrated by the fact that in Canada, for example, female personhood was only first recognized as late as 1930. See *Henrietta Muir Edwards* v. *Attorney General of Canada* [1938] A.C. 124 J.C.P.C.

Women and Moral Madness

KATHRYN PAULY MORGAN

In one of Marge Piercy's poems, 'For Strong Women,' we find the following verse:

A strong woman is a woman in whose head
a voice is repeating, I told you so,
ugly, bad girl, bitch, nag, shrill, witch,
ballbuster, nobody will ever love you back,
why aren't you feminine, why aren't
you soft, why aren't you quiet, why
aren't you dead?[1]

Similarly, we might say that a moral woman is a woman in whose head a voice is repeating words like 'immature,' 'pathological,' 'inadequate,' 'immoral,' 'evil.' What I explore in this paper are various ways in which a woman's moral voice and her sense of moral integrity are twisted and destroyed by patriarchal ideology and lived experience. I claim that, ultimately, this experience can lead to a sense of confusion and genuine moral madness which is then cited, in a patriarchal culture, to further discredit a woman's moral subjectivity.

This litany of words of moral denigration arises out of at least four different traditions and manoeuvres in the area of traditional ethical theory and moral practice. The first classical philosophical manoeuvre calls into question woman's capacity for full moral agency as a result of examining the concept of human nature. The second manoeuvre is based upon establishing a distinction between public and private morality and then claiming that only the public domain of morality, which is lived in by men, counts as genuinely moral. The third

manoeuvre is based on an ingenious set of double-binds, metamorphoses, and moral contortions which permeate the lives of women and
which lead, inevitably, to a sense of bewilderment if not outright moral
insanity. And the fourth is based on the perceived invisibility of actual
moral domains in women's lives so that often women don't even
recognize when we are being moral. I conclude with what might boldly
be called a 'Prolegomena to a Feminist Moral Heuristic.'

Women Are Denied Full Moral Agency

Women are denied full moral agency in at least three separate ways:
first, through a process of pseudo-blind gender-essentialist thinking;
second, by generating theories of women's nature that claim that
women and men are either different in degree or kind; and, third, by
alleging that women's lives are marked by a kind of moral epiphenomenalism.

The first case involves pseudo-blind gender-essentialist thinking.
Put crudely, it goes something like this. Philosophy involves the search
for the knowledge of essences. Whether we define this as the search for
the Platonic form, the paradigm case, the nature sought after by
medievalists, the elusive finite set of necessary and sufficient conditions, or the natural kinds sought after by contemporary philosophers,
the message coming through is virtually the same: that there is some
definite description which can be given which embodies essentialist
knowledge of a particular type of X (leaving aside Wittgensteinian
notions of family resemblance). The particular X that is relevant here
is, of course, the concept of human nature. Striving to adopt the
standpoint of a detached transcendental knower, many traditional
philosophers hope to define human nature in a way that is unaffected
by the vicissitudes of human history, human culture, and evolutionary
variability.[2] Often such definitions (particularly in Western philosophical thought) claim that for X to be human, X must be rational, decisive,
capable of exercising authority, theoretically oriented, and capable of
taking the moral point of view, which involves adopting a posture of
moral impartiality derived from commitment to universalizable moral
principles. Once armed with such essentialist criteria it simply remains
to discover, as a matter of empirical practice, whether any beings satisfy
these criteria for being human. It is perhaps distressing or uplifting,
depending upon one's perspective, to discover that at least half the
members of *Homo sapiens* fulfil these criteria, namely, males. Thus, one
concludes that, as simply a matter of 'pure' empirical fact, only men are

capable of full moral agency. Proponents of this manoeuvre claim that since the question of essence has been raised in a purely abstract fashion there can be no charge of bias or distortion vis-à-vis the real world.

I claim that this is a ruse. I am inclined to accept the existence of the transcendental ego about as much as that of the Great Pumpkin. As far as I can determine only empirical egos engage in philosophical reasoning, and empirical egos invariably walk about in gendered garb.[3] I suspect that many arguments (and their attendant theories of human nature) concerning abortion or sexual perversion are generated in order to support what are already assumed and fallaciously referred to as 'our moral intuitions.' I similarly suspect that essentialist thinking of this sort already presupposes its not terribly surprising patriarchal outcome and is generated to support widely pervasive social and political 'intuitions.'[4] The upshot of this method of reasoning is that women are ruled out, in a priori fashion, from the moral community.

The second method denies women full moral personhood by generating theories about the nature of woman which claim that women differ from men either in degree or in kind such that women are not entitled to full moral agency.

An example of the difference-in-degree theory is Aristotle's. As many feminist critics have noted, Aristotle maintains, in the *Politics*, that there are two necessary criteria for full moral agency: one must have a fully developed deliberative rational faculty capable of exercising authority. As he puts it, 'to be good a person must have the sort of understanding which issues in commands' (1143a8). Since, for a variety of reasons, woman's nature is such as to have only a share in deliberative faculty but not authority, the most that a woman can aspire to, from a moral point of view, is to be aligned with a fully developed man of moral integrity and to obey his commands silently (1260a4; 1260a30). The possibility of independent, self-sufficient moral integrity is ruled out for women but a life of virtue commensurate with a woman's essential moral limitations is not – provided that she is fortunate in her patriarchal associations.

This view is put starkly by Aquinas who claims, 'As regards the individual nature, woman is defective and misbegotten, for the active force in the male seed tends to the production of a perfect likeness in the masculine sex.'[5] As a result, Aquinas maintains that 'woman is naturally subject to man, because in man the discretion of reason predominates'[6] and that it is proper that women should be denied full moral-religious personhood as priests because 'it is not possible in the female sex to signify eminence of degree.'[7] One of the obvious corollaries of the impossibility of signifying eminence of degree is that women are capable, at most, only of moral mediocrity when set against the standard established by fully developed moral men. The parallel here with the work of moral developmentalist Lawrence Kohlberg should be obvious.[8] According to Kohlberg's theory of cognitive-stage moral development, women fail to advance beyond the deplorable stage of conventional morality and are thus regarded as morally immature in relation to fully developed moral men.

When patriarchal philosophers are not engaged in arguing for a difference-in-degree theory, they are often occupied in arguing for some sort of theory that postulates that women and men are different in kind. For example, in *Emile*, Rousseau argues that boys should be brought up in such a way that they become self-directed, active, strong, theoretically oriented, and capable of rational masterfulness.[9] Girls, however, should be raised in such a way as to be profoundly other-defined so that even a woman's own virtue must be constituted out of public opinion and not simply out of her private acts and intentions. According to Rousseau, women are by nature made to please, to be dominated. A woman's passivity, her weakness, her submissiveness, and her resultant reliance on guileful manipulation are taken to be marks of her moral virtue lived out by a woman who is obedient, loyal, and sentimental.[10] Rousseau assigns woman a different morality because, like many thinkers, he does not regard women as capable of theoretical reasoning. At the same time, he claims that such rationality is a necessary precondition for a self-directed moral life.

Similarly, in the chapter 'On the Distinction of the Beautiful and the Sublime,' Kant maintains that boys and men are capable of a deep understanding, of noble virtue, and of leading a life according to rational moral principle.[11] In contrast, woman's morality should essentially be one of sentiment, governed by irrational moral feelings of aversion and beauty. To compensate for the incapacity to live according to rationally understood moral principles that are chosen autonomously, women are constructed to resonate with moral feelings, sensations, and sentiments, data of consciousness which are notorious for their episodic and variable nature. While capable of moving women to action, such feelings and sentiments are, by virtue of their intrinsic character, necessarily inferior moral 'data' when compared with the permanence provided by universalizable principles. While Rousseau, Kant, and other philosophers of this ilk insist that what we have here is a kind of fundamental moral equality, it is also clear that, like other philosophers, they recommend patriarchal social arrangements. This shows an ideological bias at work. Such recommendations are inconsistent with these alleged claims to moral equality. Egalitarian complementarity would generate, at best, a heterosexual set of recommendations not patriarchal ones.

In either case the message is clear: women are ruled out as full participants in the relevant moral community. At best, a woman can aspire to be affiliated, as a kind of moral groupie, with a man of moral integrity and partake in the goodness of his moral life.

The third method of denying women full moral agency is by claiming that, at best, women are negative moral epiphenomenalists. What I mean by this is that women's bodies are interpreted as capable of acting upon the mind so as to occlude consciousness, thought, and moral feeling. And this is assumed to be an asymmetrical process, hence the epiphenomenal characterization of the process. The mind is not regarded as capable of taking control over these processes in any rational fashion. An hysterical woman is beyond the rational pale.

Sometimes the form that this theory takes is absolute, i.e., that simply by virtue of their embodiment as women, women just are closer to nature and, hence, not capable of the kind of thought that is necessary for human moral life.[12] Often these allegations concerning the afflicting nature of women's bodies are grounded in elaborate physiological theories based on an impressive array of scientific observations that war with one another in trying to decide what is the fundamental cause of potential moral disorder: the uterus, the ovaries, the softness of women's musculature, female hormones, or brain development and morphology.[13] Whatever the outcome of the debates, the claim is much the same as that of Professor Holbrook, in 1870, who said that it seemed 'as if the Almighty, in creating the female sex, had taken the uterus and built up a woman around it.'[14]

The more interesting theories are those that support episodic moral epiphenomenalism by claiming that there are various normally occurring processes that occur in women's bodies which lead to a kind of moral derangement, that for given episodes of our lives we are necessarily crazy in some respect or other because of how our healthy womanly bodies operate. In many cultures, women who are menstruating are expected to be in some deranged and dangerous physical state. Women who are pregnant are expected to behave in peculiar sorts of ways and express bizarre preferences. In the Canadian Criminal Code women who have just given birth are expected to go into a period of insanity, especially if they breast-feed their infants.[15] Consequently, murder of a newborn infant by the mother is not treated like other kinds of murder even though it may occur several months after the birth. Menopause is assumed to be a state of derangement that goes on for years.[16] Similarly, post-menopausal women are expected to be permanently disordered because of the severity of the identity crises surrounding the termination of reproductively defined womanhood.[17]

Now, pre-menstrual stress has been added to the list of morally disabling afflictions and baptized with the name of 'syndrome' in order to indicate its prominence in women's lives. In a variety of recent court cases in Britain and in North America women are claiming diminished moral responsibility for an offence because they were acting during their pre-menstrual period.[18] With all these episodic exclusions from moral life resulting from one's healthy embodiment as a woman, I reckon that we are left with approximately three to five days per month during which we can act and be held fully morally responsible. But this only occurs during our child-bearing years. Once into menopause or post-menopausal, our moral eligibility disappears altogether.

In many of these contexts women are seen either as more embodied than men or as embodied in morally damaging ways. In either case we find the fallacious inference that therefore women are less capable of full moral agency than men who achieve detachment and transcendence from their bodies and who are capable of more rational control. We need never worry about disabling testeria in men. Needless to say, these theories generate intense feelings of misogynistic somatophobia and often lead to much more external control and societal regulation of the lives of women than they do of men who are accorded moral autonomy.

The upshot of all these theories, then, is the disqualification of women from what is defined as a full moral life in what is regarded as the community of moral persons.[19] (I return to the question of the masculinist aspect of these definitions below.)

The Exclusion of Women from the Public Domain

Although various permutations occur in Western thought and practice, a sharp distinction is often drawn between public and private life. In some moral theories such as Plato's *Republic* or Hegel's theory of the state, the moral life of those with the greatest moral responsibility is entirely public. In the *Republic*, for example, the lives of the rulers are lives devoid of private property, private sexual relationships, and privatized familial relations. The publicizing of their lives, as it were, is rationally justified by the pivotal political role expected of them. In theories where life is not wholly public, it is still clear that participation in public life has pride of place.[20] Sometimes it is only the social or public domain that is accorded moral status.

However the variations occur throughout our history, the distinction between the public and the private continues to play an important contributing role to women's madness. It happens like this. We begin by postulating two kinds of morality: public morality and private morality. Public morality is the kind of morality that is expected in the moral public domain. It is characterized by its claims to universality, impartiality, reciprocity, its universalizability, and absence of emotional distortion. The proper moral agent is seen as an abstract, detached, isolated identityless autonomous individual whose actual position and identity in the just society are hidden behind a 'veil of ignorance.' Adopting these aims as one's moral ideals and striving to live according to them comes to be called 'taking the moral point of view.'

Private morality, then, pertains to the domain of the personal. It is immediate, situation specific, focused on particular individuals and relationships.[21] It is interpersonal and involves personal feelings as morally relevant factors. It is a morality that is grounded in our social relatedness to other specific individuals who are friends, or family, or preferred members of a significant social group. Girls and women are socialized into, are expected to be, are praised for being, and are gender-defined as experts in the domain of feelings because of our alleged capacity for the sensitive concrete attentiveness so important in sustaining personal relations.

So far so good. What often happens at this point, however, is morally grotesque. As I noted above, the first stage in the process equates public morality with morality per se. This equation leads to a profound devaluing of private or personal morality and undercuts its claim to moral legitimacy altogether. The second stage generates a theory which maintains that if someone does have expertise in the area of private or personal morality this is a kind of 'default expertise.' That is, often such theories will claim that it is because of women's diminished rationality and congenital incapacity for a life of principled morality that they become expert in the life of moral and psychological sentiment. This claim again devalues whatever moral excellences are to be found within this domain. Third, a woman's moral excellences, the very nature of her allegedly moral self, is transmuted into a pitiable amoral form of agency. Her sense of relatedness and connection becomes denounced as 'other-definition' or 'field-dependence' and the ground of her moral judgment is seen as involuntarily heteronomous rather than autonomous. Resulting from her feeble intellect, a woman's attentiveness to the concrete and the particular is seen to disqualify her from participation in the forms of public life and public morality.[22] Consequently, any claim to legitimate moral agency disintegrates.

Through skilful manipulation, then, of the public/private distinction women are obviously disqualified from full participation in the moral community. We are first told that there is a moral domain in which we achieve excellence. Then we are told that we can only achieve excellence in that domain. Then we are told that this domain is not a domain in which morality operates in its most exemplary way if at all. And finally we are blamed for living our moral lives in that domain while being told that we can do no other. This process must generate moral confusion if not outright madness.

The Generation of Moral Insanity

Moral Metamorphoses

Moral insanity can be generated in a variety of ways. In this section I examine two such ways: 1 / the metamorphoses of womanly vices into virtues and virtues into vices, and 2 / the setting up of feminine moral double-binds.

Womanly vices are turned into virtues in a variety of ways. One way is to socialize women into illusory or distorted moral paradigms.[23] Often these distorted paradigms are camouflaged as moral 'vocations' calling to women in the name of destiny and womanly fulfilment which require person-specific altruism of women as mothers, wives, and heterosexual lovers. As one examines these situations in detail what one very often uncovers is an appalling glorification of servility and consequent destruction of anything remotely resembling the kind of personal integrity (as distinct from autonomy) that must be preserved in any moral life.[24]

For example, works like *Fascinating Womanhood* and *The Total Woman* follow the Rousseauvian tradition and instruct women to dispense with an air of strength, ability, competence, and fearlessness and, instead, to cultivate the 'virtues' of submissiveness, frailty, fearfulness, guile, seduction, and economic dependence.[25] As one author puts it, the virtuous heterosexually fascinating woman should take as her moral role model the little canary![26]

The message that comes through is that the personal sense of power built into effective individual self-determination is morally bad; that powerlessness, self-abnegating self-sacrifice, and male-identified forms of dependence are morally fulfilling for a real woman.

An alternative twist occurs when 'liberated' women are encouraged to adopt distorted moral paradigms of independence and self-sufficiency. As Andrea Canaan put it,

By the time I was a woman, I had all the necessary external survival skills needed, supposedly, to protect me from rejection and humiliation projected onto me by white media, government, church, and social institutions. I had unending strength, ever-growing intellect, a heart as big as the heavens and earth, a soul more forgiving than gods themselves, and I accepted total responsibility for myself, my own oppressed state, the oppression of the brown man, and the sin of being both brown and woman. This super-woman veneer protected me from the external world much of the time. This super-woman veneer also warded off internal self-reflection needed to assess if indeed I was strong enough to carry such heavy burdens. The ever-growing intellect was an additional burden because the ability to think allows me to look at, if not truly see, options and truth. The open heart and forgiving soul stifled my rightful indignation, gagged my rage, and forced my fear, my needs, my rage, my joys, my accomplishments, inward. The acceptance of total responsibility, real, concrete, or abstract, for myself and others became my ultimate strait jacket, the last and strongest barrier to self.[27]

I would claim that in all these cases women are socialized into and invited to participate in forms of vice masquerading as 'womanly virtues.' And vicious they are because they destroy the capacity for moral agency in the name of its very fulfilment. They do not, however, altogether shed their identity as vices in male-defined moral schemes. As a result, women are simultaneously blamed and praised for their acquisition. This can drive us crazy.

The reverse metamorphosis – virtues being turned into vices – is equally devastating in its consequences. In the first instance, 'manly' virtues are seen as vices. What appears to be defined, in the abstract, as virtues per se often are seen as gender-incongruent in women. As a result, a virtuous woman may be regarded as 'deviant' and her dispositions to behave labelled vices. If a woman is publicly acknowledged to be rational, to be strong, to be powerful, to be courageous, to be decisive, she is labelled 'masculine' and seen to be lacking in womanly excellences. She cannot simultaneously display these moral strengths and be a woman. Or if she displays some subsets of these abilities, such as rational decisiveness and strength, she is often cast, in mythological contexts, as evil. The images of Eve, of Pandora, of the various active mothers and stepmothers in the Western fairy-tales come immediately to mind.[28]

In the second instance, characteristically womanly virtues are regarded as vices. Nurturing, helping, and sustaining the growth of others – the morally worthy aspects of altruism – are cited as evidence of woman's normal but pathological masochism.[29] Even though a woman's open emotional expressiveness may put her in a better epistemic position to make moral judgments than practising postures of emotional closure and denial, this very expressiveness is cited as a disqualification for moral responsibility. Ironically, a finely developed empathic imagination is noted as a reason for eliminating women from positions that require sensitive moral reflection on the grounds that the alleged requisite of hyper-detachment cannot be achieved. Receptivity becomes labelled passivity and denounced while simultaneously encouraged. A woman's refusal to compete in situations which entail someone else's failure and her tendency to prize co-operation over domination are described as her deplorable 'fear of success.'[30]

Finally, mediating gender coding takes its toll. Classical moral theory would have us believe that certain actions or certain intentions simply are, in themselves, intrinsically moral or immoral, or, if circumstances affect this judgment, those circumstances are objectively pertaining states of affairs in the world. So goes the ideology but not the practice. Often our moral assessment is gender-dependent. Consider the following anecdote:

Buckingham Palace has announced that 19-year old Prince Charles of England, the demure English rose and heir to the throne, has become engaged to Lady Diana Spencer, the 32-year-old, worldly woman who has been seeking the 'right' royal husband for ten years. (It has been stated by reliable sources that Charles is still a virgin. It is acknowledged in royal circles that Lady Diana has had several affairs over the past ten years.) When interviewed, Charles blushed sweetly over his engagement ring, and giggled happily on the TV news. The Queen had happily assented to Lady Diana's request for Charles' hand in marriage. Because of Diana's age and the fact that she is a self-proclaimed opponent of men's liberation, it is expected that the quiet prince will merge his identity with hers.[31]

At the time that the analogous column appeared in the media, groans

of traditionalism were heard but no particular moral outrage was
expressed at the thought that Diana would merge her identity with his.
But this inversion of the situation does prompt such moral reactions in
addition to the amusement derived from the ludicrous gender
incongruence in the passage in question. But why should gender
mediate our moral judgments?

Consider similar gender-mediated moral assessments in an administra-
tive context where, presumably, the identical behaviour is assessed
in a praiseworthy way when the moral agent is male and in a
blameworthy way when the moral agent is female. His behaviour is
praised for being aggressive and assertive; hers is denounced as pushy.
He is praised for his attention to detail; she is reprimanded for her
pickiness. He is seen as steadfast; she is seen as dogmatic and hard. He
is valued for his firm judgments; she is deplored for her prejudices and
biases. He is admired for his courageous frankness and straightfor-
wardness; she is labelled mouthy and strident. He is seen as witty; she is
experienced and blamed for being sarcastic. And so on. What are
virtues in him are, invariably, vices in her. In each case, gender is
mediating the judgments and personal assessments in the situation.
Thus, it would appear that even if women try to emulate men who are
seen as fully developed moral players in the game of morality, women
will still fail because such emulation, *per impossibile*, cannot literally be
seen or experienced as the same moral behaviour.

I conclude, then, that in all three types of moral metamorphoses
women are put into the impossible moral position of simultaneously
being moral and immoral, virtuous and vicious, for the same dispositions and behaviour. To try to understand this situation from the
inside, to try to live out these moral prescriptions, is to live in a situation
not only of moral chaos but of moral madness.

Moral Double-Binds

It is clear that women can become morally insane as a result of these
metamorphoses. But this is not the only pressure bearing upon us. In
many societies, women are socialized to aspire to life situations that
involve them in self-destroying moral double-binds. In Western
societies, two such situations are leading a life committed to romantic
love and having recourse to personal manipulative power as a
life-defining power strategy.

The situation of romantic love is a morally paradoxical and deeply
threatening one for woman. It is morally paradoxical because it

requires submission to and identification with another in the name of one's own growth and identity realization. It is deeply threatening because, almost by definition, it entails identity-destroying servility as its operating dynamic and underlying moral principle.[32]

There is a long tradition of Western thought that celebrates the suggestion that loving is a woman's central vocation, that it is her highest purpose in life and that which most confirms her womanliness. What is particularly prized in this loving devotion is its unconditional character as a commitment to person-specific altruism. Whether you examine the lyrics of the familiar song 'Stand by Your Man' or Rousseau's admonitions to Sophie the message is clear: the loving woman's moral obligation is to stay committed even in situations of manifest injustice and violence. Through loving, a woman hopes to realize her identity, stabilize her locus of value, acquire significance as a woman, integrate her eroticism, and live a life of moral self-respect gained through her commitment to her lover. One consequence of this moral commitment is that the woman comes to feel that any self-regarding intention or act is a selfish betrayal of her commitment to her lover. In this powerful way, then, gender and morality become inextricably intertwined for a woman in love.

Because of the totality of the commitment required women are taught to seek out a superior person to whom they will make this commitment. The commitment is honestly undertaken in the name of growth, of fulfilment, of realization of value. But the very dynamic and commitment chosen to achieve these goods rules out their realization. Ultimately, in many cases of romantic commitment, the situation degenerates into one of abject servility. As the woman in love becomes more and more aware of the vulnerability of her position she engages in tactical behaviour that can have only a negative outcome. If she succeeds in gaining control over her lover (thereby reducing her terrifying metaphysical vulnerability), he or she loses status in her eyes and is no longer worthy of her commitment. If she fails in her manoeuvres, then she is even more powerless than prior to her attempt and can only become more abject in the situation. Moreover, insofar as romantic love is an asymmetrical identification relationship of a woman becoming absorbed into the identity of her lover, the very dynamic itself eliminates the conditions of the possibility of genuine love.

Thus we see that two moral double-binds are at work here. 1 / In attempting to create and realize her own identity in the name of moral self-determination, the woman in love enters into precisely a kind of relationship that, by its very nature, will make that moral self-determination impossible and that will likely lead to terrifying servility on her part. What promises her fulfillment ends up destroying her. 2 / the love that is sought after, as a genuine moral good, is rendered impossible by the very dynamic that promises to deliver it.

Women also experience moral double-binds with respect to the use of manipulative power. Manipulative power can be distinguished from other sorts of power, such as coercion, reward power, expertise power, or positional power attached to a social role or position.[33] It differs from all these other forms because it is not publicly acknowledged, and often one assumes that some covert form of management is taking place.

Women are driven to use manipulative power for a variety of reasons. First, women who exist in situations of poverty, of racial or heterosexist oppression, or who live under conditions of personal or political violence often have recourse to manipulative power because it is the only form of power available to them. Second, even when women do have access to other forms of power, we are not perceived by others or even by ourselves as genuinely having access to power. Attribution theory in psychology documents all too easily the tendency of women to attribute our success to factors outside ourselves, e.g., luck, the position of the moon, some chance event, rather than claim it as a form of power within. Third, as women we are expected to be manipulative; it is gender congruent. Whether we look at the images of women in Homeric literature or the *Malleus Maleficarum* or Rousseau or the instruction books on *Total Womanhood*, it is clear that women are assumed to be naturally seductive, cunning, guileful, and manipulative. Such gender congruence becomes an important factor in a society such as ours where access to and practice of virtually all the other forms of power threaten to be coded as 'masculine' and labelled deviant when exercised by women. And the penalties for gender deviance are severe. Remember the line in the Piercy poem, '... bitch, nag, shrill, witch, / ball-buster, nobody will ever love you back, / why aren't you feminine ...?'

The double-binds involved in the use of manipulative power are multiple. It is generally agreed that the most effective way to exercise manipulative power is by simulating a position of weakness and vulnerability. What is problematic about this for women is that it gives actual support to a long patriarchal tradition that already regards women as 'the weaker sex' both intellectually and morally. In addition, it sustains that very perception of the woman who is simulating weakness in order to gain power. While her manipulative tactic can gain her some immediate good, it almost invariably weakens her position in subsequent situations. Moreover, role-playing is a powerful psychological mode in which, as social learning theorists point out, role-engulfment is an ever-present danger. This means that all too easily the manipulative woman can come to see herself as weak and defenceless as well as encouraging this public perception of her. She is thereby effectively eliminated from a search for more publicly acknowledged collective forms of power by both private and public perceptions of herself. A further difficulty with the use of manipulative power is that it is seldom cumulative. Again, a woman is encouraged and expected to behave in such a way that the very means she uses to gain power in the name of independent self-determination weaken her both publicly and privately and rule out, in principle, genuinely moral intercourse to the extent that such manipulation is covert.

To the extent, then, that women are socialized into lives of romantic love and restricted to the use of manipulative power, to that extent will our lives be filled with moral paradoxes and double-binds that contribute to our sense of moral madness.

The Invisibility of Moral Domains

The last factor contributing to women's moral madness is what I refer to as the invisibility of women's moral domains. What I mean by this is that very often only certain domains of human life are accorded moral status. As a result, it is difficult for women and men, literally, to see certain dimensions of women's lives as worthy of moral consideration. As a result, we become confused about whether what we are doing has any moral worth whatsoever and whether there are any operative moral standards. Consider the following anecdote. In a university class, the instructor asked the students to say a little bit about themselves by way of introduction to their class-mates. Various interesting narratives followed but none was quite as instructive as that of a woman in her early fifties who said that she 'raised seven children and then [she] went back to work'! It was instructive because it highlighted two of the important domains in women's lives that are not accorded moral worth and significance: maternal practice and domestic labour.

Although mothers are standardly blamed in the current clinical literature for well over seventy problems ranging from sleep-walking, ulcerative colitis, hyperactivity, peer avoidance, delusions, poor language development, to inability to deal with colour blindness, maternal practice is, nevertheless, a morally camouflaged process.[34] Hidden under the conceptual umbrella of 'maternal instinct,' mothering is regarded as a natural process that arises spontaneously between biological neonate and female parent between whom there is assumed to be a powerful bond that triggers mothering in normal cases. As a result, crucial questions of a social, political, and moral nature are not raised with respect to this human artefact called mothering. While some moral content must be assigned to such normative terms as 'perfect mother,' 'smothering mother,' or 'bad mother,' little moral subtlety is to be found.[35] And historically and theoretically, the domain of mothering and reproductive labour has been seen, at best, as a deficient and devalued moral domain involved with concerns that are individualized, private, and infantile. This realm is necessarily insignificant when compared with the transpersonal, universalizable domains of public institutional life. As a result, it is not surprising, then, that women not only do not accord themselves moral worth for good mothering, but describe themselves as not even engaging in morally worthwhile actions at all. Meanwhile they experience the agonies bound up with the absence of moral criteria for good mothering.

Similarly, domestic labour has been morally camouflaged as 'labour of love' performed by an 'angel in the household.' When performed well it is, literally, unseen, as Blum et al. point out.[36] Because women are encouraged to perform domestic work and provide sexual service in disconnected and privatized ways, both their exploitative character and intrinsic connection to institutional forms of patriarchy remain hidden. Rather than seeing either the morally destructive dimension of this work or the morally worthy aspect of nurturing and supporting the growth of other moral subjects, women are encouraged to describe this as 'doing nothing' while exhausting themselves in the process of trying to prove that they are gender-stable 'real women.' Sometimes the domain of domestic labour becomes an area for double moral oppression when immigrant women or women of colour are employed, under exploitative conditions, to work for women who themselves exist in a situation of moral exploitation. But it is also a potential domain for moral and political revolution. As Marge Piercy puts it, 'Burning dinner is not incompetence but war.'

In this section, then, I have tried to show how complete moral domains of women's lives are rendered invisible and then ideologically removed from the sphere of human morality so that we do not even realize that we are engaged in actions capable of generating moral worth. As a result, we often feel morally worthless when we should, in fact, be celebrating our moral worth. I take this to be the final stage of advanced moral madness.

Prolegomena to a Heuristic for Feminist Ethics

A Prediction

I predict that there will be no Rawls, no Nozick, no 'star' of feminist moral theory. There will be no individual singled out for two reasons. One reason is that vital moral and theoretical conversations are taking place on a large dialectical scale as the feminist community struggles to develop a feminist ethic.[37] The second reason is that this community of feminist theoreticians is calling into question the very model of the individualized autonomous self presupposed by a star-centred, male-dominated tradition. Thus there is a committed meta-level of shared consciousness among feminist moral theorists that would militate against the competitive aspiration for an individual achievement. We experience it as a common labour, a common task.

Sketch of a Heuristic: Some Central Issues

Feminist ethics must have its critical and its substantive aspects. As a moral critique, it is important to carry out the following tasks: It must critique any allegedly empirically grounded theories of moral human nature, sifting out that which is true from that which is false, distorted, or compromised by skewed a priori assumptions built into the conceptual framework, the methodology, and the results. We need to exercise a vigilant deconstructionist attention to sexist, racist, hetero-sexist, and class presuppositions. Second, aimed at generating new moral paradigms, a feminist ethic must call into question previously accepted 'full moral paradigms' in order to identify and expose those moral paradigms that are treacherously incomplete or twisted. Third, a feminist ethic must explore and analyse moral double-binds arising in the lives of women in order to determine which ones correspond to situations of genuine moral conflict and which are spurious, resulting from patriarchal ideological camouflage and oppressive practices. A fourth, important critical task is to dis-cover and render visible the hidden moral domains of women's lives while establishing women's claim to the full human spectrum of moral action and character, whether good or evil.

As a substantive radical moral theory, feminist ethics challenges the model of the moral subject as an autonomous, detached, rational subject, often seeing this hyper-masculinist ideal of the moral self as both psychologically and morally flawed. We can expect new models of the self, perhaps pluralistic in nature, to emerge. Whether these will call for a unitary quasi-essentialist model of the self remains to be seen; it may be that a looser, more open-textured notion of human consciousness will be necessary and that our epistemic paradigms will be similarly challenged in this process.[38] However they are described, I would expect such models literally to incorporate a sense of moral imagination, moral empathy, and moral feeling into an integrated, other-connected self.[39] (Whether such selves would be, necessarily or voluntarily, gendered will continue to be a lively matter for debate, I suspect.) Correlatively, what will count as a legitimate moral 'reason' will shift.

Second, after identifying the pernicious aspects of the public/ private distinction as it has been applied to women and other oppressed groups consigned to the private domain, feminist moral philosophers can be expected to blur this corrupt distinction. One way to do this is by continuing to explore the radical politicizing of the allegedly personal domain and the simultaneous personalizing of the allegedly deperson- alized public domain. An important corollary of this process will be a questioning of the relationship between the moral and the political. It will be important to ask whether either set of considerations has primacy, or whether they are, necessarily, bound up in some dialectical process in relation to feminist values and collective, feminist revolu- tionary practice. Again, this would particularly challenge all those moral traditions and practices that have assumed that genuine moral principles are universalizable over context. Finally, feminist moral theory must identify and reclaim our genuine womanly virtues as fully human virtues, rescuing them from the odious swamp of inferior vices. This process is necessary whether virtues will come to be theoretically understood as dispositions to act or as part of a looser moral repertoire of a moral self conceptualized and experienced in some more radical way.

A Poetic Criterion of Adequacy

It would seem that any worthy moral theory must meet criteria of adequacy. I do not pretend to know what a complete set of such criteria are in the present context. It is too early to tell. Nor am I entirely convinced that the question even makes sense. Nevertheless, I have a fierce moral conviction that no moral theory is worthy of the name 'feminist' unless it can account for the following moral 'facts' of a strong woman's life. I close by citing Marge Piercy once again:

A strong woman is a woman who loves
strongly and weeps strongly and is strongly
terrified and has strong needs. A strong woman is strong
in words, in action, in connection, in feeling;
she is not strong as a stone but as a wolf
suckling her young. Strength is not in her, but she
enacts it as the wind fills a sail.

What comforts her is others loving
her equally for the strength and for the weakness
from which it issues, ...
... Strong is what we make
each other. Until we are all strong together,
a strong woman is a woman strongly afraid. ('For Strong Women')

NOTES

1 Marge Piercy, 'For Strong Women,' reprinted in Jane Thompson, ed.,
 Learning Liberation: Women's Response to Men's Education (London:
 Croom Helm, 1983), p. 7
2 In his recent book, aptly entitled *The View From Nowhere* (Oxford: Oxford
 University Press, 1986), Thomas Nagel rejects this transcendental definition of individuality as unworkable in science and ethics, although he
 does suggest that saints and mystics can achieve it. Thus it seems to
 function as a kind of supererogatory moral ideal.
3 In an interesting essay, another committed Kantian theorist, Robert Paul
 Wolff, struggles with the aspirations of Kantian moral theory and their
 seeming irrelevance when juxtaposed to his actual life. See Robert Paul
 Wolff, 'There's Nobody Here but Us Persons,' in *Women and Philosophy:
 Toward a Theory of Liberation*, ed. Carol Gould and Marx Wartofsky (New
 York: G.P. Putnam's Sons, 1976).
4 Virtually all of this thinking has been carried out by men in situations in
 which the labour of women under conditions of patriarchal oppression
 has made possible the philosophical enterprise itself.
5 Aquinas, *Summa Theologica*, Part I, question 92, Reply to Obj. 1 (West-
 minster, MD: Christian Classics, 1981)
6 Ibid., Reply to Obj. 2
7 Ibid., Part III, question 39, Reply to Obj. 3
8 Kohlberg is a widely published author. See, for example, Lawrence Kohlberg, 'Moral Stages and Moralization; The Cognitive-Developmental

Approach,' in *Moral Development and Behavior: Theory, Research, and Social Issues*, ed. T. Lickona (New York: Holt, Rinehart and Winston, 1976); also *The Philosophy of Moral Development* (San Francisco: Harper and Row, 1981). Kohlberg's best-known feminist critic is Carol Gilligan, *In a Different Voice: Psychological Theory and Women's Development* (Cambridge, Mass: Harvard University Press, 1982).

9 Jean-Jacques Rousseau, *The Emile of Jean-Jacques Rousseau*, trans. William Boyd (New York: Teachers College, 1962). Originally published in 1779.

10 Ibid. See Book v, concerning the education of Sophie.

11 See Immanuel Kant, *Observations on the Feeling of the Beautiful and Sublime*, trans. John Goldthwait (Berkeley, Ca: University of California Press, 1960), pp. 76–96.

12 For two feminist discussions of this notion, see Simone de Beauvoir, *The Second Sex*, trans. H.M. Panohley (New York: Vintage, 1952), especially chaps. 1 and 9 (de Beauvoir discusses both the drawbacks and the potential power of such an identification); and Sherry B. Ortner, 'Is Female to Male as Nature Is to Culture?' in *Women, Culture and Society*, ed. Michelle Zimbalist Rosaldo and Louise Lamphere (Stanford: Stanford University Press, 1974).

13 See Brian Easlea, *Science and Sexual Oppression: Patriarchy's Confrontation with Woman and Nature* (London: Weidenfeld and Nicholson, 1982), chaps. 3 and 5; also Marian Lowe, 'The Dialects of Biology and Culture,' in *Biological Woman: The Convenient Myth*, ed. Mary Sue Henifin and Barbara Fried (Cambridge, Mass: Schenkman, 1982).

14 Barbara Ehrenreich and Deirdre English, *For Her Own Good: 150 Years of Experts' Advice to Women* (New York: Doubleday Anchor, 1978). p. 120

15 See Martin's *Criminal Code*, 1983, art. 216: 'A female person commits infanticide when by a willful act or omission she causes the death of her newly-born child, if at the time of the act or omission she is not fully recovered from the effects of giving birth to the child and by reason thereof of the effect of lactation consequent on the birth of the child her mind is then disturbed.'

16 In a recent judgment in British Columbia a 'Menopausal Woman' (note the use of this phrase as a kind of proper name) was removed from jury duty – one of the exercises of moral-political rationality – on the ground that she was unfit to serve because she was in menopause.

17 See Rosaline Barnett and Grace Baruch, 'Women in the Middle Years: Conceptions and Misconceptions,' in *Psychology of Women: Selected Readings*, ed. Juanita Williams (New York: W.W. Norton, 1979), pp. 479–87. This article exposes patriarchal twisting of research findings on the alleged 'empty-nest syndrome.'

18 For a critical discussion of this and similar decisions, see Hilary Allen, 'At the Mercy of Her Hormones: Premenstrual Tension and the Law,' *M/F* 9 (1984).
19 For an acute theatrical discussion of this move, see Marilyn Frye, 'Male Chauvinism,' in *Philosophy and Sex*, ed. Robert Baker and Frederick Elliston (Buffalo: Prometheus Books, 1975). For an extended historical analysis of the philosophical tradition, see Genevieve Lloyd, *The Man of Reason: 'Male' and 'Female' in Western Philosophy* (Minneapolis: University of Minnesota Press, 1984).
20 For two representative discussions of this distinction, see Hannah Arendt, *The Human Condition* (Chicago: University of Chicago Press, 1958); and Jean Bethke Elshtain, *Public Man, Private Woman: Women in Social and Political Thought* (Princeton: Princeton University Press, 1980); also Lloyd, *The Man of Reason*.
21 For a recent discussion of this distinction see the essays by Stuart Hampshire, 'Morality and Pessimism' and 'Public and Private Morality,' in *Public and Private Morality* (Cambridge: Cambridge University Press, 1978). Hampshire discusses, among other things, the challenges presented to the concept of public morality by Machiavellian models of public life.
22 Even a thinker as emancipated as John Stuart Mill succumbs to this kind of thinking, though not as the result of an essentialist line of thinking. See J.S. Mill, *The Subjection of Women*, reprinted in *Essays on Sex Equality*, ed. Alice Rossi (Chicago: University of Chicago Press, 1970).
23 Blum et al. discuss the notion of distorted paradigms. See L. Blum, M. Homiak, J. Horseman, and N. Sheman, 'Altruism and Women's Oppression,' in *Women and Philosophy*, pp. 222–47.
24 I distinguish moral integrity, which entails a moral and particular sense of connectedness and definition through others, from what I see as a pathological notion of transcendent detached individual antonomy, which pervades much of traditional ethical theory.
25 Helen B. Andelin, *Fascinating Womanhood* (New York: Bantam, 1974); Marabel Morgan, *The Total Woman* (Markham, Ont: Simon & Schuster, 1975)
26 Andelin, *Fascinating Womanhood*, p. 270
27 Andrea Canaan, 'Brownness,' in *This Bridge Called My Back*, ed. Cherrie Moraga and Gloria Anzaldua (Waterton, MA: Persephone Press, 1981), p. 233
28 See Andrea Dworkin, 'The Fairy Tales,' in *Woman Hating* (New York: E.P. Dutton, 1974), chaps. 1 and 2; Madonna Kolbenschlag, *Kiss Sleeping Beauty Good-Bye* (New York: Bantam, 1981).

29 For an extended analysis of this move, see Paula Caplan, 'The Myth of Masochism,' *American Psychologist* 39, no. 2 (1984): 130–9.

30 For an excellent discussion of these metamorphoses, see Jean Baker Miller, *Toward a New Psychology of Women* (Boston: Beacon Press, 1976), especially chaps. 4 and 5.

31 I am grateful to Norma Shearer and other students in my Philosophy of Feminism class for providing me with this example.

32 For an extended analysis of this experience and ideology of love, see Simone de Beauvoir, 'Women in Love,' *The Second Sex*; and my essay, 'Romantic Love, Altruism, and Self-Respect,' *Hypatia* 1, no. 1 (Spring 1986): 117–48, reprinted in *Women and Men*, ed. Greta Nemiroff (Toronto: Fitzhenry and Whiteside, 1986).

33 For a discussion of these forms of power, see 'Women and Interpersonal Power,' in *Women and Sex Roles*, ed. J. Parton, P. Johnson, D. Ruble, and G. Zellman (New York: W.W. Norton, 1978), pp. 301–20.

34 See Paula Caplan and Ian Hall McCorquodale, 'Mother-Blaming in Major Clinical Journals,' *American Journal of Orthopsychiatry* (July 1985).

35 Ruddick has, of course, done much to fill the vacuum in this area. See Sara Ruddick, 'Maternal Thinking,' *Feminist Studies* 6, no. 2 (Summer 1980): 342–67; reprinted in an important anthology, *Mothering: Essays in Feminist Theory*, ed. Joyce Trebilcott (Totowa, NJ: Rowman & Allanheld, 1984).

36 Blum et al., *Women and Philosophy*.

37 Feminist theorists working in the area of feminist ethics include Kathryn Pyne Addelson, Annette Baier, Mary Daly, Marilyn Frye, Carol Gilligan, Beverley Harrison, Barbara Houston, Sheila Mullett, Nel Noddings, Adrienne Rich, Carol Robb, and Susan Sherwin.

38 For a discussion of how an epistemic shift might work, see Evelyn Fox Keller, *Reflections on Gender and Science* (New Haven: Yale University Press, 1985), especially 'Gender and Science,' 'Dynamic Autonomy: Objects and Subjects,' 'Dynamic Objectivity: Love, Power and Knowledge,' and 'Cognitive Repression in Contemporary Physics.'

39 The most sustained critique of gender-labelling of this notion grows out of the work of object-relations theorists such as Jane Flax and Nancy Chodorow. See, for example, Nancy Chodorow, *The Reproduction of Mothering* (Berkeley, Ca: University of California Press, 1978). For an application of this work see Nel Noddings, *Caring: A Feminine Approach to Ethics and Moral Education* (Berkeley, Ca: University of California Press, 1984). This research, which emphasizes an essential sense of personal connectedness, runs through much of feminist moral theorizing. It calls into question the adequacy of Isaiah Berlin's theory of two concepts

of liberty and the alleged illegitimacy of other-directedness in moral agency (the horrible spectacle of the heteronomous moral agent). Subtler distinctions are called for here. See Isaiah Berlin, 'Two Concepts of Liberty,' in *Four Essays on Liberty* (Oxford: Oxford University Press, 1969).

Gilligan and the Politics of a Distinctive Women's Morality

BARBARA HOUSTON

In this paper I undertake to examine certain political issues associated with any attempt to establish the existence of a distinctive women's morality. What I am interested in is the *possibility* of a distinctive women's morality. Carol Gilligan's work is rich enough to at least suggest that possibility.[1] However, I want to make clear at the outset that I do not rest my case on whether Gilligan has correctly identified gender differences in morality. For my purpose it does not matter whether Gilligan is correct or not. I want to use her work and the criticism of it to *illustrate* what I take to be *problematic* criticisms of her enterprise – criticisms that, if heeded, would prematurely foreclose on the discovery of a distinctive women's morality.

From the context of our current sexual politics I characterize the criticisms I discuss as political, not in respect of their motive, but from the point of view of their impact. Of course I do not intend the mere political labelling to justify the objections I raise. Nevertheless, my arguments against these criticisms do not stand apart from political considerations. In many cases my arguments draw out the political implications of the criticisms and are intended to remind the reader that there can be no convincing distinction drawn between the political implications of the considered criticisms and their merit.

Several of the criticisms of Gilligan's work that I discuss are coincidental with the concerns which some feminists have raised about cultural feminism.[2] In my discussion I shall indicate which criticisms fit under the rubric of a complaint about cultural feminism. Thus, my discussion of Gilligan will attempt to be responsive to two different political perspectives: the sexual politics of contemporary North American society and the internal politics of recent feminist theory.

One further note: Gilligan claims to describe 'a different voice,' a moral voice that she says is 'characterized not by gender but theme.'[3] Nevertheless, she acknowledges that 'it is primarily through women's voices that I trace its development.'[4] Thus, for our purposes, to register the political nature or impact of certain criticisms, I will *assume* that the 'different voice' belongs to women. Only with this assumption will we be able to see what impact the criticisms would have on the possibility of establishing a distinctive women's morality.

The Politics of Dismissal

Gilligan's work was initially conceived as a criticism and a corrective to Lawrence Kohlberg's theory of moral development, so I propose to begin with an examination of Kohlberg's response to Gilligan's work. Criticisms of Gilligan's work are more or less overtly political. Kohlberg's responses to her research are among those which are not *obviously* political but I think they can be appropriately filed under the heading 'The Politics of Dismissal.'

Kohlberg: Is Women's Moral Thinking Non-rigorous and Too Personal?

Kohlberg allows that Gilligan's research provides us with some reason for thinking that although both women and men use both a justice orientation and a care orientation in solving moral problems, women prefer to use, and will more frequently use, a care orientation. That is, a care orientation can be said to take prominence in their moral thinking.[5] However, in response to these acknowledged findings, he tells us that he still thinks it inappropriate to alter his moral-reasoning tests to capture this phenomenon for two reasons.

The first reason he offers is that the care and response orientation does not yield the same 'hard stage' characteristics as does justice reasoning. Thus, even though he admits that, for some subjects, a care orientation may be a spontaneous and preferred orientation, he leaves his test such that it 'pulls for the justice orientation.'[6]

The interesting point about this response is that it leaves Kohlberg open to the charge that he thereby relinquishes the basis of his claim to be studying the *moral* development of his subjects. In the face of the discovery that some of his subjects do not always choose to perceive moral problems from the point of view of justice, he inconsistently abandons two of the three formal criteria he uses to characterize moral judgments categoreally. Kohlberg initially defined moral judgments formally in terms of (a) universalizability, (b) prescriptivity, and (c) overridingness.[7] On his understanding of these criteria, a spontaneous and preferred orientation (or structuring of thought) would surely qualify as moral in the categoreal sense on the grounds of prescriptivity and overridingness. However, it is clear that Kohlberg abandons these two criteria when he refuses caring full entry into the moral arena on the questionable and unsubstantiated grounds that caring is not universalizable.

Notice that now Kohlberg is reduced to using only universalizability as a criterion for moral thought. This means that he is measuring only the cognitive skills, not moral ones, of those subjects who prefer to use a care orientation. Universalizability by itself is not a feature peculiar to moral reasoning.

Suppose a subject interprets a problem as a moral problem because it involves someone getting hurt, sees herself as responsible for preventing harm in the situation, and resolves to solve the problem by determining how to care for those persons involved. One cannot measure the moral reasoning of this subject by considering her thinking to be irrelevant, insisting that she perceive the problem from the point of view of justice, and persevere in testing her ability to discriminate rights and universalize some maxim of action if the subject herself does not want to perceive the problem and solve it in this way. One might appear to be measuring moral reasoning inasmuch as it is justice reasoning competence one 'pulls' for, but it is, in an important sense, not *this subject's moral* reasoning, for she regards herself as reasoning morally about it when she reasons in some other way.

The second reason Kohlberg offers for rejecting the suggestion that his moral development tests should be restructured to incorporate care orientation is this: he claims that care orientation is most properly categorized as part of what we in North America call personal morality; that is, it typically has to do with 'the spheres of kinship, love, friendship, and sex,' and with the 'affectively tinged' notions of loyalty and love.[9]

However, Kohlberg too has difficulty defending a clear distinction between personal and proper morality, just as do those who invoke the distinctions between the personal and the political, the private and the public. He says that personal morality has to do with special relationships, including relations to family, to friends, and to groups of which the self is a member.[10] If I were to conceive of myself as a member of the human community as, for example, in the way in which Margaret

Laurence articulates in her 'Open Letter to the Mother of Joe Bass,' so that I acknowledge that at some point I too am responsible for the world we live in, one could hardly find my loyalties and love too narrow and only a 'personal' concern.[11]

In Kohlberg's labelling of the care orientation as 'personal,' there is a trivialization of important moral matters. It is not as though such concerns were, as the term 'personal' suggests, non-serious or not of overriding concern or not concerns of everyone. Oddly then, Kohlberg dismisses some moral considerations that may be of more concern to women than to men on the ground that they are not impersonal enough to be representative of human moral development. As Boyd points out, 'If these two different moral concerns [care and justice] are differentially related to gender ... this neglect or misinterpretation is not surprising, but sadly fits the universal pattern of the ideals seen as feminine being assigned secondary status within cultures.'[12]

There is yet another way in which women's moral concerns become trivialized in Kohlberg's consideration of Gilligan's work. Kohlberg has dismissed the care orientation as a central part of moral development on the grounds that it may simply be more accurate to see this orientation as a part of women's ego development, part of women's personal development.[13] It is not entirely clear what Kohlberg means by ego development, but whatever he means by it he has overlooked the obvious question, 'Does ego development involve a moral struggle for women?' Any moral theory that places respect for persons close to its centre, as does Kohlberg's, will take a special interest in the development of persons, for on such a theory, becoming a person and learning to see others as persons are moral tasks of paramount importance.

Within a sexist culture, within a society that oppresses women and exploits them, it just may be that 'ego development' is related to seeing oneself as a person: it may also be true that this involves a moral struggle for women, a struggle requiring immense courage. If Kohlberg lived in Canada he would know this. Feminists in Canada do not consider the development of women into personhood as a non-moral, merely personal matter. In fact, we have an annual celebration we call Persons Day. This is a celebration of the day in 1929 on which women, as a group, won a hard-fought political and moral battle to be officially recognized as persons. The battle had to be taken to the British parliament when our own government declared we were not to be counted as persons who were recognized as 'persons' eligible to hold public office.[14] At least in Canada then we have no doubt that the development into and the struggle for personhood involves a moral struggle and important moral development for women collectively and individually. Given the oppression of women in most cultures this struggle can be a heroic one.

But now let me pass to a more subtle criticism of Gilligan by another critic, one which I think can also be filed under the heading of 'The Politics of Dismissal.'

Broughton: Are Women Self-Deceptive in Their Moral Thinking?

John Broughton has raised criticisms of Gilligan's work, which, if accurate, would substantiate a claim that Gilligan's account of moral development subscribes to the view Joan Ringelheim has characterized as cultural feminism. Broughton charges that Gilligan has in fact given us a theory that 'perpetuates the status quo, affirms the established division of labour, and forecloses on the possibility of a radical transformation.'[16] In particular, he argues that by discounting the possibility of self-deception in her subjects, Gilligan, in her account of women's moral experience, may simply be reinforcing sexist notions of femininity. He says:

[Gilligan,] by limiting women's morality to the conscious conflict-free
sphere of the developing ego ... denies the possibility of self-deception, she
ignores the Freudian revelation that we have an interest in not knowing
ourselves and so hides from sight women's collusion in their own oppression
(the latter being 'projected' onto the male morality of mastery). As long as
Gilligan asks her subjects only what they think of themselves, and accepts
what they say at face value, she cannot distinguish insightfulness from
defensiveness, knowledge from wishful thinking, fact from fantasy. In trying
to restore the subject to cognitive structuralism, she has collapsed subjectivity and objectivity into a flat, one-dimensional psychology. It is an idealist
psychology, in which self and self-concept are assumed to be identical.
Small wonder that Gilligan's women offer little resistance to traditional views
of what women are and what their place is. Much as her interview offers
them no way to penetrate their own self-mystifications, it offers them no way
to penetrate the mystifications of femininity. They are left without reason
or desire for emancipation.[17]

There are in this criticism some fundamental misconceptions and significant dangers that can be easily revealed if we simply take the criticism to heart and attempt to describe its suggestions positively as to how we might better conduct research into women's moral thinking. The suggestions appear to be that we should assume that: 1 / women's morality excludes tasks of ego development and is not primarily a function of their rational consciousness; 2 / women collude in their own oppression and this oppression is not attributable to the male morality of mastery; 3 / what women say about themselves and their moral lives is defensiveness, wishful thinking, or fantasy, as opposed to insight, knowledge, and fact; 4 / women have self-mystifications and our interviews with them should offer them ways to penetrate their own self-mystifications and the cultural mystification of femininity; 5 / women have the reason and desire for emancipation.

When they are put in their prescriptive form we can immediately see the misconceptions and dangers inherent in Broughton's criticisms. First, we can notice Broughton's mischaracterization of Gilligan's subjects as women with conflict-free egos pursuing their own development. If there is anything clear from the protocols of her subjects, it is that these women experienced a great deal of conscious, moral conflict in deciding whose interests they should attend to most assiduously. These women cannot be accurately characterized as having conflict-free egos. Nor, for reasons I have already mentioned, can we confidently assert that ego tasks such as 'disentangling self from conformity expectations' are not moral tasks for women.[18]

Notice, too, that Broughton criticizes Gilligan for adhering to one of the basic presuppositions of moral agency, viz. that morality is largely characterized by the intentions, reasons, and deliberations the agent *consciously uses*. It is this feature of moral agency that allows us to be held accountable for our actions. Why should we think it inappropriate to continue with these assumptions about moral agency and accountability when investigating women's moral thinking?

A further, yet more troubling, implication of Broughton's criticism is that it asks us, in our research on women, to set aside another basic presupposition of most human intercourse, viz. that we assume that an individual will tell us the truth *until we have reason to think otherwise*. It is telling that Broughton does not offer us any interview statements to illustrate the point he wants to make. While I sometimes find Gilligan's protocols disheartening because they exhibit little political consciousness of women's situation, I would say that the protocols are more self-revealing than self-deceptive. It is one thing to recognize and claim that women are ignorant of their social-political situation and quite another to claim that they are practising self-deception.

In this context it is ironic that Broughton appeals to the importance of Freud's 'revelation' that we have an interest in not knowing ourselves. It is more likely the case, as Jeffrey Masson argues, that Freud had an interest in not knowing women or their experiences.[19] Freud's so-called revelation has caused untold damage to women by assuming that their accounts of sexual abuse and rape were forms of self-deception, wishful thinking, and fantasy.[20]

In all of this, unhappily, we have more than enough evidence to show that the far greater danger lies in not taking what women say seriously. And the greater moral negligence lies in a refusal to see women themselves as the best judges of how they construe their moral experience, of what it means to them. It may be that the moral thinking of most women *is* without political consciousness. But the point is, we need to have accurate information about what it is *as it is*. It is precisely this that we have had so little information about because women have been left out, or what they have tried to say about themselves has been discounted or denied for some 'reason' or another. There is a danger here of rejecting any possibility of the knowledge of what women's morality is because it is not a full-blown feminist ethic of the sort we would like.

The point at issue here is important. Let us consider it once again, from the point of view of a researcher. In entertaining Broughton's suggestion that women are self-deceptive we notice that (a) there is a proven danger in mistakenly adopting the hypothesis that women are self-deceptive; (b) the charge of self-deception entails a moral judgment, and arguably a moral criticism; and (c) judgments of self-deception are extremely difficult to prove and usually require first-person confirmations. Thus, it is clear that before suggesting and certainly before adopting a self-deception hypothesis, one would reasonably expect a researcher to consider other hypotheses or explanations for the phenomena.

In this case there are other, more obvious, simpler hypotheses at hand. The women in Gilligan's studies (and any future studies) may be ignorant of women's political situation, or even more simply, they may have adopted moral values and ways of thinking coincidental with their socialization. Neither of these hypotheses entails deceit.

But now we come to the crux of the objection against Broughton's criticism. In wanting to suggest that women are self-deceptive, Broughton is clearly assuming that the moral thinking expressed by Gilligan's subjects is, in some way, bad. This is the implicit judgment made, for which there is no justification offered, in suggesting that their thinking is a result of self-deception. Thinking the women self-deceptive, defensive, or engaged in wishful thinking implies that there is something wrong with their thinking, that there are other values they might espouse that are better. But this is precisely what is under debate. Thus, Broughton's urging that we dismiss Gilligan's findings, that we entertain the hypothesis that women are self-deceptive in their moral thinking, begs the question. We do not easily, or readily invoke an hypothesis of self-deception in dealing with male subjects; why should we hasten to do so with women?

The Politics of Subsumption or Separatism

I turn now to a criticism which is somewhat more complex than those we have considered, a criticism that charges that there are some devastating political consequences to Gilligan's account of women's moral development.

Walker: Does Gilligan's Account Commit Us to Separatism?

James Walker, in a recent issue of *Social Research*, claims that Gilligan's theory, given her use of Chodorow's account of gender-identity formation, commits her to the view that women are the obligated bearers of certain intrinsic values even if this obligation results in or augments their oppression. He further claims that Gilligan's theory entails a morally objectionable separatist politics.[21] I want to consider Walker's criticisms in some detail since I think his objections to Gilligan's work illustrate several mistakes that are often made in discussing the implications of the differences between women and men, and because the spectre of separatism is one that keeps many from giving due consideration to accounts of women's experience, moral and otherwise.

Walker argues that Gilligan's explanation for the different moral voice we hear in women's accounts of their moral reasoning, inasmuch as it relies on Chodorow's account of gender-identity formation, entails a view he calls 'female essentialism.' He also contends that Gilligan's account entails what he calls a 'moral essentialism.' The consequence of these two elements is a commitment to what Walker calls 'cryptoseparatist politics.'

The worries that Joan Ringelheim and others have raised about cultural feminism are precisely concerns about the assumptions that Walker has called 'female essentialism' and 'moral essentialism' and the consequences to which they appear to lead. Thus, my remarks about

Walker's criticisms of Gilligan can be taken as an answer to the charge that Gilligan is a cultural feminist.

In its simplest, most straightforward form, Walker's argument comes to this:

P1. Gilligan, to the extent that she relies on Nancy Chodorow's account of general identity formation, is committed to a 'female essentialism' in her account of the production of the 'different voice' which, by implication, means that the different voice is one that is inevitably female.[22]

P2. Gilligan, in addition, holds a form of moral essentialism, i.e., she separates the qualities of care and connection from their context of inequality and oppression and demands that they be considered in their own right, according to their intrinsic merit.[23]

P3. Gilligan's 'female essentialism' combined with her 'moral essentialism' gives us the unhappy consequence that 'women become the obligated bearers of moral value, regardless of whether they are treated equally or oppressed as a result, or more likely as the cause.'[24]

P4. A further consequence of Gilligan's claim that certain desirable human qualities, such as intimacy, integration, solidarity, and selfishness, are primary in women and causally contingent on female psychosocial and moral development is that they require 'a recognition, protection and cultural valuation of female development' and this further entails that 'women who *ex hypothesi* understand these best, should organize to ensure that their voice is heard, understood and heeded, and that conditions for its development and exercise are secured.'[25]

P5. But then, 'since intimacy, integration, and solidarity are contingent upon as yet irreducible sex differences, the maintenance of such relational patterns presupposes an infrastructure of independence (of women as a group, not as individuals), of separate female development.'[26]

Conclusion: Thus, Gilligan's theory entails a 'cryptoseparatist' politics.

If Gilligan's theory does indeed lead to the unpalatable consequences Walker claims it does, we have reason to reject it. I think Walker's account of these matters is highly misleading, full of equivocation, and rests upon several mistaken assumptions. None the less, it addresses equivocations, mistakes, and questions that are too common in our discussions of the implications of sex differences so that it is worth our while to attend to how he goes wrong.

Walker: Is Gilligan a Female Essentialist?

Given its central role in Walker's argument, it is of primary importance to assess the claim that Gilligan is a female essentialist by virtue of her reliance on Chodorow's work. Walker's central argument for the premise that Gilligan is committed to a female essentialism in her account of the production of the 'different voice' occurs in the following passage:

The irreducible ... anatomical sex differences we noted in Chodorowian account of the Oedipus complex lay an essentially female bias for the production of feminine gender, for the reproduction of mothering, and for the female moral psychology and morality. (Likewise, *mutatis mutandis* for males.) Although this account is not 'biologically determinist' in the sense that gender, mothering and morality are the products of biological factors and these alone, it is an account in which such biological factors are ascribed an essential role. Whatever the sociocultural form taken by the development of gender, mothering and morality, there is a trans-historical, biological, essentially female ingredient in female development – at least in sociocultural patterns in which the Chodorow-Gilligan theory is applicable. This female essentialism has consequences of which neither Chodorow nor Gilligan appear to be aware.

Is Gilligan a female essentialist by virtue of her reliance on Chodorow? No. Walker's charge here rests upon a simple equivocation on the term 'essential.' In one sense it means required or necessary. In another sense it means something like inevitable. Walker's argument trades on a slide from saying that femaleness in the sense of anatomical differences plays a *required* role in Chodorow's account of possible sex differences in relational capacities to claiming that femaleness plays an *inevitable* role in the generation of certain relational capacities or moralities.

It certainly is the case that in Chodorow's account there is a *required* reference to anatomical differences because it is *about* females and males and that just is how we delineate these two groups. However, in her reference to anatomical differences Chodorow is not an essentialist in any worrisome sense. Without due reason, Walker is dismissing the crucial point in Chodorow's theory. Chodorow makes it clear in her account that the *trauma* involved in male separation and individuation from the mother occurs because of the public social devaluation of

women and the social devaluation of women's characteristics, especially for men.[28] Without this devaluation, we would have more boys
identified with their mothers for longer periods in a non-traumatic
fashion who could then learn the relational capacities we think have a
moral importance. This means that anatomical differences *in themselves*
are not related to anything we take to be central to human moral
development. If they are related it is because these differences are
mediated through a cultural meaning that can, of course, be altered.
The fact that we now assign these anatomical differences a meaning
which is inimical to parallel development in women and men is not
evidence of essentialism but of contingent development that is, of
course, female and male development. I think then, all we can say
about the inevitablility of femaleness in Chodorow's account stops with
our saying that it is inevitably *about* females and males.

Walker: Is Women's Distinctive Morality a Morality That Men Can't Have?

Without his saying it directly, I think Walker has another notion in
mind when he addresses the issue of female essentialism. He wants to
claim that in Chodorow's theory femaleness plays an essential role in
this sense: women are claimed to develop relational capacities that men
cannot have. This is one of the possible meanings of 'a distinctive
women's morality.' But Chodorow's theory does not support this
interpretation either.

In one obvious sense it would be odd to say that a morality was
distinctive in the sense that only certain persons could have it. Our
sense is that inasmuch as something is *a morality*, inasmuch as it is
attitudes, beliefs, concepts, motivations, and actions we are dealing
with, these would have to be available to anyone, including men. A
morality is just that sort of thing – appraisal, assessment, modes of
thinking and feeling that are available, possible for anyone to have or
acquire.

What is interesting in the debate about Gilligan's account of a
distinctive women's morality is that this issue is never discussed in terms
of the limits there are on the notion of a morality, i.e., that whatever
else a morality is, it has to be something that is accessible to everyone.
This approach strikes me as the most interesting, and obvious, one to
take in this discussion. Kurt Baier accurately points out the one sense in
which morality is characterized by a universality: 'Morality is not the
preserve of an oppressed or privileged class or individual ... An esoteric
code, a set of precepts known only to the initiated and perhaps

jealously concealed from outsiders, can at best be a religion, not a morality ... "Thou shalt not kill, but it is a strict secret" is absurd. "Esoteric morality" is a contradiction in terms.'[29]

Drawing out the implications of this feature of universality, Baier rightly claims that morality must be teachable. Whatever is to be offered as a morality must satisfy what he calls 'the condition of universal teachability.'[30] Thus, one could legitimately object to a distinctive women's morality on the grounds that it was not teachable to men. But this is not the case with the ethic of care as it is described in Gilligan's work, nor does her use of Chodorow commit her to any such undesirable conclusion.

However, let us suppose that it is true that women do have a distinctive morality in the sense that they invoke attitudes, thinking, concepts, values that men do not. Let us further suppose that Chodorow is correct in recognizing and identifying the conditions that give rise to a different moral psychology in women and men. Let us take it for granted that in the formation of a sense of self as a gendered person there are certain relational capacities built into our sense of self as women which we call upon in our parenting practices and our moral experience. There is nothing in Chodorow's account that claims that this is the *only* way in which women can acquire these relational capacities. And certainly Chodorow is clear enough in her account that she does not think that if we acquire them in this way, then this is *the best, most desirable way* to acquire them. In fact, Chodorow claims that the development of these relational capacities is available to both women and men, if we alter the social organization of our primary parenting. We can arrange it so that both women and men can acquire a gender identity within an affectional relation that is not devalued in the culture, nor singularly intense.[31]

Walker's charge that the Chodorow-Gilligan theory entails undesirable political consequences rests upon two mistaken assumptions. First, Walker thinks that because these desirable moral capacities (traits) are now produced in a particular way in women, this is the *only* way in which they *can* be produced in women. Second, he assumes also that since men do not acquire these moral capacities (traits) *in the way that women do now*, they cannot acquire them *at all*.

To be fair, Walker accuses Gilligan and Chodorow of a de facto separatism because they do not explain in detail just how one might develop these relational capacities in men.[32] But this seemingly more sophisticated criticism will not wash either: it is an appeal to ignorance. Walker admits that the theory does not commit one to the

impossibility of men developing capacities[33] but he claims, nevertheless, that since neither Gilligan nor Chodorow explains, in detail,
precisely how to develop these capacities in men, the theory then
commits one to separatism. Absence of details in a theory on how to
solve a particular problem (the development of certain moral traits or
capacities in men), which is not the focus of the theory, cannot justify
the claim that the theory entails the adoption of a particular controversial solution to the problem, nor can it justify a claim that the theorist is
committed to that particular controversial solution.

In point of fact, Chodorow's theory entails neither of the assumptions Walker makes. What we are committed to, if we want to argue that
Gilligan's ethic of care is a *morality*, is that it is an ethic that is teachable.
Nothing in Gilligan's or Chodorow's account, so far as I can see,
indicates that an ethic of care is not teachable. And if, *per impossibile*, it
were true on Chodorow's account that women learned it or acquired it
in ways that men could not, it would still be open to us to save the ethic
of care, *as a morality*, by having women teach it to men.

Walker: Is Gilligan a Moral Essentialist?

In another crucial premise of his argument Walker has charged that
Gilligan is a moral essentialist. But as I read her, Gilligan does *not*
subscribe to care and responsibility in any sort of essentialist way. She
makes some significant distinctions among kinds of caring and suggests
that one may 'advance' within this orientation.[34] She also, explicitly and
frequently, warns that inequality is the danger of an emphasis on only
the values of care and responsiveness to others.[35] It is true that she does
not *always* take account of the political context in which these
characteristics are formed, but from the fact that she often says nothing
about the context we can draw no conclusions about what she would
say. Nor can we conclude what her theory entails about this question
without, again, appealing to ignorance.[36]

But there is a more obvious, and more serious, objection to be made
to Walker's argument; it is invalid. From the two premises, even if we
grant them, that Gilligan is a female essentialist, and Gilligan is a moral
essentialist, we cannot get the conclusion Walker offers as premise
three, that on Gilligan's theory women must be the obligated bearers of
intrinsic moral values even if it means the continuance of their
oppression. To get this conclusion one would have to assert that
Gilligan thought the values of care, connection, and responsiveness
were the *only* intrinsic values. In short, we would have to attribute to

her a moral monism. But this she clearly rejects. She in fact argues that moral maturity requires both a justice and a care orientation and, as I have already noted, she recognizes justice as an important corrective to what she calls the 'danger of inequality.'[37]

Walker: Does Gilligan's Theory Suppose That Women Have a Problem Only They Can Solve?

Finally, we come to the spectre of separatism that haunts most discussions of sex differences. But now Walker forces us to address it directly for he boldly and unequivocally concludes that Gilligan's theory entails a radical separatist politics. We have already demonstrated that Walker's argument rests upon false premises and dubious inferences but it is worth persisting with an examination of his separatist charge if only to clarify the radically different political implications that are seen to follow from different descriptions of the same problem.

In charging that Gilligan's theory entails a radical separatist politics Walker means that she holds a theory that insists that it is not possible to identify (a) those who have a problem, (b) the causes of the problem, or (c) the solution to the problem, without appealing to a necessary component of femaleness. Nor is it possible for her to stipulate conditions under which it would be possible. In contrast, Walker describes and supports what he calls integrationism, a view that 'denies and avoids insistence on sex-specificity.'[38]

Given his meaning of radical separatism, Walker's charge comes to this: since, for Gilligan, femaleness is a part of the cause of women's problems; since femaleness is a differentium of the group of problem possessors; and since femaleness is the basis for an epistemic privilege to decide who can participate in the business of solving women's problems; therefore, Gilligan's theory entails a separatist politics.

But we have already seen that Gilligan's theory in using Chodorow's account of gender-identity formation is not essentialist because it declares that female anatomical differences are mediated by a social meaning that devalues the characteristics for some persons of a particular anatomy. That is, femaleness is not a part of the cause of the problem except insofar as we contingently make it part of that cause.

Furthermore, femaleness is not the differentia of the group of problem possessors. Whether one thinks this or not will depend upon what one takes the problem to be. Walker, following Gilligan, claims that the problem is that women are seen as deviant or defective in men's

moral developmental psychology and suffer as a result. But he takes
her too literally here. There are other descriptions of the problem
Gilligan acknowledges, e.g., that we do not have adequate knowledge
of women's moral development, and the 'we' here includes men. In
short, the 'problem possessors' are men as well as women.

Is femaleness the basis for the epistemic privilege to decide who can
participate in the business of solving 'women's problems'? Well, I do
think it worth bearing in mind John Stuart Mill's advice that women
themselves will have to tell us what their nature is. Women certainly are
in a privileged position in terms of telling us what they think and feel,
and how they themselves construe their own moral experience – how it
is from their point of view. But even if women do have a 'privileged'
position in this sense, it does not follow that women are, or must be, the
only persons able to contribute to the solution of *our* gender-related
difficulties once these problems have been articulated.

In answer to the concerns raised by Gilligan, Walker presents us with
only two alternatives: separatism or assimilation (and immaturity). He
concludes: 'If the argument for interpreting Gilligan as a female
essentialist and a moral essentialist stands, then the complementarism
remains misleading surface rhetoric – an ideology for cryptoseparatist
theory and practice. If the argument for such an interpretation does
not stand, then the different voice may turn out to be not so different
after all, though just as diffident. It will sound, as Kolhberg has
suggested, like an immature cry from a group of people arrested at an
early stage of development.[39]

The Politics of Silence

These alternatives of subsumption, immaturity, and separatism are
depressing enough, but there is yet another alternative offered us by
the critics of Gilligan: silence.

Nails: Should We Be Silent about Women's Differences?

Debra Nails, mindful of the scientific racism that flourished in the
atmosphere of acclaim for IQ testing, notes that 'social-scientific sexism
grows strong on claims that females by nature or by nurture, have an
intellectual or moral make-up or development different from that of
males.'[40] She claims that Gilligan's description of women's moral
development, especially as it is elaborated in *In a Different Voice*, 'can
and will be used as evidence of the inferiority of women unless (i) males

are shown to undergo the same development, or (ii) the female morality is proven superior, or (iii) the entire enterprise is undermined as fallacious and unreliable.'[41]

Noting that other critics have addressed the first and second points, Nails takes up the task of trying to show that 'the entire enterprise is ... fallacious and unreliable.' She critically examines Gilligan's method (presentation of data and interview procedures) and her presuppositions (reification of moral maturity, scaling from negative to positive, and measurement of moral rather than cognitive skills), and she concludes with some remarks about the danger of generalizing for groups and applying one's generalizations to the individuals within a group.

It is somewhat unclear from Nails's comments whether she intends to dismiss as fallacious and unreliable *Gilligan's* attempt to describe sex differences in morality or whether she intends to dismiss *any* such enterprise. I think we can fairly understand her to be dismissing *any* such attempt from the following passage:

A danger of the *Gilligan-type* description of female moral develpment is
that it has the power to exaggerate existing differences, or even create expectations that reward particular behaviours. It does not much matter whether
one who believes in the accuracy of Gilligan's descriptions believes as well
that the differences occur through hereditary or environmental causes.
The description itself can erect a set of boundaries for female moral development, a set of limits on behaviour; a girl child who sees a moral dilemma as
sort of like a math problem with humans (a response of one of Gilligan's male
sixth graders) is viewed as somewhat less feminine than one who emphasizes
the relationships among the various characters of a hypothetical dilemma.
And it does not matter whether the researcher herself or himself has the
good intentions of giving voice to a disadvantaged group.[42]

She adds, 'Let the red flags go up in warning; this type of research is social science at sea without an anchor, and no one is out of danger.'[43]

Nails has of course correctly identified the problems we all fear with research on sex differences, reinforcement of stereotypes, and sex roles. But her warning focuses attention on only one of the points of view of the individual. We need other possible points of view of the individual. We need to consider what happens if we fail to address issues of sex difference and the gender relatedness of certain morally relevant characteristics or kinds of moral thinking. The landscape from this point of view is also bleak. If we simply ignore gender differences, we run the danger of continuing to induce in girls and women a state that Kathryn Morgan eloquently describes as 'moral madness.'[44]

In effect, Nails, and Walker too, with his integrationist view which eschews any reference to sex-specificity, are issuing what Louise Marcil-Lacoste has called an 'imperative of silence' on a description of sex differences. Marcil-Lacoste clarifies the notion: '[I]mplicit in the sexually neutral notion of validity is the idea that a statement is valid by virtue of its silence on sexual variables. Silence is thus here an epistemological imperative and plays the role of what I. Lakatos calls a "negative heuristic," the paths which must be avoided in research.'[45] She too warns us of dangers: 'The most important point is that by the imperative of silence, the delineation of well designed procedures to see where the limits of abstract reasoning are situated in such matters is made impossible, let alone desirable.'[46]

If, as a result of Nails's warning, we were to adopt 'the imperative of silence' as a heuristic against bad consequences, the tacit assumption that in moral development there are no sex differences would entail the claim that in moral development women are repeating men. And whether 'women would repeat men *qua* human beings or *qua* males is systematically unverifiable.'[47] As Marcil-Lacoste notes: 'In other words, the gist of the imperative of silence is not so much the claim that in a sexually neutral notion of validity males and females are indistinguishable. Rather it is the claim that for all epistemologically valid purposes it must remain so.'[48]

The undesirable options of subsumption, immaturity, and separation urged on us by Walker are enlarged by Nails – silence appears to be yet another alternative. But let me remind you again of the problem Gilligan sees and tries to address. She claims that ordinary women face a problem created for them by the failure of our theories to 'represent their experience or by the distortion in its representation.' As a consequence, 'Women come to question whether what they have seen exists and whether what they know from their own experience is true. These questions are raised not as abstract philosophical speculations about the nature of reality and truth but as personal doubts that invade women's sense of themselves, compromising their ability to act on their own perceptions and thus their willingness to take responsibility for what they do.'[49]

There is something particularly perturbing about Nails's imperative of silence when it comes to an investigation of women's morality precisely because it is women's morality she is cautioning us to be silent about. One's morality is intimately tied to one's sense of self, one's sense of agency, and one's sense of oneself as a responsible agent. If we are to silence ourselves about this aspect of ourselves, we will fail to acquire self-knowledge of the most important political sort.

If we agree to this imperative of silence, we lose the opportunity to know whether statements made about morality are issued in our name. We lose the opportunity to test the hypothesis of universality (and universalizability). In short, we lose the opportunity to challenge our oppression in our own way and for our own reasons. And when one loses this, one has lost the opportunity to challenge one's own oppression *tout court*.

Conclusion

I do not know whether Gilligan has accurately characterized women's morality. Nor do I know whether this moral orientation she has described as an ethic of care and responsibility is one that is shared by many men. But I do know that some women have felt that it described their moral struggles and that it has given some women precisely what Gilligan intended it to, it has given them their own voice. If one does not have a voice, one cannot speak on one's own behalf. But has she given women the right voice? Is the voice saying what is politically correct? Is the voice asking questions, political questions, about whether or not this morality serves women's oppression? Not yet, certainly not as Gilligan has thus far described it. But voices, once heard, have a strange way of generating unpredictable utterances. The point is, one has to start somewhere. If women are to come to political consciousness, they have to come to it as a form of self-consciousness. Hearing and recognizing one's own voice is a beginning – a necessary beginning.

My remarks in defence of Gilligan are not so much a defence of Gilligan's theory and her expression of our voice, rather, they represent a commitment to her enterprise, the enterprise of trying to describe how women themselves understand their own morality. And, now my own politics become clear. In the face of these considered criticisms, I advocate the politics of persistence.

NOTES

For their helpful assistance and criticism, I am grateful to Kathleen Okruhlik, Maryann Ayim, Vicky Spelman, Joan Ringelheim, and especially Ann Diller.

1 Carol Gilligan, *In a Different Voice: Psychological Theory and Women's Development* (Cambridge, Mass: Harvard University Press, 1982)

2 For a historical analysis of the development of cultural feminism with attention paid to its conceptual structure and its impact on both theory and political action see Brooke, 'Retreat to Cultural Feminism,' in *Feminist Revolution, Redstockings of the Women's Liberation Movement* (New York: Random House, 1975), pp. 79–83; Ti-Grace Atkinson, 'Le Nationalisme Feminin,' in *Nouvelles Questions Feministes* 6, no. 7 (Printemps 1984): 35–55, issue titled *Les Femmes et l'Etat*. For an interesting discussion of the possibly pernicious influences of cultural feminism on feminist research into women's experience see Joan Ringelheim, 'Women and the Holocaust: A Reconsideration of Research,' paper presented to the American Philosophical Association Meetings, New York City, December 1984. In this paper Ringelheim presents an honest and rigorous examination of her own previous research on women survivors of the Holocaust and attempts to show through this examination of her own work what is problematic about cultural feminism.

3 Gilligan, *In a Different Voice*, p. 2

4 Ibid.

5 Lawrence Kohlberg's most recent and most fully considered response to Gilligan's work appears in L. Kohlberg, C. Levine, and A. Hewar, *Moral Stages: A Current Formulation and a Response to Critics* (New York: Karger, 1983), especially chap. 3.

6 Ibid., p. 130; see also p. 125.

7 Specifically, Kohlberg says, 'Like most philosophers from Kant to Hare ... we define morality in terms of the formal character of a moral judgment or a morality in terms of the formal character of a moral judgment or a moral point of view, rather than in terms of its content. Impersonality, ideality, universalizability and pre-emptiveness are among the formal characteristics of a moral judgment.' 'Stages of Moral Development,' in *Moral Education: Interdisciplinary Approaches*, ed. C.M. Beck, B.S. Crittenden, and E.V. Sullivan (Toronto: University of Toronto Press, 1971), p. 55. Kohlberg also contends that 'prescriptivity and universality' are the formal criteria of moral judgment which parallel the psychological criteria of differentiation and integration allowing him to map the *justification* for a move to a higher stage of moral thinking onto the psychological *explanation* for this move. 'From Is to Ought: How to Commit the Naturalistic Fallacy and Get Away with It in the Study of Moral Development,' in *Cognitive Development and Epistemology*, ed. Theodore Mischel (New York: Academic Press, 1971), p. 216; see also p. 215. Kohlberg's most recent writing confirms the importance he places on

universalizability and prescriptivity as formal criteria of moral judgments. On some readings, prescriptivity entails overridingness. See *Moral
Stages*, pp. 19f.

8 Kohlberg, Levine, and Hewar, *Moral Stages*, pp. 20 and 22–3
9 Ibid., pp. 22 and 20
10 Ibid., p. 20
11 Margaret Laurence, 'Open Letter to the Mother of Joe Bass,' in *Heart of a
Stranger* (Toronto: McClelland and Stewart–Bantam Ltd., 1976), p.
225
12 Dwight Boyd, 'Careful Justice or Just Caring: A Response to Gilligan,'
*Philosophy of Education 1982: Proceedings of the Philosophy of Education
Society* (Normal, Ill.: Illinois State University, 1983), p. 68. For an extended discussion of this point, see *Women, Culture and Society*, ed. Michelle
Zimbalist Rosaldo and Louise Lamphere (Stanford: Stanford University
Press, 1974).
13 Kohlberg, et al., *Moral Stages*, pp. 22–7 and 141. See also the discussion of
'A Distinction between Soft and Hard Stages,' in *Moral Stages*, p. 298.
See also John Broughton's article, discussed below, for a discussion of this
same criticism.
14 'The Persons Case is the name commonly used to designate the contest
waged by Emily Murphy and her four associates from Alberta to prove
that women are eligible for appointment to the Canadian Senate. The
name is derived from the fact that eligibility hinged upon the legal
interpretation of the word "person" as found in Section 24 of the British
North America Act.' The case was decided in favour of women being
recognized as "persons" in the eyes of the law in October 1929 by the
Privy Council in Great Britain. Catherine Cleverdon, *The Woman Suf-
frage Movement in Canada* (Toronto: University of Toronto Press, 1950), p.
141.
15 Ringelheim, 'Women and the Holocaust.'
16 John Broughton, 'Women's Rationality and Men's Virtues,' *Social Research*
50, no. 3 (October 1983): 626
17 Ibid., p. 633
18 Gertrude Nunner-Winkler, 'Two Moralists? A Critical Discussion of an
Ethic of Care and Responsibility versus an Ethic of Rights and Justice,'
in *Morality, Moral Behavior and Moral Development*, ed. William Kartines
and Jacob Gerwitz (New York: John Wiley & Sons, 1984), p. 358.
19 Jeffrey Masson, *The Assault on Truth: Freud's Suppression of the Seduction
Theory* (New York: Farrar, Straus and Giroux, 1984)
20 For an account of the damage done to victims of incest and sexual abuse,
and a discussion of Freud's theorizing about the matter, see Florence

Rush, *The Best Kept Secret: Sexual Abuse of Children* (Englewood Cliffs, NJ: Prentice-Hall, Inc., 1980).

21 James Walker, 'In a Different Voice: Cryptoseparatist Analysis of Female Moral Development,' *Social Research* 50, no. 3 (October 1983), p. 667

22 Ibid., p. 688

23 Ibid., p. 689

24 Ibid., p. 690. On this same page Walker states the point even more bluntly: 'If my interpretation of Gilligan is so far correct, Gilligan is demanding the right for women's essentially female voicing of moral essentials to be heard, although it claims the right – no: asserts the responsibility – of women to preserve their commitment to, their very identity in, caring, nurturing networks of connection, oppression and exploitation notwith-standing. Women would have not only the right but the moral duty to demand to be oppressed if this were the only way they could preserve their essential femaleness and bestow their gift of caring relationships on the world.'

25 Ibid., p. 667

26 Ibid.

27 Ibid., p. 688

28 Nancy Chodorow, *The Reproduction of Mothering: Psychoanalysis and the Sociology of Gender* (Berkeley, Ca: University of California Press, 1978), pp. 182–4

29 Kurt Baier, *The Moral Point of View* (New York: Random House, 1965), p. 101

30 Ibid., p. 101. It should be noted that this is a somewhat more stringent requirement than the claim that morality must be learnable. This latter requirement would also satisfy the general presupposition that 'ought' implies 'can,' but I think Baier is correct to insist on the stringent criterion.

31 Chodorow, *The Reproduction of Mothering*, pp. 217–18.

32 Walker, *Social Research*, p. 694

33 Ibid., p. 693. Walker explicitly mentions the possibility that these good qualities might be cultivated in males through the influence of women but inexplicably excludes this as an obvious or desirable route open to Chodorow and Gilligan.

34 Gilligan, *In a Different Voice*, pp. 126–7 and 149

35 Ibid., pp. 149 and 174

36 It should be noted that Gilligan, in one sense, is addressing the political context. She is reminding us that recent influential theories of human development are *not* about humans, as they purport to be, but are about men, not women.

37 Ibid., p. 274
38 Walker, *Social Research*, p. 683
39 Ibid., p. 695
40 Debra Nails, 'Social-Scientific Sexism,' *Social Research* 50, no. 3 (October 1983), p. 643
41 Ibid., p. 644
42 Ibid., p. 663
43 Ibid., p. 664
44 Kathryn Morgan, 'Women and Moral Madness,' this volume
45 Louise Marcil-Lacoste, 'The Trivialization of the Notion of Equality,' in *Discovering Reality: Feminist Perspectives on Epistemology, Metaphysics, Methodology, and Philosophy of Science* (Boston: D. Reidel Publishing Co., 1983), p. 128
46 Ibid., p. 129
47 Ibid.
48 Ibid.
49 Gilligan, *In a Different Voice*, p. 49. Nicole Brossard noted that the essence of this problem is captured in the remark, 'Darling, you're imagining things.'

Self-Abnegation

BONNELLE LEWIS STRICKLING

My principal purpose in this paper is to discover whether self-abnegation, long supposed to be a virtue and now, especially in feminist circles, widely questioned, has value. In order to do this, we must first ask ourselves what is meant by self-abnegation. The following definitions appear under 'abnegation' in the *Oxford English Dictionary*: '2. Denial (of anything) to oneself; self-denial; renunciation of rights, claims, things esteemed). 3. Self-abnegation; renunciation of oneself, self sacrifice.'[1] Two kinds of self-abnegation emerge from these definitions taken together: first, there is the denial of one's rights, claims, and/or things esteemed, which may not necessarily involve a loss or renunciation of self; Second, there is the loss or denial of oneself altogether.

The first kind of self-abnegation, hereafter called moral self-abnegation, involves only the renunciation of rights, claims, and/or things esteemed, and I think we can add 'desires' to this without distortion. Although the OED does not specify any moral motive, nevertheless 'renunciation' usually suggests giving up something for moral reasons. Otherwise, we might describe giving up some proposed plan of action or set of desires as simply changing our minds or deciding not to do something; renunciation is quite a different matter. Again, the OED does not specify whether this renunciation is temporary or permanent; let us look at examples of both. We might temporarily renounce necessities for ourselves for the sake of our children or loved ones, and we might permanently renounce our intense desire to have the last word. Often, we even renounce such things as self-concern in the sense of attention to ourselves or our desires for the sake of acting morally, as in this passage from Iris Murdoch's *The Nice and the Good*:

'It's a rather important decision which affects this person's whole life, and I feel particularly rotten about having to make it as I'm feeling at the moment so – jumbled and immoral.'

'Jumbled and immoral.' Mary repeated this curious phrase as if she knew exactly what it meant. 'But you know how to make the decision. I mean you know the machinery of the decision?'

'Yes. I know how to make the decision.'

'Then shouldn't you just think about the decision and not about yourself? Let the machinery work and keep it clear of the jumble?'

'You are perfectly right,' he said.[2]

Here, one renounces one's own psychological difficulties, preoccupations, moods, or interests in order to allow one's principles to work unimpeded for the sake of the good of others.

The second sense of self-abnegation that suggests itself is more obscure in the sense that we do not know precisely what is lost; nevertheless it is frequently described by mystics as a loss of self. Bernadette Roberts describes precisely that in *The Experience of No-Self*:

I turned my gaze inward, and what I saw, stopped me in my tracks. Instead of the usual unlocalized center of myself, there was nothing there; it was empty; and at the moment of seeing this there was a flood of quiet joy and I knew, finally I knew what was missing – it was my 'self'.[3]

The experience that initiated this journey was the permanent silencing or closing down of the reflexive mechanism of the mind, with the result that it became impossible to remember myself. I could no longer reflect backward or inward, and though I strove with all possible energy to remain self-conscious, my mind kept falling back into the silence of no-self-consciousness. When this occurred, I blacked out because there was nothing there anymore – there was no thinker of thoughts, no doer of doing. Not only as an object had self disappeared, but as a self-conscious mechanism, self had become an impossibility.[4]

I propose calling the foregoing metaphysical/epistemological self-abnegation since the experience is usually described as if there were something that is genuinely lost or given up, or at least one experiences something as lost or given up. It is not voluntary to quite the same extent as moral self-abnegation is, in that it is far more difficult to give up a self than it is to give up a desire or claim. Nevertheless it is often the object of intense spiritual effort, which is voluntary. In fact, moral self-abnegation is often seen as a technique leading to, among other things, metaphysical/epistemological self-abnegation (hereafter called m/e self-abnegation).

In order to assess the value and point of self-abnegation, we must first ask ourselves whether self-abnegation serves any purpose in human life. It is, after all, possible that self-abnegation will turn out to be a practice better dispensed with. What in the human condition could be improved with self-abnegation?

Let us examine one prominent possibility. It can be argued that, if human beings are basically self-interested, the willingness to put aside one's own interests in favour of the interests of others is absolutely necessary if we are to enter into relationships of care and love with one another. One of the defining traits of at least one kind of love seems to be that the person who loves is willing to set aside her/his interests in favour of the loved one. Thus the willingness to engage in self-abnegation is connected to an interest in the welfare of others. Given a picture of basic self-interestedness, self-abnegation can be seen as a kind of achievement, a renunciation of one's own interests that cannot be easy. In fact, if we argue that, all things being equal, self-interest is persistently and consistently far stronger than interest in others, self-abnegation on any scale could be seen as a major moral undertaking for which one deserves major moral credit. However, we must be cautious in assigning this credit; not just any sort of self-abnegation will do.

Consider the sort of self-interested person with a strong ego, plenty of self-esteem, work to do, and interests to pursue. Such a person might be said to be engaging in self-abnegation if she/he were willing to enter into a relationship in which she/he put aside activities and interests that concerned only herself/himself and focused to a greater extent on shared activities. In doing so, one might become more willing to co-operate rather than wishing to dominate, to find things that both like doing rather than insisting on one's favourite activities at all times; one may consult the tastes of the other in housing, decoration, life-style in general, and consider the feelings of the other when tempted to take out frustrations on her/him, or to do things that frighten and upset her/him. All these changes involve a certain amount of self-denial, but most of us would be unwilling to call this true self-abnegation, simply because so much pleasure and so many benefits accrue as a result of doing these things. Most of us find having relationships preferable to not having them, and these are the minimal requirements for keeping a reasonably comfortable relationship alive without tension and resentment. Self-abnegation for which we give moral credit ought not to involve, one feels, so much reward in contrast to such small renunciations. It might even be argued that, when one considers the desires and interests of others in the ways mentioned above, one may be putting aside one's interests in one sense, but in another one is ultimately increasing one's gratifications by bringing relationships into one's life. Therefore let us move on to a practice that is a more plausible candidate for genuine self-denial, entering into sympathy with another as opposed to simply considering the other person's interests as equal in importance to one's own.

Entering into sympathy with another involves a deeper sort of self-denial, denying that one's own way of seeing the world is the only possible way. This is a view cherished in secret by the majority of us, and it is most difficult to transcend. It is particularly difficult to transcend in the case of emotional response; e.g., to admit that something that enrages one is seen by someone else as perfectly reasonable or even natural is so difficult as to be, often, the cause of ruptured relationships. This sort of disagreement and failure to understand usually occurs in the context of deeply ingrained psychological attitudes. Some people, for example, consider it quite ordinary to be possessive, to be affronted if one's partner wants to do things alone, and to be demanding about quantity of time spent together. To renounce this attitude, to try to see the question from one's partner's point of view, can be extremely painful and not very rewarding, since one may not change one's attitude in doing so, but only try to resist it through reason and/or forswear expressing it. This is certainly a case of self-sacrifice with small rewards; one's partner may regard this behaviour as just the decent thing to do with no particular credit deserved, and one may be able to understand one's partner's desires and attitudes without being able to change one's own, thus having to make continuous efforts. All this becomes especially acute when the desires under consideration are not one's partner's but one's children's. Parents tend to be firmly attached to certain pictures of how their children should be, based in part on their own family histories, psychological attitudes and/or class position. It may require a really exceptional amount of psychological self-sacrifice to forswear one's fear and anxiety about activities or life choices that seem to one's children infinitely desirable. In general, the more one cherishes a rigid and detailed picture of how others should behave and respond based on one's own desires and fantasies, the more difficult and admirable the kind of self-abnegation involved in supporting the decisions of others and attempting to develop a genuine understanding of their feelings and desires will be. Total self-abnegation would of course involve completely entering into the views of others or putting aside one's interests altogether for the sake of the other, but this would defeat the purpose for which, presumably, one engages in the kind of self-abnegation described above; what one wants is a relationship in which the interests and feelings of both are taken into consideration, and each enters into the world-view of the other. Complete self-abnegation, even if possible, would no more promote such a relationship than complete self-interestedness.

This brings us to the point of self-abnegation. It would, I think, be true to say that a certain amount of self-abnegation is necessary in order to have relationships. But we need to be more precise about what exactly is accomplished through self-abnegation. Perhaps the main thing that is accomplished through the kind of psychological self-abnegation described above is an increase of sympathetic understanding between and among persons. This is especially important if a reason for wanting to have a relationship is that one wishes to have an alliance, a sense that one's partner and/or one's friends are on one's side and share one's most cherished values. At the same time, too much self-abnegation will not increase but undercut these desirable relations. There is a difference between feeling that one has an ally and that one has an uncritical fan; an ally is a source of strength, but a fan is a responsibility, since continuous self-abnegation usually takes place only in the context of the belief that the person for the sake of whom one engages in self-abnegation is superior. Furthermore, the resentment created by the demand that someone be utterly self-abnegating and become a fan is so considerable that, very often, rather than having a fan or an ally, one has in the end an enemy, as the emotional outcomes of the traditional relations between men and women so often show.

Another reason for supposing self-abnegation to be a virtue is that it is generally taken to be necessary for entering into a life focused on service to others. It seems at first self-evident that service to others would require self-abnegation; if one's declared purpose is service to others, by implication one's goal is not service to oneself. Nevertheless, we need to know more about how self-renunciation helps us serve others. In *How Can I Help?* Ram Dass and Paul Gorman suggest the following:

While some self-images are more likely to facilitate the expression of our compassion than others, it is also true that *any* model of the self, positive or negative, will limit our capacity to help.[5]

When our models of who we are fall away, we are free simply to meet and be together. And when this sense of being encompasses all – one another, the park, the rain, everything – separateness dissolves and we are united in compassion.[6]

As we become less identified with any single aspect of the separate self against another, we're freer to know which among them all is most appropriate for a given situation. It's as if we can be anyone to anyone ...

The awareness that allows us to rest behind ego, moreover, also gives us a far greater ability to listen to others, to hear what's really needed.[7]

Throughout their book, Ram Dass and Gorman offer many examples of instances in which the personal desires, needs, and fantasies of those who were attempting to help impeded their understanding of what was needed, which in turn interfered with their ability to help. For Ram Dass and Gorman, this difficulty is considerably lessened by a loosening of one's attachment to the self. The self, which seems to consist of self-images, the organizing ego, and a strong sense of separateness from others, is not abandoned altogether but transcended. Clearly, it is m/e self-abnegation that is being recommended here. We do not renounce the self altogether, but it takes on relative insignificance, so that we renounce its importance. Thus we can see that self-abnegation plays a role not just in the cultivation of sympathetic understanding, but also in the sort of action that is often taken to be the highest expression of principle, service to others. We can also see that these two kinds of self-abnegation, though separate, are related: in the case of sympathetic understanding, we have the kind of attention to the desires and feelings of others that requires us to put aside our own conflicting desires and feelings, at least temporarily; in the case of service to others, we also put aside our own desires and feelings and, in addition, we put aside the source of at least some of those desires and feelings, our sense of being a particular self. All of this would seem to suggest that self-abnegation, all things being equal, is worthwhile indeed. Before we commit ourselves to this, however, let us turn to one of the sources of current interest in the question of self-abnegation.

In Carol Gilligan's *In a Different Voice*, she points out that the gender models offered to women result in their having quite a different picture of what has moral significance than men do. Whereas men tend to think in terms of justice as fairness and the respect for and preservation of rights of individuals, women tend to think in terms of responsibility to and helping of others, not causing pain, and willingness to give up their own desires in order to accomplish these things. In short, one is strongly tempted to see what women learn to do and to value as self-abnegation. Consider the following: 'If I could grow up to be like anyone in the world, it would be my mother, because I've just never met such a selfless person. She would do anything for anybody, up to a point that she has hurt herself a lot because she just gives so much to other people and asks nothing in return. So, ideally, that's what you'd like to be, a person who is selfless and giving.'[8] Gilligan found that many women, in addition to holding the view that one ought to help others, avoid causing them pain, and generally take responsibility for considering their feelings and even making them happy, also believed that they themselves did not have the right to these same attitudes and behaviour from others; they believed they did not have an equal right to consideration, that their own pain and/or unhappiness was relatively unimportant, and that they ought to be willing to deny themselves fulfilment of their own desires for the sake of others. In this sense, they saw selflessness as a virtue, and any claims of their own to equal rights as selfish. While this sort of self-denial may fit the OED definitions and appear to be the sort of attitude that could promote sympathetic understanding and/or service to others, there are good reasons to doubt that this is so. To see why, let us turn briefly to Steven Hendlin's paper 'Pernicious Oneness.' In it, Hendlin argues that a certain level of ego-development is necessary before one can successfully reach the self-transcendent spiritual states achievable through meditation, and that many people fail to distinguish between an undeveloped sense of self and transcending an already-developed self: 'The most pervasive trap at the ego level appears to be the disrespect, discounting, and denigration of the ego itself. The primary self-deception is that one has *already* transcended ego, with the assumption that one has *already* firmly established this individual ego and therefore no longer needs or wants to acknowledge ego as having anything to offer in one's quest. It is nothing less than an *attempt* at premature disidentification with all that makes up one's sense of identity, belongingness, security, self-esteem, and so on.'[9] This attempt often involves the denial of the importance of one's own emotional responses, and lack of respect for one's intellectual abilities. Hendlin's views seem to me important here because his description of a false spirituality, leading to the withdrawal, blankness, and even disintegration and despair that he calls 'pernicious oneness,' bears a strong resemblance to the kind of self-denial practised by some of Gilligan's subjects, with the same disastrous results if persisted in. Gilligan argues that, at certain crisis points, one must see oneself as having rights and one's desires as being important, or fall into despair. And if this is so, what we have here is at least not the kind of self-abnegation that can bring about the increased sympathy and joyful service to others that would appear to give self-abnegation its value. If one gives up one's desires and claims to the extent that one fails to develop one's own sense of self, the attempt at self-abnegation will lead at worst to despair, at best to enormous resentment and anger. Therefore, what Gilligan's subject describes, and what women are taught to value insofar as this subject is representative, seems to me to be false self-abnegation; to engage in genuine self-abnegation, one must first have a self to abnegate.

But what exactly is it that women are taught? The guiding model offered is not, I suspect, clearly and sharply either moral self-abnegation or m/e self-abnegation; often the two are confused, and this confusion leads to a certain amount of corresponding confusion about what is expected as well as a vulnerability to manipulation. Furthermore, what is expected of women as participants in romantic love and sexual desire is inconsistent with either kind of self-abnegation. Let us consider these points in order.

In order to see how moral self-abnegation and m/e self-abnegation are confused in the traditional roles set for women, we must look first at what ideals and virtues are offered to women, then at the conditions under which one could achieve them.

In Gilligan's work, one attitude is expressed by women many times: it is wrong to hurt people, it is important not to hurt anyone but ultimately one does not count oneself as part of 'anyone' since it is oneself that is hurt in order to bring about comfort and happiness for others. This willingness to renounce consideration of one's self as a person who deserves equal consideration, this concern with the happiness of others insofar as it can be produced by this renunciation, is representative of the ideals traditionally offered to women. All of this is old news by now, but worth reminding ourselves of for the sake of this argument: traditionally, women have been asked to be helpful, loving without expectation of return, emotionally dependable, supportive, and generally nurturing to both children and husband both physically and in the sense of nurturing their respective senses of self, all without complaining. I am not suggesting that women have actually managed to do all these things, but certainly women have been expected to do these things, as well as many others. And, taken together, these expectations comprise the expectation of self-renunciation on an extremely large scale. For, in a household that involves husband and children, a woman's life can be completely taken up with being helpful, nurturing, supportive, and so on. What would a person who could do all this without complaining, and presumably without the hidden complaining involved in resentment and frustration, be like? She would have to be a person who does not accumulate resentment and frustration because her own desires and needs are neglected; in particular, she would have to be the kind of person who would not feel resentful about the fact that, although some individual selves are nurtured (husband, children), she is not. In short, she would have to be a person who is self-abnegating in the m/e sense. Only if one has no self, or at least no attachment to a self, can one give oneself to a life of service to others who are themselves permitted to be self-concerned. There would be no resentment only if one had no self to feel resentful on behalf of, were not an individual in the usual sense of a particular idiosyncratic individual with an ego to nourish and a sense of self-esteem to be cultivated.

Of course, this is not the picture overtly offered to women. Usually, insofar as self-abnegating behaviour is clearly demanded in relationships, it is seen as moral self-abnegation, which may involve setting aside some desires or goals, but does not necessitate the loss of or renunciation of the self in a general sense. For one thing, traditionally marriage is supposed to be gratifying to women as well as men, satisfying our natural desires for children and being cared for. Candidacy for sainthood is not seen as a qualification for marriage, since women are supposed to feel special pride and pleasure in our homes, the love of our husbands, and the achievements of our children. Nevertheless, I suspect that the image of m/e self-abnegation is never far away; consider Freud's description of the satisfactions available to the mothers of sons. Only a person without a self or without an attachment to whatever self there might be could experience the kind of vicarious pleasure in the life of another that Freud describes without experiencing intense resentment and frustration:

The difference in a mother's reaction to the birth of a son or a daughter shows that the old factor of lack of a penis has even now not lost its strength. A mother is only brought unlimited satisfaction by her relation to a son; this is altogether the most perfect, the most free from ambivalence of all human relationships. A mother can transfer to her son the ambition which she has been obliged to suppress in herself, and she can expect from him the satisfaction of all that has been left over in her of her masculinity complex. Even a marriage is not made secure until the wife has succeeded in making her husband her child as well and in acting as a mother to him.[10]

Only an utterly self-abnegating person could accept this curious substitute for a penis without feeling some resentment and frustration over the fact that, son or no, she still does not have the highly valued (according to Freud) penis and all the rights and privileges its ownership has traditionally bestowed. This example illustrates a general point: although women are presented with the requirement of some self-abnegation, there is in fact a hidden expectation that, in the normal course of motherhood at least, women will be expected to perform large numbers of self-abnegating, supererogatory acts. I suggest that one reason this expectation is not entirely overt is obvious: if it were, many women would never marry and have families. Nevertheless the presence of this hidden expectation can be detected through the frantic efforts many women are willing to make in order to fulfil it. Consider, for example, the many studies that have shown that women who work full time outside the home experience very little help with the housework from their husbands, so that these women have, essentially, two full-time jobs. Why do they continue to make these noble and exhausting efforts? Why do they consider it 'less trouble' to do it themselves than to teach, bully, nag, or otherwise assert themselves in the direction of their husbands? Because women are psychologically prepared for enormous personal sacrifice as a moral duty, so that when it is exacted they may feel exhausted and resentful but nevertheless that they've done their duty.

If the only problem with self-abnegation for women were the ambiguity of the concepts involved and the suffering that has often resulted, we might nevertheless say that the problem is a serious one. But there is more; at one and the same time, women are expected to be both self-abnegating and to be the sorts of beings who are capable of enthusiastic participation in romantic love. That is, we are expected to be persons sufficiently developed to be able to form strong attachments to particular others, not just the human race or the needy. We must be capable of experiencing strong emotional and sexual attractions for a particular person, and be willing and able to endow that person with all sorts of enhancing fantasy qualities. This means that we take an interest in some people and virtually no interest at all in others, but not for moral or spiritual reasons; rather, we take this interest and indeed base choices that determine what sorts of lives we lead on this interest. Nothing could be farther from the ideals of either moral or spiritual self-abnegation than cultivating the image of oneself as an object of desire, and the ruthless personal preference that is one of the characteristics of romantic love. Women do make considerable sacrifices in romantic relationships, but the informing ideal is usually a rich mixture of romantic self-obliteration and the belief that such sacrifices will make us more desirable. These two sets of ideals taken together are extremely confusing; many women feel they are never as self-abnegating or as sexually desirable as somehow they ought to be. Since each of these ideals precludes the other, the resultant confusion is not surprising.

Is self-abnegation a virtue? Only sometimes, when one has reached a certain level of self-development. As Hendlin has pointed out, we cannot transcend ourselves without first becoming somebody. Is self-abnegation as traditionally conceived for women a virtue? I argue that it is not, that women experience sufficient loss and/or under-development of self that our attempts at self-abnegation cannot lead to the good results self-abnegation can bring. One must first develop a sense of self, then ask oneself whether traditional forms of self-abnegation – e.g., giving up work in the world for the sake of work in the home, taking complete responsibility for the home, attempting to produce happiness in husband and children – in fact increase human happiness in the form of sympathetic understanding between persons and the actions that follow and/or service to others without at the same time creating resentment, anxiety, and despair. Furthermore, one must ask how self-abnegation fits with the other ideals we embrace, whether these ideals form an internally consistent whole or are in conflict. Finally, we may well discover that, when the demand for it is made consistently and in the same way for both sexes, certain forms of suffering through insufficient self-development and corresponding self-sacrifice will disappear.

NOTES

1 *Oxford English Dictionary*, s.v., 'Abnegation.'
2 Iris Murdoch, *The Nice and the Good* (London: Chatto and Windus, 1969), p. 270
3 Bernadette Roberts, *The Experience of No-Self* (Boston: Shambhala, 1982), p. 23
4 Ibid.
5 Ram Dass and Paul Gorman, *How Can I Help?* (New York: Alfred A. Knopf, 1985), p. 26
6 Ibid., p. 38
7 Ibid., p. 49

8 Carol Gilligan, *In a Different Voice: Psychological Theories and Women's Development* (Cambridge, Mass: Harvard University Press, 1982), p. 136

9 Steven Hendlin, 'Pernicious Oneness,' *Journal of Humanistic Psychology* 23, no. 3 (Summer 1983): 65

10 Sigmund Freud, *New Introductory Lectures in Psychoanalysis* (Harmondsworth: Penguin, 1975), p. 168

Notes on Contributors

Lorraine Code is a Canada Research Fellow with the Department of Philosophy and the Women's Studies Research Group at York University. In addition to numerous published articles in theory of knowledge, ethics, and feminist theory, she is the author of *Epistemic Responsibility* (University Press of New England, 1987), for which she was awarded the Brown University Press First Book Prize Award; and is co-editor with Sandra Burt and Lindsay Dorney of *Changing Patterns: Women in Canada* (McClelland and Stewart, 1988). She is currently writing a book on knowledge and gender, which will be published by Rowman and Littlefield.

Jacqueline MacGregor Davies graduated from Queen's University with a Bachelor of Arts and Master of Arts in philosophy. Currently employed by the Elizabeth Fry Society of Kingston, she works with women in conflict with the law, and reads philosophy and feminist science fiction in her spare time.

Marsha P. Hanen is Professor of Philosophy and Dean of the Faculty of General Studies at the University of Calgary. She has published numerous articles in philosophy of science, philosophy of law, and feminist theory and is co-editor of *Science, Pseudo-Science and Society* (Wilfrid Laurier, 1980) and co-author of *Archaeology and the Methodology of Science* (New Mexico, forthcoming). Her current research interests are in legal theory, feminist theory, and interdisciplinary education.

Barbara Houston teaches philosophy and women's studies at the University of Western Ontario and the University of New Hampshire.

Her current research interests are gender identity, an ethics of care, feminist ethics, and a gender-sensitive approach to moral education. She has published articles on these topics in various journals and anthologies.

Kathryn Pauly Morgan is Associate Professor of Philosophy and Women's Studies at the University of Toronto. She is the author of various articles on romantic love, sexuality, androgyny, feminist pedagogy, manipulative power, and issues in women's health. When she is not caring for her new son, she is working on a collection of essays entitled *The Metaphysical Politics of Gender*.

Sheila Mullett is Associate Professor of Philosophy at Concordia University, where she has been teaching since 1969. She is currently publishing articles on ethics, feminist ethics, and philosophy of leisure.

Christine Overall is Associate Professor of Philosophy and Queen's National Scholar at Queen's University. Her published papers are in the areas of philosophy of religion, feminist theory, and biomedical ethics. She is the author of *Ethics and Human Reproduction: A Feminist Analysis* (Allen & Unwin, 1987), and the editor of an anthology of papers on reproduction by Canadian scholars (Toronto Women's Press, forthcoming). She is currently working on a book tentatively entitled *Women, Sexuality, and Feminist Theory* (Allen & Unwin, forthcoming).

Susan Sherwin is Associate Professor of Philosophy at Dalhousie University. Her major interests are in the areas of philosophy of feminism and bioethics; in particular, she is exploring the dimensions and implications of a feminist approach to ethics.

Bonelle Lewis Strickling teaches philosophy and women's studies and is co-ordinator of the philosophy department at Vancouver Community College. She is also a feminist therapist in private practice.

Petra von Morstein is Professor of Philosophy at the University of Calgary. She has published philosophical articles in German and English, translations, art criticism, and poetry. Her most recent publication is *On Understanding Works of Art* (Mullen Press, 1986).

Articles on philosophy in literature, and on the self are forthcoming. In 1987 she founded the Apeiron Society for the Practice of Philosophy in Calgary. This society, which aims to integrate professional philosophy in everyday life, offers regular seminars and individual counselling.